Lean Acres

Also available from ASQ Quality Press:

Profitability with No Boundaries: Optimizing TOC, Lean, Six Sigma Results
Reza (Russ) M. Pirasteh and Robert E. Fox

The Logical Thinking Process: A Systems Approach to Complex Problem Solving
H. William Dettmer

The Executive Guide to Understanding and Implementing Lean Six Sigma: The Financial Impact
Robert M. Meisel, Steven J. Babb, Steven F. Marsh, and James P. Schlichting

The Certified Six Sigma Black Belt Handbook, Second Edition
T. M. Kubiak and Donald W. Benbow

Six Sigma for the New Millennium: A CSSBB Guidebook, Second Edition
Kim H. Pries

The Certified Six Sigma Green Belt Handbook
Roderick A. Munro, Matthew J. Maio, Mohamed B. Nawaz, Govindarajan Ramu, and Daniel J. Zrymiak

5S for Service Organizations and Offices: A Lean Look at Improvements
Debashis Sarkar

Lean Kaizen: A Simplified Approach to Process Improvements
George Alukal and Anthony Manos

Lean for Service Organizations and Offices: A Holistic Approach for Achieving Operational Excellence and Improvements
Debashis Sarkar

Lean ISO 9001: Adding Spark to your ISO 9001 QMS and Sustainability to Your Lean Efforts
Mike Micklewright

Root Cause Analysis: Simplified Tools and Techniques, Second Edition
Bjørn Andersen and Tom Fagerhaug

The Certified Manager of Quality/Organizational Excellence Handbook, Third Edition
Russell T. Westcott, editor

To request a complimentary catalog of ASQ Quality Press publications, call 800-248-1946, or visit our Web site at http://www.asq.org/quality-press.

Lean Acres

A Tale of Strategic Innovation and Improvement in a Farm-iliar Setting

Written by
Jim Bowie

Illustrated by
Madeleine E. McGraw

ASQ Quality Press
Milwaukee, Wisconsin

American Society for Quality, Quality Press, Milwaukee 53203
© 2011 by ASQ
All rights reserved. Published 2011
Printed in the United States of America
17 16 15 14 13 12   5 4 3

Library of Congress Cataloging-in-Publication Data

Bowie, Jim.
  Lean acres : a tale of strategic innovation and improvement in a farm-iliar setting /
written by Jim Bowie ; illustrated by Madeleine E. McGraw.
    p. cm.
  Includes bibliographical references and index.
  ISBN 978-0-87389-809-6 (soft cover : alk. paper)
  1. Organizational effectiveness. 2. Cost control. 3. Quality control. 4. Industrial
efficiency. 5. Industrial management. I. McGraw, Madeleine E. II. Title.

  HD58.9.B685 2011
  658.4'012—dc23   2011019128

ISBN: 978-0-87389-809-6

Publisher: William A. Tony
Acquisitions Editor: Matt T. Meinholz
Project Editor: Paul O'Mara
Production Administrator: Randall Benson

ASQ Mission: The American Society for Quality advances individual, organizational,
and community excellence worldwide through learning, quality improvement, and
knowledge exchange.

Attention Bookstores, Wholesalers, Schools, and Corporations: ASQ Quality Press
books, video, audio, and software are available at quantity discounts with bulk
purchases for business, educational, or instructional use. For information, please
contact ASQ Quality Press at 800-248-1946, or write to ASQ Quality Press,
P.O. Box 3005, Milwaukee, WI 53201-3005.

To place orders or to request ASQ membership information, call 800-248-1946. Visit our
website at http://www.asq.org/quality-press.

 Printed on acid-free paper

Quality Press
600 N. Plankinton Ave.
Milwaukee, WI 53203-2914
E-mail: authors@asq.org

ASQ **The Global Voice of Quality**™

Dedication

To my Lord and Savior, Jesus Christ. I am nothing without you. Thank you for saving me and teaching me how to love and live forever.

To my incredible wife Dana, for all of your love, support, and encouragement when I was convinced that the well was dry. Thank you for reinforcing and refueling my passion and imagination every second of every day. I love you.

To my children, Vivian, Evelyn, Big Jimmy, and Little Jimmy. *Yes, I named both of my sons Jimmy. I'm an efficiency expert, and they are two years apart. If I call for one, I probably need both.* Thank you for refusing to let me grow up. You guys are awesome, and you inspire me every day. I love you guys more than you will ever know. Thank you for sacrificing months of playtime. Now, let's break out the Lincoln Logs!

To my Dad: Thanks for *Monster Matinee* Saturdays, Ray Bradbury and Stephen King books, and the nights we spent peering into the *Twilight Zone.* You taught me how to wonder and believe.

To my Mom: I never thought I'd say this, but thank you for being an active and diligent homework enforcer. All those nights spent rewriting reports and essays at the kitchen table made a difference, and you made me better.

With special thanks to:

Tim Leary for a second set of eyes and a sanity check, Jeff Booth, Joe Leppo, Bill Harris, Rose Sage, Bob Jamison, Doreen McMahon, Jim Henson, Paul Williams, Stephen King, Shel Silverstein, Ridley Scott, Robert Rodriguez, Terry Gilliam, Takashi Miike, James Horner, Howard Shore, and Randy Newman.

And to Poolesville, Maryland, as you used to be when there were Wesmond, Summer Hill, and Westerly alone. Selby's and High's at the center of it all. A simple country town that was anything but, and a small, close-knit community with depth beyond measure. When there were farms and fields, family and friends, fireflies and fantasy. I remember the smell of your crisp autumn mornings and the feel of your clear summer nights. When I was raised there, I came to know the best people this world had to offer. As much as a man can love and thank a people and a place, this is for you.

Table of Contents

Pretest:
What Do You Know?

Test score:

This is a preliminary exam that will set a baseline, or a starting score. If you score incredibly low, don't worry about it. In fact, celebrate it. The fact that you picked up this book and want to learn more about performance improvement moves you to the head of the class. When you finish reading this book, there will be a second test titled "What Have You Learned?" Hopefully, when you compare the scores of that test with this one, you will see marked improvement in your understanding of basic performance improvement principles. So—here we go:

1. The *lean* methodology is focused on reducing or eliminating _____ in a process.

    a. Variation

    b. Waste

    c. Work

    d. People

2. In order, the five principles of lean are:

    ___ Pull

    ___ Flow

    ___ Value stream

    ___ Perfection

    ___ Value

3. When engaging in a project using the *theory of constraints,* one is looking to increase:

    a. Inspection

    b. Inventory

    c. Operating expenses

    d. Throughput

4. The Six Sigma methodology is focused on reducing or eliminating _____ in a process or product.

    a. Variation

    b. Waste

    c. Work

    d. Expenses

5. _____ is an improvement methodology that proposes radical transformation of current processes and a fundamental shift in operations in order to increase efficiency and efficacy.

    a. Six Sigma

    b. Lean

    c. Business process reengineering

    d. Theory of constraints

6. From a project perspective, the individuals or groups who have interest in or are impacted by the results of an improvement effort are the _____.

7. Which of the following is not one of the 7 S's?

    a. Salvage

    b. Standardize

    c. Security

    d. Safety

8. Which of the following is not one of the nine "wastes":

    a. Motion

    b. Transportation

c. Injury

d. Reporting

9. A process running at a Six Sigma performance level produces a yield of:

a. 95%

b. 99%

c. 100%

d. 99.99966%

10. Which of the following factors does the theory of constraints *not* focus on?

a. Operating expenses

b. Inventory

c. Throughput

d. Efficiency

Now, turn to the Test Answer Key (page 235), evaluate your answers, and record your score. If you scored 100%—great job! Explore the pages ahead for new applications of the knowledge you possess. If you scored below 100%—great job! The following pages will present new information for you to absorb, digest, and apply in your world. Either way, have fun and press on.

Foreword

Change can be hard. This is a profoundly true statement, and I'm not the first to say it. It is often difficult to conceive performing tasks in a different order, in a different place, at a different time, with different resources, or in a different manner altogether. Change is difficult enough for the individual. When we talk about organizational change, the difficulty increases with each individual that is added to the equation, introducing new personality traits, perspectives, and experiences. Over the last century, we have seen the birth of organizational improvement methodologies focusing on quality, process, relationships, and strategy. We have seen total quality management, lean manufacturing, Six Sigma, project management, customer relationship management, and the multiple iterations of strategic planning, to name a few. As disciplines, each of these is difficult to implement. As concepts, they are difficult to understand. There are too many books on the market today that are written as if the average reader is an expert. There are too many dissertations and not enough instructions. There are not any commonsense, practical publications that answer the "how to" or the "so what." Until now.

The bottom line up front is this: we are engaged in a war on waste. As complicated as our world becomes, with globalization and technological advances that increase at an exponential rate, there are simple truths, basics in attitude and application that can drive us forward to victory. The following passage comes from the *Hagakure* (or *Bushido: The Way of the Samurai,* its English translation):

> I have found the essence of Bushido: to die! In other words, when you have a choice between life and death, then always choose death: this is all you must remember. It is neither troublesome nor difficult. You have only to go on with a clenched stomach. Any other ideas are unnecessary and futile.

In his original translation, Minoru Tanaka is relating the wisdom of Tsunetomo Yamamoto, a famous samurai who lived in eighteenth-century Japan. While at first the words and ideals in the passage seem disturbing and suicidal, further review will reveal the disciplined dedication that Yamamoto is encouraging. As a warrior, choosing to die removes fear. This is not suicidal action, but instead, complete and uninhibited devotion to the battle—living as a true warrior will. The true purpose of a warrior is to kill, not to live. Self-preservation comes in many forms and complicates the decision process. This allows the opportunity for excuses and actions that are outside of the mission of the samurai. This is a clear message about leadership, and a concise example to follow. It is a living form of communication that does not require emphasis or reimagining or reconsideration. By choosing death, the samurai will have incredible opportunities for honor by targeting the most difficult battles without hesitation. How does this relate to business? Let's revisit the passage post-editing (*by me*):

> I have found the essence of *Business:* to *evolve*! In other words, when you have a choice between *status quo* and *evolution,* then always choose *evolution:* this is all you must remember. It is neither troublesome nor difficult. You have only to go on with a clenched stomach. Any other ideas are unnecessary and futile.

In order to survive and thrive, organizations must evolve, and evolve on a regular basis. Evolution is, of course, referencing positive change, yielding positive results for the organization. In business, a simple definition of evolution should include *improvement*. There are some, both in the past and today, who will argue that they "don't have time for improvement efforts" when the fact of the matter is that they don't have time because they haven't engaged in improvement efforts. Others will argue that they "can't afford to change." The question I return is this: "Can you afford *not* to?"

Before we go any further, a few comments on *process improvement*. This is a fallacy, and the name alone has driven countless programs into the ground. Do not focus on *process* improvement! There . . . I said it. That felt pretty good. One more time? Well, if you insist. Do *not* focus on *process* improvement! The problem does not always lie in the process. It is *performance* improvement that takes organizations to the next level. The issues within your organization might start in the environment, the equipment, the training, the funding, or, dare I say, the management. Yes, all of you managers who are reading these words—you could be the problem. And you, the shop floor worker—it could be you. If we focus on performance improvement rather than process improvement, results rather than activity, we begin to consider a strategic, holistic picture of our services, and this enables us to apply a balanced set of solutions that are complementary instead of competitive.

So, why have so many organizations failed when it comes to continuous performance improvement program implementation? Simply put (as is the intent of this entire book), they have abandoned or skipped the basics for more advanced and "sexier" techniques. They have substituted automation or IT solutions in place of the principles of the core methodologies. This is a critical mistake. While technology-based capabilities can complement organizational or performance improvement endeavors, a lack of understanding or engagement of these basic principles and practices leads to disaster. You have to understand the core of the methodologies, and while there are some shared benefits, the basics are:

- *Lean* and *business process reengineering* (BPR): efficiency and velocity

- *Six Sigma:* quality

- *Theory of constraints:* throughput

A more detailed explanation follows in the graphic on the next page, something that I like to call the *performance improvement scope.*

You must understand your problem and desired result in order to accurately select and apply the appropriate methodology, but recognize that each of the approaches is driven by and focused on the customer. A quick note and a point of contention of my own: Please do not think of these approaches as distinct programs that operate in parallel to your day-to-day activities. That is not the intent. Instead, consider these methodologies as different ways of approaching the work that you already have. Don't initiate a Lean Six Sigma deployment and go searching for or generating projects. Apply the tools to the issues you face now, and achieve sustainable results with real impact. In other words, don't *do* lean, but *become* lean. Don't *do* Six Sigma, but *achieve* Six Sigma performance levels.

I have planned and constructed the chapters in this book to isolate the essence of each methodology and apply them to targeted situations that are integrated across a larger enterprise. Chapter 4, for example, is ordered by the first five steps of the *seven alpha* (7A) approach that I have developed. The seven A's represent an iterative deployment cycle framework that is intended for organizations of all sizes, types, and ages. Chapters 5 through 9 are outlined around the remaining two steps in the cycle. The 7A approach includes:

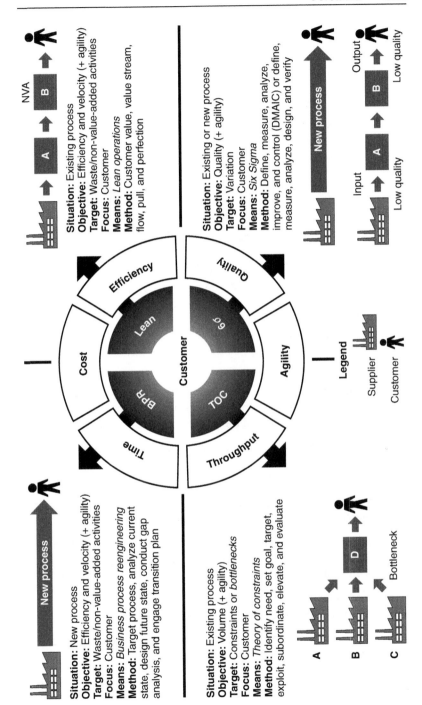

Situation: New process
Objective: Efficiency and velocity (+ agility)
Target: Waste/non-value-added activities
Focus: Customer
Means: *Business process reengineering*
Method: Target process, analyze current state, design future state, conduct gap analysis, and engage transition plan

Situation: Existing process
Objective: Efficiency and velocity (+ agility)
Target: Waste/non-value-added activities
Focus: Customer
Means: *Lean operations*
Method: Customer value, value stream, flow, pull, and perfection

Situation: Existing or new process
Objective: Quality (+ agility)
Target: Variation
Focus: Customer
Means: *Six Sigma*
Method: Define, measure, analyze, improve, and control (DMAIC) or define, measure, analyze, design, and verify

Situation: Existing process
Objective: Volume (+ agility)
Target: Constraints or *bottlenecks*
Focus: Customer
Means: *Theory of constraints*
Method: Identify need, set goal, target, exploit, subordinate, elevate, and evaluate

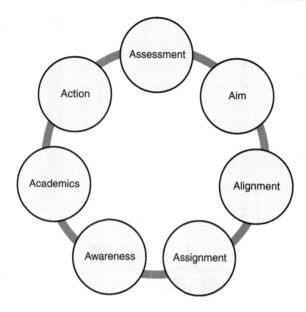

1. *Assessment:* Comprehensive (recommended) third-party review of environment, strategy, and operations—includes training program evaluation

2. *Aim:* Strategic: refining or designing strategic plan—includes VOC (voice of the customer) and executive/champion training, and the establishment of the *mission, values,* and *vision*

3. *Alignment:* Which business units play what roles in accomplishing the vision (vertical and horizontal), and how will they contribute to the vision through specific objectives and targets

4. *Assignment:* Designation of responsibility and accountability and tactical-level initiatives to achieve objectives and targets

5. *Awareness:* Vision and methodologies: communicating strategic plan, methodologies to utilize, and leadership support—also "What's in it for me," or WIIFMs

6. *Academics:* Methodologies and leadership: formal training sessions, team designations, and project selections

7. *Action:* Implementation: targeted deployment of resources to yield results that support the vision

The 7A approach is a program-centric approach versus DMAIC or the five principles of lean, which are essentially project-centric. The 7A approach incorporates strategic planning and project management with *targeted continuous performance improvement* (T-CPI) in order to best integrate practices to facilitate effective organizational change.

What are the keys to success? Some will say *attitude*. Some will say *determination*. Others still will say *passion*. They are all wrong. *Dissatisfaction* and *discontent* are the true keys to success. These aspects ignite any true improvement initiative. The fuel to success is the willingness or the desire to change or improve.

My intent for this book and my hope for you, curious reader, is this: that you will enjoy the story and be able to apply these examples directly and immediately in your workplace. I hope that whether you work in a manufacturing plant, a church, a service center, a hospital, a bank, or a restaurant, you will see the Barnyard, the corn carts, the Shearing Shack, the Hen House, and the Milk Parlour mirrored in your organization. I hope that you will see, remember the approaches described here, and apply the methods. I hope that you will benefit—now.

Another note: This book has been written for the "pracademic." This is the person who has the ability to apply what they learn in order to better the world around them. The "practicals" will not take the time to read this, and the "academics" won't pick up a book that contains less than 500 pages. So you are a "pracademic." Congratulations. You are highly sought after in our global economy.

Every chapter ends with a Rest/Reflect/Relate (R^3) section. This affords you, the reader, the opportunity to apply the subject matter and situations in the chapter to your world and from your perspective. This is not intended to be a test. Rather, it is a journal for you to reflect on and learn from as you move forward in your own continuous performance improvement journey. Hopefully, you will revisit these sections over time, revising your responses and sharing them with family, friends, and colleagues.

Merriam-Webster defines a fable as: *a narration intended to enforce a useful truth; especially one in which animals speak and act like human beings*. And that is exactly what we have here. This story is not untrue, but it is not fact either. The group dynamics are real, the problems are valid, and the solutions are legitimate. And yes, the animals talk.

Consider a complex environment with multiple classes interacting between functional units with requirements that are perceived as exclusive and unique, and personalities that reinforce presumed boundaries. Also, this environment exists solely to deliver value to a customer base while optimizing resource utilization and increasing product and service volume and delivery capability. This is not a multinational conglomerate. This is not a massive corporate entity.

Consider Lean Acres Farm.

The Boo-chair—A Forbidden Tune

(As sung in secret stolen whispers by the animal children on Lean Acres Farm.)

Don't be lazy, don't sit on your butt

Or the Boo-chair will come, and you'll get cut

Dripping red fingers and bright shiny steel

He'll come for you, the nightmare is real

Collect every egg and harvest the crops

A productive paw will escape the chops

Busy yourself with milking and shears

For there's only one way to avoid the tears

So spread the word, stay clear of harm

Tell every animal on Lean Acres Farm

Don't be lazy, don't sit on your butt

Or the Boo-chair will come, and you'll get cut

Chapter 1

The Narrator

I have always been driven to buck the system, to innovate, to take things beyond where they've been.

—Sam Walton

Please allow me to introduce myself. I will be the Narrator. I have been with humankind since the Creation, and will be until the End. I was there when man tamed the flame. I was there when the catapult changed the battle. I was there when the first clock "tocked." I was there when the telescope brought the stars that much closer. I was there when the cotton gin transformed industry. I was there when electricity was harnessed in a bulb. I was there when the phone rang out. I was there when Henry developed the assembly line. I have flown with astronauts, and I wove the Internet.

We are not strangers, you and I. We have met before, and we will meet again. I am almost invisible to those who suffer from shortsightedness and pessimism. Dreamers stare into my eyes. I am fluid and difficult to grasp, like a smooth stream of water. When I am directed appropriately, I can carry the impact of a tidal wave. Wherever I go, strong leadership and effective change management must reside, or my stay will be brief.

My parents are Discontent and Necessity. My brother is Invention, and my sister is Creativity. I am a close cousin of both Transformation and Imagination. I am married to Evolution. I am a part of every success story throughout history. I am *Innovation*.

I can be difficult, but I do not have to be confusing. While my effects are incredible, it is often best to see me in the simplest of settings. It is there that you, dear reader, can observe the fundamentals of my essence and relate them to your own world. Look for the core, the basics, and apply them deliberately. It is better if I show you. There is a beautiful spot right around the corner where you will see what I mean. I am on my way there now, and you are coming with me. Let me take you to Lean Acres Farm.

Rest/Reflect/Relate (R³)

1. List three innovations that have occurred anywhere on earth in the last five years that have impressed you or filled a personal, specific need (or both).

2. For each of the innovations you have listed, what unique characteristic(s) does each have that makes it special?

3. List three innovations that have occurred at your place of work in the last five years that have impressed you or filled a specific need.

4. How does your company encourage innovation to stay?

5. Is there anything that discourages innovation in your workplace? If yes, list these factors, and potential countermeasures that would alleviate the issue.

Chapter 2
Farm-iliar Territory

*Nothing like a farm. Nothing like being around
animals, fixing things. There's nothing like being
in the field with the corn and the winter wheat. The
greenest stuff you ever saw.*

—Robert Redford as Roy Hobbs, *The Natural*

You may have never been to a farm. I understand. But certainly you have read about them or listened to stories framed in this rural setting. The point is this: to explain the core of my being, I believe that a simple, clear approach is best. I could have taken you to an automobile manufacturing plant or a pharmaceutical testing facility, but we might have lost each other in the lobby. Let's go to a place where we can see the entire picture, studying and enjoying its attributes at the same time.

Lean Acres

In the state of Perfection, Lean Acres Farm is picturesque: a little barn, rust red; a quaint yet robust white house, resting on an overlooking hill; animal pens teeming with life and activity; healthy, vibrant crops growing in the most fertile, dark soil. When the wind blows, the rustling of leaves and stalks is reminiscent of a world-class orchestra playing for everyone. The sun shines, the moon glows, and the rain gently falls when it is needed.

Lean Acres Farm provides several key resources for the citizens of the state of Perfection. The wool is used for all of the clothing in the territory, and is known as the "Cloud 9" brand due to its white, soft, and "fluffy" characteristics. The eggs are enjoyed in every household, and are in constant high demand. Milk from the Lean Acres cows is renowned for its sweet taste. And the crops from the fields serve a dual purpose: they are used within the farm to feed the animals on Lean Acres and sent to market where buyers pay a premium.

The Farmer

 Did I mention? There is a Farmer. It wouldn't be a farm without one. And there are animals, as I know I have mentioned before. The Farmer understands the farm and all of its workings from the perspective of his house on the hill. The Farmer is not concerned with the details of the day-to-day operations—how the crops are gathered or which cows are milked. Instead, the Farmer's attention stays with "the books," watching intently as the incoming checks balance with the bills. The Farmer will give direction and guidance when the Farmer feels it is needed, but the Farmer trusts the animals to produce results. The Farmer is supported by the work performed by others. Thus, the Farmer wants to take care of his animals. But, if the crop yield is low (after the animals have taken their share), if the wool is thin, or if the eggs and milk fall short, there is a corresponding increase in animal "turnover." In other words, if the animals do not meet expectations, the Farmer will make "cuts" in order to reduce losses, and send one or several of the animals off to the "Boo-chair" (or at least, that is the way it is pronounced amongst the pens—the scary sound of the destination is not half as scary as the reality). Animals who go to the Boo-chair do not return. If the Farmer ever has to "cut" too many animals, Lean Acres will have to be sold to the competition.

The F.A.T.

The animals work the farm, trying their best to translate and execute the Farmer's intentions and desires. They work together under the Farm Animals Team, or F.A.T. They are divided into smaller teams, or pens, that are grouped solely by species. All of the pigs work together, all of the chickens, all of the cows—you get the idea. Each pen functions as a unique unit of the farm. Communication within each pen is rapid and effective. The Dog brings word from the Farmer, and the information is disseminated throughout the ranks of each pen as he stops to translate the message. Communication between the pens, however, is another story.

Personalities aside, pigs have trouble listening through a chicken's accent, and horses find the Sheep's drawl unbearable. Each pen is primarily concerned with its own needs above all others, including the needs of the farm. Furthermore, if you can catch pieces of any conversation through the hustle and bustle of the day, each pen is convinced that they are the most important and that Lean Acres could not exist without them.

Now let's take a closer look at the F.A.T.

Observe the *Dog*. The Dog obeys the Farmer's commands. The two communicate directly with each other, and the Dog does his best to act in a way that will fulfill the Farmer's intent. There is no bureaucracy between them. It is simply one-way communication. To the animals, the Dog is the voice of the Farmer. They are one and the same. The Dog also understands how to lead groups of animals, no matter the type. He is a model manager.

Examine the *Bull*. This is an experienced supervisor. The Bull is powerful, established, and obstinate. The Bull does not like change, and will always stand his ground. However, the Bull can be led in a different direction through a very specific approach. The approach must be tailored for each individual bull. The approach must be subtle, so that while you are gently pulling the ring in their nose, they believe that they are leading the way.

Look upon the *Rooster*. Roosters are time-oriented, wizards with numbers, and very specific. This helps the entire farm to stay on track. They are excellent schedulers but must be coaxed to travel beyond their functional area (the Hen House). The Rooster can not hold anyone accountable by himself.

Mind the *Horse*. The Horse is an extremely hard worker but needs guidance on a periodic basis. This is the source of product transportation on the farm. The Horse can perform a given task over long periods of time and will not think to question how the task is performed. The Horse is not the most creative animal, but its loyalty and determination are instrumental to the success of the farm.

Regard the *Pig*. The Pig assists with all of the tasks on the farm, but does not produce anything by itself. When working, the Pig consumes a great deal of resources. Pigs are dangerous because they move in one direction at a time and as a herd. They do not acknowledge the benefits of diversification or mul- titasking. However, pigs are also highly intelligent. They can be of great benefit to the farm. Pigs are keenly aware that they are typically the first to be sent to the Boo-chair when production is low. This creates apprehension on their part, and a desire to stress their own importance to the success of the farm (whether valid or not).

Perceive the *Cow*. Cows are not difficult animals. They are producers. They are, however, slow to move, and lack any sense of initiative whatsoever. They require strong direction and leadership. When they act in concert, they are a force to be reckoned with. Just be certain that when they act, they are moving in the right direction.

Inspect the *sheep*. These animals go with the flow. They are not *bah-thered* by issues facing the farm, and they have neither influence nor decision-making capabilities. They are producers, and do provide valu- able services to the customer. They require supervi- sion and regular, low-level goals.

Consider the *Chicken*. Chickens are producers. Chick- ens react with great energy when anything happens that is "out of the norm." While the connotation of the name indicates fear, in reality these animals function with a high level of energy that can be positive or neg- ative. The more specific the information as it relates to the impact on the chickens, the more focused the chickens are in their required performance. Also, squawking and feather loss are minimized.

Witness the *Cat*. Cats are extremely detail oriented, and myopic in nature. They maintain a short-term perspective, and are easily occupied with single- focused, minuscule tasks. They are excellent inspec- tors, having the natural ability to detect the slightest changes in taste, smell, texture, sound, or appearance on a localized level. They are not concerned with large-scale change, just as long as specific tasks remain that require their utmost attention. Cats enjoy the now and do not consider the future.

See the *Jackass*. This animal is a hard worker, in its own mind. This animal has great big ears that don't quite work. They function, but they only listen selectively to opinions or ideas that they agree with. All others are mute. This animal has an even bigger mouth. The Jackass is quick to put down ideas that vary from the norm, and will silence smaller animals with its overpowering, yet often nonsensical, braying. It is extremely skilled in explaining why things can't be done, and can not speak to how to accomplish a goal. Typical statements include: "We've already tried that before" and "This will never work." This animal is a negative influence, and can only be redirected through personal intervention by the Bull or the Dog. It never opens its mouth in the presence of the Farmer.

Watch the *Owl*. The Owl remembers everything spanning years and years. The Owl has fantastic vision and observes with objectivity, flying from place to place learning more at each location. Believe it or not, the Owl also works closely with mice (well, some mice). The Owl is a knowledge repository, and can be a great source for advice when the animals get into a jam. His counsel does come at a cost, but the guidance that he provides often leads to lasting solutions. He relies on the Woodpecker to record information as required.

Notice the *Mice*. These miniscule mammals have tremendous value. They are blind, and they live with severed tails due to an unfortunate incident with the Farmer's wife. However, they are astute listeners (large ears) and through their vast networks they can communicate information over great distances by means of verbal relay. Mice are everywhere (as unsettling as that might be), listening to the animals on Lean Acres, the vendors at the market, and the customers in their homes. Due to a long-standing treaty with the Owl (that does not include moles), the Mice are able to move rapidly and freely about Lean Acres in exchange for the information that they possess.

While the descriptions above might fit your perception of certain individuals, these animals are not meant to describe anyone in your organization.

At different times in our lives (and sometimes in a single day), we all display attributes of each of the animals listed above. As leaders, it is our job to pay attention to our attitudes and behaviors and to be able to act accordingly in order to minimize detrimental impact and maximize positive gains.

The Farmer and the animals are content on Lean Acres Farm. Each member of this community puts in what they consider to be extraordinary effort every day to contribute to the survival of the collective. There is tremendous satisfaction in their exertion. There are times when some of the crops spoil before they can be shipped, and there are eggs that go ungathered. What can you do? Sometimes the milk runs a little bitter, and no one minds (or at least complains about) pitching in to shear the sheep, even if it is not their assigned job. It is all part of living and working in a small community. What is the worst that could happen?

There are new farms in the area, and each provides similar products to the state of Perfection using a specialized approach. These farms operate faster and cheaper than they do on Lean Acres. Milky Ways is selling more dairy each day. Cumulous Hills is shearing more wool. The eggs from Shelley's Shack are sharing the supermarket shelves. And Cornelius's Crops is delivering more grain every day.

The dreaded Boo-chair has been buying underperforming farms, and the Boo-chair does not sell crops, eggs, milk, or wool. The Boo-chair deals in flesh at the highest cost. He does not discriminate in his dealings, and can use any animal in all of his products. The animals don't know that for all of their efforts and all of their intentions, Lean Acres has been losing money over the past few years. They don't know that the worst can happen, and that survival is not mandatory.

The animals don't know it, but there is a man standing on the wooden porch of the Farmer's white house. The wind is blowing colder. The man is at the door, standing with a deep red dripping from his gloves and splashing gently to the floor. The man knows that Lean Acres has a fading pulse and that the farm can not survive much longer. The man smiles through stained teeth and twisted lips as the Farmer answers the door. The Farmer doesn't have much choice.

The animals don't know it, but the Boo-chair is offering to buy Lean Acres Farm.

Rest/Reflect/Relate (R³)

1. Describe the functional divisions ("pens") in your organization. If applicable, label each with an animal type of your choosing that best exemplifies each functional area's operational manner. Be objective here. Don't label these areas based on emotions.

2. What are three to five communication boundaries that exist between these functional areas?

3. What are three to five communication enablers that exist between these functional areas?

4. Do you use any "mice," or a communication network that ties your organization to its target market(s) and its customer(s)?

5. Do you have any owls? What benefit have they provided to your organization in the last year? Be specific here with hard, quantifiable results.

6. Who is your Farmer?

7. Who is your Boo-chair? Is there more than one?

Chapter 3

Losing the Farm

*There is no comparison between that which is lost
by not succeeding and that lost by not trying.*

—Francis Bacon Sr.

The Bark Is Worse . . .

The chill afternoon has become a cold evening. The Dog has called a meeting in the barn, and all of the animals are reluctantly gathered close together, clucking and murmuring with nervous anticipation. As the Dog climbs to the top of a crate in the center of the group, the room settles into an uneasy silence.

"We have a problem," he begins.

"Tell us something we don't know!" shouts a pig from the rear. The barn explodes with chaotic conversations, each animal talking past the other with increasing volume and intensity.

"*Listen!*" barks the Dog, breaking through the chatter, "I have heard the Farmer talking to the telephone. He told it that if we can't improve milk, egg, wool, and crop output, he will have to send all of the animals to the Boo-chair."

The last word, that name, cuts through the air with steely precision. Dead silence falls over the barn.

"What do you mean by *improve*, Dog?" The Bull has stepped forward toward the front. "I've been here longer than you. What is wrong with the way we do things now, when we have always done it this way and we have survived?"

"Agreed," whinnies the Jackass. "If it ain't broke, don't fix it!"

"Things have changed," continues the Dog. "There are new farms in Perfection, including one farm that makes sweeter milk." The cows moo their disagreement. "And one farm that can deliver more eggs, another more wool, and yet another more corn while using fewer animals to do the work." The chickens and sheep sit stunned. "If we can not better utilize our resources and raise our performance above the competition, animals will get *cut*. The Farmer needs us to work together in order to find solutions. And frankly, we are at a point where we can not afford to continue with *busy-ness* as usual. As of today, there is no second place. No one comes back from the Boo-chair. We need to change for the better."

"What can we do?" grunts a pig.

"If each pen is willing to donate a portion of their feed, their time, and their effort," replies the Dog, "then I recommend that we call on the Owl. His experience is broad and deep, and we could use his wisdom now."

The animals reluctantly agree, grumbling to themselves and to each other about the high costs of the Owl's services and whether or not the perceived threat on the horizon could ever rise to become reality.

The Dog asks the Mice to contact the Owl, and dismisses the animals for the remainder of the evening. No one sleeps well that night.

To Listen and To See

The following day is uncommonly quiet on Lean Acres Farm. The animals carry on with their chores as they have since any can remember, but without a grunt or a bah. Today they are all wondering if and how things will change in the near future, and if they even have a future. Word is out that the Owl will be arriving that evening, and that he has requested to meet with representatives from each pen in the barn. The sun races across the sky, and the night arrives without hesitation.

The Rooster sounds the call for the meeting. Animals gather in the barn once again, only this time it is a smaller collective with one animal from each pen in attendance. The Dog is with the group, and the crate stands empty before them in the evening shadow.

"Do you know where he is?" the Bull asks the Dog.

' "I am here," whispers a voice from the rafters.

With a rustling of feathers, the Owl descends upon great wings spread wide. He settles effortlessly on the crate and looks out at the animals before him. He sees their apprehension and understands their concerns.

"I am the Owl," he begins, "and I am happy to be here to help you. I have traveled from farm to farm across the land. I have worked with countless animals in a myriad of pastures, solving problems and improv-

ing situations. Throughout my life and all of my adventures, I have learned. I have learned to see. I see animals with unique and shared needs. I see the value as it flows through the activities that animals perform on farms. I can only see this value, this invisible aspect, because I have also learned to listen. I listen to my friends, the Mice. They can hear what the humans say. They know what the humans love about your goods and what they despise about them. They provide me with direct, unfiltered feedback from within the humans' homes. I am here to teach you to listen and see. Then I will teach you to act."

"Thank you for coming, Owl." It is the Dog that steps forward. "We are in dire need of your services. We must avoid the Boo-chair at all costs. How can we begin?"

The Owl replies, "I need to know more about Lean Acres and the individuals in this room. If you please, let us go around the barn one animal at a time. Tell us all who you are and what you do. Then detail one strength that you see in the farm, followed by one weakness." "This is my friend the Woodpecker," he continues. "He will be recording our discussions on wood surfaces around the farm. He will not contribute to our conversations, but will to our success."

The Woodpecker steps out nimbly from behind the Owl, a stealthy and silent bird. He flits across the open air to the side of the barn and perches near some spare wooden boards.

"I'm set, boss," he tells the Owl, and the Owl nods in his direction.

"Dog," continues the Owl, "let us start with you as the leader of this team."

"Okay," begins the Dog. "As you all know I come from a long line of my breed that has been here as long as the Farmer's ancestors. While my brothers and sisters were sold to humans, as is tradition, the Farmer selected me to stay and to serve at his side. I bring information from the house on the hill, including work requirements issued directly by the Farmer. One strength that I see in Lean Acres is that we are especially good at communicating within each pen. One weakness would be that we are not so good at communicating between pens."

"If I may," hoots the Owl. "Let us keep the introductions moving along and save any feedback until the end. There are no wrong ideas here, just opinions based on experience and point of view. Dog, you believe that communication across the pens needs improvement?"

"Yes, I do," replies the Dog.

"Thank you," returns the Owl. "The Woodpecker has recorded your input, and will continue for each member of the group. How about you, Chicken?"

"Who me?! Okay, okay . . . I'm a chicken, and I make the eggs!" sputtered the Chicken. "The volume of production in the Hen House is fantastic! I just think that the pigs could move faster in clearing them out and getting them to market!!"

"Now, wait a minute," grunts the Pig. "We work our little tails off . . ."

Again the Owl interrupts. "Pig, there are no wrong answers. Please hold your comments for now. You will have a turn to speak as well, and the other animals will afford you the same courtesy."

"So, Chicken, you believe that the Hen House produces a large volume of eggs, but transportation velocity within the house and between it and the market could be better?" asks the Owl.

"Yes! Yes! Absolutely!" blurts the Chicken.

"Very well," says the Owl, "What do you say, Rooster?"

"As you all know, I ensure that we stick to our schedules as needed in order to get the work done for the Farmer," states the Rooster. "We always meet our deadlines, and that is a key strength. That is, except for the corn harvesting. The horses never seem to be able to get the corn to the trucks on time, and that worries me."

"We pull more weight around here than anyone, " shouts the Horse, but the Owl intervenes.

"Please, Horse, these are distinct opinions, each with its own value. Just ideas, and we need them."

The Horse settles back with a frustrated lip flurry, abiding by the Owl's guidance.

"So," the Owl continues, "are you saying that the harvesting process could be faster, Rooster?"

"I believe that it could," the Rooster responds.

"Very well," replies the Owl. In the background, the animals can hear the Woodpecker hard at work, capturing their thoughts within the grain of the loose planks.

"How about you, Jackass?" the Owl continues.

"I work with the horses at times, sometimes with the cows, I'm really a jack of all trades," begins the Jackass. "Basically, I help to hold the farm together."

Some of the animals balk at the last statement. Visibly annoyed, the Jackass continues. "A strength that I see is that we have been able to maintain our operations without significant change for the last 50 years."

"That's not true," whispers the Cow.

The Owl reminds everyone to hold their comments.

"As I was saying," the Jackass goes on, "if we have any weakness, which I don't believe is true on a significant level, it would be that our customers don't know what they want."

"Could you please expand on that last statement?" requests the Owl.

"Sure!" says the Jackass. "These humans don't know how they want their milk to taste or how many eggs they need. We are the experts. We produce what they need. They might say that they want sweeter milk, but they'll come around. They have to." The Jackass sneers at the other animals in the group, confident in his superior understanding and the value of his contribution.

The Owl keeps the conversation moving. "Thank you, Jackass. What say you, Cow?"

The Cow blushes for a moment and hooves at the dirt on the barn floor. "I try to help out around the farm where I can, but spend most of my time making milk. In my humble opinion, we are especially good at cooperating as a team here on Lean Acres. Though all of us in the Milking Parlour have noticed that the corn tastes different, a little bitter."

"Thank you for your contribution, Cow," states the Owl. "Is there anything else that you would like to share?"

"No, not right now. Thank you all for your time," the Cow says with a hushed voice.

"All right. Bull, you are up," announces the Owl.

"I work with the Dog, and you all know that. I have to make sure that everyone knows what they need to be doing, that they stay on task; and I work with the Rooster to make sure that these tasks get done on time," the Bull states sternly. "We are strong at Lean Acres, working as hard as we can to complete the jobs we are assigned. The problem I have is that

I know when we are done with our chores, but I have no way of tracking progress throughout the day. This is information that I need to have if we are going to increase our performance and output levels."

"So you are saying that the only progress indicator you currently have is the confirmed completion of a job?" asks the Owl.

"Yes," answers the Bull, "in a painfully simplistic manner, yes."

"Thank you for your input," replies the Owl. "Sheep, you are next."

"Well, my main job here is to let my wool grow thick and fluffy. We regrow our wool every night after we've been sheared. When I have time to spare I help where I can around the barnyard," bleats the Sheep. "The animals here on the farm that help with the shearing process are extremely careful and very skilled. My brothers and sisters and I have not been nicked or cut in any way over the last five years. This is a great safety record. But we are exhausting ourselves hauling away the grain that does not make shipment to the market. It is stressing some of my family members to the point where their wool is thinning, and at an extremely early age. This concerns us."

"Thank you," says the Owl.

"I'm next," shouts the Pig. "I work all over this farm, shearing sheep, gathering eggs, milking cows, and helping with the harvest. Do you want to know our strength? We gather more product than any other farm, and we're proud of it. We are a hardworking team, and results show it. I don't know of any obvious areas for improvement, but I have heard that the milk is coming out a little sour lately."

The black-and-white cow turns a new shade of embarrassment red.

"So, if I have heard you correctly," says the Owl, "you produce volume like no other, but the milk is supposedly developing a sour taste."

"That's it!" grunts the Pig. "You've got it."

"Great!" says the Owl. "Thank you for your perspective. Cat, you are next."

"My family and I keep an eye on the products here at Lean Acres. We inspect the eggs for cracks, gauge the sweetness of the milk, test the fluffiness of the wool—you get the idea," starts the Cat. "We are a quality-focused family, and that is an asset to an operation as large as ours. Due to this strength, I have begun to notice an increase in cracked eggs as of late, and I don't know what's causing it."

"Thank you," the Owl responds. "We will come to a conclusion with the Horse. Are you ready?"

"Absolutely. My brothers and I move the heaviest loads around the farm and to the market," touts the Horse. "We are in constant demand, especially when it comes to harvesting corn. This chore takes up most of our time. We have so many different animals with so many different skills that it's hard to find something that we can't do. As far as a weakness is concerned, I have to say that our barnyard is a mess. As I make my rounds hauling corn, I constantly have to weave between the animal pens as I try to walk the shortest distance with the least amount of effort. To this day I have not yet found the best solution."

"Has anyone else on the team encountered issues with the physical setup of the barnyard?" asks the Owl. Animals mutter together in agreement.

"All right. I want to thank each of you for participating in this creative session. Let us take a look at what we have so far," hoots the Owl, and he motions with one great wing toward the large plank of lumber that the Woodpecker has used to inscribe each of the group members' thoughts.

The animals on the team read over the information, and are each pleased to see their unique contributions noted on the board.

"There are a great many ideas listed here, both strengths and weaknesses. Ideas, however, do not provide a solid foundation in and of themselves. We will need to validate our suspicions with data and careful analysis," advises the Owl.

"It looks like we need a plan," says the Bull.

"We don't need *a* plan. *A* plan will not help Lean Acres. We need *the* plan that will ensure your survival and your success," says the Owl. "I can help you, if you desire."

The majority of the animal representatives agree that they need the Owl. Even the doubtful minority reluctantly abides the decision.

The Dog steps forward. "Owl, we need your help and would like you to stay. We need you to help us see this through, to guide us along this journey."

"Good," hoots the Owl. "Most of the time it is not big efforts that save the day, but the smaller efforts that add up cumulatively and evolve individually. The best part is that we have already started. Go back to your pens and get some rest. I will see you tomorrow."

Rest/Reflect/Relate (R³)

1. If *Ignorance = Bliss,* then it stands to reason that *Bliss = Ignorance.* If you are content with your operations in their current state and at their current performance level, then you should be afraid. Remember, it is discontent that leads to innovation and improvement. Is your organization's leadership content with its operations? In all areas? Is there performance discontent in any key operations? Is the discontent leading to improvement or destruction?

2. The term "burning platform" has been used to describe circumstances or the state of an organization that demands action, including radical reform. The "platform" is so dangerous that the members of the organization are willing to jump into somewhat unknown solutions and situations to avoid catastrophic exposure. What is the burning platform at Lean Acres Farm? Is there a burning platform in your organization? What is it?

3. What are some of the strengths in your organization? What are some of the weaknesses? Consider only internal factors.

Chapter 4

Growing a Strate-Tree

The best time to plant a tree is twenty years ago.
The second-best time is now.

—Ancient proverb

The night passes slowly over Lean Acres. The animals do not sleep well, if at all. Then again, who would? With the future of the farm uncertain, rest is an elusive commodity. Their minds (and their stomachs) are turning with anxiety and anticipation, half from an outright and mysterious fear of the Boo-chair, half from hope—albeit a brief spark at first—from the Owl.

The members of the F.A.T. know that they have two choices, and only one of them has a pleasant outcome. They can continue to coexist on the farm, working in their functional areas, and hope to avoid "cuts," but hope is not a strategy. They all know that this will not work in the long run. The fact that survival is not mandatory is becoming clearer to them as the world around and within Lean Acres lurches forward into the future. As a team and as individuals, the animals must choose to collaborate across their pens and eliminate the need for "cuts" altogether. To do this, they must strive for growth. They begin to understand that they need a unifying strategic plan in order to survive and, eventually, to thrive.

This is not to say that Lean Acres does not have a strategy in its current state. Every individual, every group, and every organization has a strategy. It might not be focused properly or communicated effectively, it might not be clearly articulated and there may be no accountability, but every action—no matter how disjointed and chaotic it might appear—occurs with intent. As resources and effort are applied within this intent to achieve a certain goal, a strategy is executed.

There certainly are poor strategies, just as there are great ones. And what separates the two? In the most basic sense, a "poor" strategy does not have a clear focus or direction, it is not aligned and cascaded through all levels of stakeholders, its goals are not measurable (some would call these "soft" or "fluffy" goals), and there is no accountability or designated actions that will contribute to the achievement of the higher and initial intent. A "good" strategy is formulated, communicated, and executed quite differently, and it produces outputs that include continuous organization-, group-, and individual-level performance improvements. This strategy includes the seven A's: *assessment, aim, alignment, assignment, awareness, academics,* and *action.*

So—how do we get there? Let's check in with our friends on Lean Acres Farm.

The Strate-Tree

As the sun crests the horizon, cutting through the murk of a sleepless night, the Rooster calls everyone to work. For some of the animals, this means returning to the barn. The animals are silent today. Hoofs, paws, and claws drag forward across the dirt floor as each of their minds scurries in different directions, guessing at what to do next. The Owl is waiting for them, resting on the crate and acknowledging each animal as they settle. The Woodpecker is poised in his precarious position above the planks, prepared with purpose to peck precise points as they are presented.

"Good morning to you all," the Owl begins. "I want to thank each of you for your contributions yesterday, and I look forward to our session this day."

There is an attempted return of courtesy from the local animal mass, but it comes under sighing breath and bowed heads.

"Discouraged, are we?" asks the Owl. "No need for that. The information you provided last night is extremely valuable, as you will soon see. Let us take a look at what we have so far."

The team members gather around the notes that the Woodpecker captured on the wooden boards, and the Owl continues.

"As you can see, we captured each of your comments from yesterday's discussion. It looks like you communicate well within your pens, or functional areas, but not so well between them. You produce high volume here at Lean Acres, but at times the transportation is slow and the product is not of the highest quality. You have a highly capable workforce, but you have no way to track your progress as you work through your chores. And finally, while you have been operating in your current state for a long time,

Strengths	Weaknesses
1. Communication within pens	1. Communication across pens
2. High volume of egg production	2. Slow egg collection/ transport to market
3. Always meet deadlines	3. Slow corn harvesting
4. Long history of operations in current state	4. Unclear expectations between producers and customers
5. Teamwork	5. Flat wool
6. Hard workers	6. No task progress tracking—only complete or working
7. Skilled shearers	7. High volume of rotten grain
8. High overall production volume	8. Inconsistent milk taste
9. Expert quality inspectors	9. Cracked eggs
10. Diverse, skilled workforce	10. Disorganized barnyard
	11. Not enough goods to market

the expectations from your customers are unclear, and the barnyard is not the easiest piece of ground to negotiate. Did I summarize your thoughts from last night correctly?"

"It sounds like you've been here a while," says the Dog. "I'd say you've hit most of our problems on the nose."

The rest of the team agrees, and is encouraged by the Owl's ability to help them focus on the key issues.

"What now?" snorts the Pig.

"Now we are going to use your knowledge and experiences to build what the humans call a *strategy*," states the Owl.

The Pig and the Chicken step on each other as they ask, "What's a strategy?"

"In the most simple terms, a *strategy* is a set of carefully planned and coordinated activities that when executed will help you to reach a desired destination," replies the Owl. "It requires a great deal of effort to develop a robust strategy, but those who have dedicated the time and the resources to it have realized great benefits."

"Can you show us what a strategy looks like?" the Dog begs. A few other animals look from the Dog to the Owl, longing to understand through sight.

"There are different ways to display a strategy," the Owl responds. "Some folks create a map, while others develop a book. With the Woodpecker's assistance, we are going to grow a *Strate-Tree*, and we have an example for you right over here."

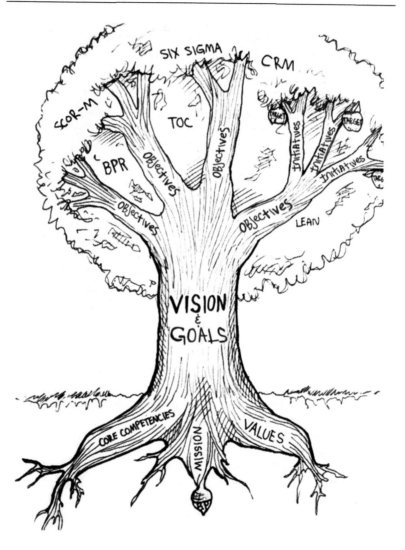

The Owl turns completely around and gestures to the rear face of the supporting crate. The animals shuffle to the other side and peer at the image carved into the wood.

"So *that's* a Strate-Tree," the Chicken gasps from the front of the group. The animals gather around the picture and explore each element.

"Let me walk you through the growing process," the Owl answers, and with wings wide, he glides down to the barn floor and begins describing the image. "There are three stages involved in cultivating the Strate-Tree. In the first stage, we plant a seed deep within data- and information-rich soil and sprout roots. This helps us to define where we are now. The second stage involves the growth of a trunk, which represents where we are going. During the third phase, the trunk produces branches, which work together with the leaves to produce fruit. Each of these components symbolizes how we are going to move from the present into the future. We have already planted our seed. This is the driving reason for the Strate-Tree, and some humans call this a 'burning platform.' We want to avoid any and all future cuts, and stop the Boo-chair from purchasing Lean Acres. Now we are getting ready to dig into the soil. The soil must be rich and fertile, full of nutrients to help our Strate-Tree to grow tall and strong. We ensure this by conducting different forms of assessment, some of which include capturing the voice of the customer (VOC), measuring customer and/or workforce engagement, securing input from leadership, engaging in stakeholder analysis, delving into process and system management, developing a SWOT (strengths, weaknesses, opportunities, and threats) analysis, looking at our work results, and evaluating our performance against another farm or some recognized set of criteria for excellence. Many humans rely on someone named Malcolm Baldrige, and call this a *benchmark*."

"What about the roots?" asks the Horse. "I've had to pull a few stumps in my day, and I know that strong, deep roots can keep an ordinary tree in place through just about anything."

"The same is true with the Strate-Tree," replies the Owl. "The three roots that we will develop provide a stable base for our strategy. The first is our *mission,* a statement that answers the question 'Why are we here?' The second root is made up of our *core competencies,* and these answer the question 'What do we need to do well?' And the final root is composed of our *values,* or what we believe are the most important principles for animals to exhibit and adhere to here on Lean Acres. If we develop these too quickly or without sufficient depth, and hastily spawn too many branches or strategic objectives, the Strate-Tree will topple."

"Where are we going with all of this?" the Rooster calls.

"Exactly," answers the Owl. "Where we are going is described in the trunk of our Strate-Tree, or the vision and goals. The *vision* is a statement that we will develop together describing what we want this farm to be in the future. The *goals* will help us to measure our progress in achieving the vision. As with any tree, the trunk will branch off in different directions. These main branches will represent our *objectives,* and we will need to fulfill these in order to achieve the goals, which in turn help us to reach our vision. The objectives take us from the *as-is* to the *to-be*, from the present to the future. Now, the objectives will produce fruit."

"Fruit?!" The Pig is now fully vested.

"Yes, fruit," continues the Owl. "On the Strate-Tree, the fruit, or apples specifically, represent measurable results, or *targets,* that we are attempting to attain with our objectives. The color of the apple serves as a visual indicator concerning its status. A red apple is making little to no progress, an amber apple is working but might need some help, and a green apple is moving full steam ahead without any issues. All of our apples will be red at first, but we are looking for Granny Smiths here. And while the objectives bear this fruit, the fruit is also nourished by the leaves of the Strate-Tree. These grow on the smallest branches of all, the *initiatives.* The initiatives are the projects that you will engage in—the work that you will actually do—in order to complete the objectives. The leaves symbolize the different *methodologies* that we will use in each initiative to hit the objective targets. Some examples include lean operations, Six Sigma, and the theory of constraints, but we will discuss these soon enough. Now, do you truly see the picture, and are you ready to move forward?"

The Jackass scoffs at this and hollers, "We don't have time for a strategy or a Strate-Tree. We're overrun with the here and now." Some of the other animals voice their agreement.

"You have it backwards, Jackass," responds the Owl. The barn goes silent. "You are overrun with the here and now because you do not *have* a strategy. And I think that you will all find the journey toward a strategy more pleasant than a journey to the Boo-chair, at least in the end." All ears perk up at the sound of the horrible name. "Our first step involves *assessment.*"

Step 1: Assessment

SWOT

"When we build a strategy, we need to understand the world we work in as best we can," the Owl explains. "Now, we already have a good idea what Lean Acres Farm looks like from the inside, thanks to all of your contributions from yesterday. The strengths and weaknesses that we discussed are all internal to the farm. What we need now is a view of the world beyond our fence line, a look at the external factors we will need to consider. We need to understand the opportunities and threats for the farm."

"Owl, I believe that you have a network of Mice that bring in word directly from the homes of our customers," offers the Cat. "At least, that is what some of them have told me. I let them go, of course."

"Thank you, Cat," replies the Owl. "Thank you for your insight, and thank you on behalf of the Mice that you let free. The Cat is on to something here, something that we all need to consider."

"Our resources for information?" asks the Bull.

"Precisely," the Owl responds. "Horse, while you have never ventured beyond the gate, you have been to the market, correct?"

"Of course," replies the Horse.

"Have you ever seen animals, carts, or products there from other farms?" the Owl inquires.

"All the time," the Horse says.

"Have you seen what the humans are buying, what they are not, and heard the other farmers talking about busy-ness?" continues the Owl.

"Well, of course I have, but . . ." and the Horse stops. He begins to understand. He begins to see, as do other animals in the barn.

"Maybe we do know something about the outside world here on Lean Acres," interjects the Bull. "How do we use what we know?"

"By applying it to the rest of our SWOT analysis," states the Owl.

"Our what?" asks the Chicken. "What is this SWOT analysis thingy?! It sounds complicated?! Is this new?! Should we have already started?!"

"Relax, Chicken. We are half of the way through it already," assures the Owl. "SWOT is an acronym for *strengths, weaknesses, opportunities, and threats.* The analysis is a tool that provides a framework for discussion concerning the current state of an organization, like your farm. In our *strategy*, we will need to build upon our strengths, to overcome our weaknesses, to exploit opportunities, and to mitigate threats. As I have mentioned before, the strengths and weaknesses are internal, and the opportunities and threats are external. These are what we need to talk about now. So, take your time, dig deep, and tell the group what you know about the opportunities that are available to Lean Acres Farm, and the threats that loom on the horizon."

"Horse," calls the Rooster, "whenever you return from the market, you always say that we hardly ever fill all of our bins at the stand, right?"

"Well," the Horse ponders the Rooster's question, "yes, I suppose I do. We empty our carts, which are never completely full, and leave at least half of our allocated bins empty. There is always space left over."

"Sounds like an opportunity for us to sell more product," the Cow adds. "Is this right, Owl?"

The Owl nods with a smile, and the Woodpecker is ticking and tacking at the boards.

"That is all well and good," offers the Pig, "but I've noticed more and more farmers and carts at the market as well. Seems like more of 'em each time we go."

"Do you believe that this threatens the future of Lean Acres, Pig?" asks the Owl.

"You're darn right it does! What do you think . . ." the Pig pauses for a frustrated moment, then realization hits. "Yes, Owl, I understand. We have more competition now, and this is a threat. Alright."

"While we can't seem to fill all of our bins, what we do fill sells out on a regular basis, right?" inquires the Sheep.

"It does," answers the Bull. "And usually before midday. If we could get more product out there, there is a very good chance that it would sell."

"Yeah, but remember, we're not the only ones selling out early," counters the Cat. "I've heard that the Boo-chair sells out of whatever it is that he sells on the other side of the market, too. If he is doing well, that is not good for us."

"Why do you say that, Cat?" poses the Owl.

"Well," the Cat continues, "I think that if the Boo-chair gets more and more green paper, he will have more to offer to the Farmer for Lean Acres."

"A very valid conclusion, Cat," returns the Owl. "Thank you for your thoughts."

"I've heard something at the market," utters the Cow. "I've heard the humans talking about something called *rester-unts*. Apparently a great deal of the corn, eggs, and milk that we harvest here goes on to these places. And I've heard that they're really catching on in Perfection. In fact, I've heard that they are popping up everywhere, and I guess that they will need our goods."

"Sounds like an opportunity to me!" spouts the Chicken.

"Yeah, but also for the Boo-chair," counters the Pig. "Don't forget, whatever it is that he sells, the humans eat it, too."

"Can that happen?! Can that be?! Can something be an opportunity and a threat, Owl?! Can it?!" the Chicken frantically appeals.

"Yes, it can," the Owl responds. "An opportunity is not always inherently or exclusively ours. Sometimes our competitors share that opportunity, making it a threat as well. This does not negate or cancel out this factor, and it will appear in both columns that the Woodpecker is using to record your inputs. Does anyone else have ideas on opportunities or threats?"

"I have heard that the humans are opening a new building in Perfection, something called a *fact-story,*" declares the Sheep. "And at this fact-story, they use wool to make the different pelts that the humans use to cover their skin each day. We make wool, so this could be good for us, right?"

"Absolutely," responds the Owl. "This is definitely an opportunity for you."

"And I have heard something as well," the Dog solemnly submits. "I have heard the Farmer talking to the telephone, and he has told it that the Boo-chair is opening a new, second store this winter. Again, more work for the Boo-chair is a threat to us."

"And that is correct, Dog," the Owl replies. "Take a look at our SWOT analysis. Does anyone else have anything more to add?"

Strengths	Weaknesses
1. Communication within pens 2. High volume of egg production 3. Always meet deadlines 4. Long history of operations in current state 5. Teamwork 6. Hard workers 7. Skilled shearers 8. High overall production volume 9. Expert quality inspectors 10. Diverse, skilled workforce	1. Communication across pens 2. Slow egg collection/ transport to market 3. Slow corn harvesting 4. Unclear expectations between producers and customers 5. Flat wool 6. No task progress tracking—only complete or working 7. High volume of rotten grain 8. Inconsistent milk taste 9. Cracked eggs 10. Disorganized barnyard 11. Not enough goods to market

Opportunities	Threats
1. Open product space at market 2. Product selling out on regular basis 3. New rester-unts 4. New fact-story	1. More farmers and carts at market 2. Boo-Chair is selling out on regular basis 3. New rester-unts 4. Boo-Chair is opening new store

The barn falls silent with concerned thought as the animals read over the carefully carved words, each in their respective columns.

After a brief time, the Cat speaks. "Are there supposed to be fewer opportunities and threats, or did we do something wrong?"

"That is a great question, Cat," the Owl replies, "And no, you did not do anything wrong. Opportunities and threats are typically more difficult to come up with because they are external to our operations. The strengths and weaknesses are internal, and thus we are often intimately familiar with them. Sometimes more than we would like to be."

"Yeah, okay. But really—who cares about all this?" the Jackass interjects.

"You are exactly right, Jackass," answers the Owl.

The Jackass is happy with himself.

"*Who* cares? That is what we need to explore next. The *who* are our stakeholders—they have interest at varying levels in what it is that we do here because they are affected by what we do. They are those humans and animals who care. Let us figure out who our stakeholders really are, how they affect us, and how we should treat them. But first, I am sure that you could all use a break. Go out and grab some feed, clear your minds, and I will see you in one hour."

The animals disperse into the bright day's sun through the doors of the barn. As they walk to their respective pens, they are beginning to see the farm in a different light.

Stakeholders

It's now well past noon (according to the Rooster's crow), and the animals gather in the barn once more. The Owl greets each team member as they arrive. They are all talking amongst themselves about farm busy-ness, and of course, their pen-mates' reactions to their activities in the barn. The last animal has taken a seat, and the Owl continues their ongoing session.

"What is a stakeholder?" the Owl asks.

The Cow responds, "You said a stakeholder is anyone who cares about Lean Acres."

"And that is correct!" returns the Owl. "So, to quote the Jackass, 'Who cares?' Let us have a discussion. Anyone can begin."

The Woodpecker nods and prepares to peck.

"Well," starts the Bull, "then we are stakeholders, all of the animals on the farm."

"And don't forget the Farmer. He might be the most important stakeholder," adds the Dog.

"We will get to rating the stakeholders later, Dog" the Owl comments, "but great contribution! Who else might care about your work?"

"The people! The people at the stand who buy our goods! They're from all over the state! They're stakeholders, right?!" exclaims the Chicken.

"And the people who own these rester-unts and fact-stories," the Cat mentions. "They use our products and serve the people of Perfection. In fact, the latest word from the market is that these humans are buying up more product than all of the other humans put together."

"This is great!" exclaims the Owl. "Can you think of anyone else?"

Several minutes pass without a contribution, and the Owl speaks. "Let us take a look at what we have."

The Woodpecker stands to the side of his work as the animals gather around. The Owl has joined them on the barn floor, and as he approaches the boards he turns and faces the team.

"It looks like Lean Acres has four primary stakeholder groups. We have the Farmer and you, of course, the farm animals. And then we have the rester-unt and fact-story owners, as well as the citizens of Perfection. Take a good look at this diagram and tell me if you see any similarities between any of the stakeholder groups."

"We are the only animals in there," declares the Pig. "The rest are all humans."

"Good point," responds the Owl. "What else do you see, species aside?"

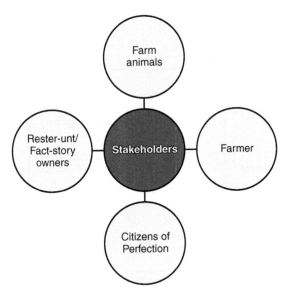

"It looks like us and them," the Bull reports.

"Please explain yourself, Bull. What do you mean by 'us' and 'them'?" the Owl prods the Bull on.

"We are the *us*, the stakeholders here on the farm. The Farmer and us animals who provide," says the Bull. "*They* are the humans who use our stuff."

"I see what you are saying, Bull," adds the Horse. "And if we look at these two groups from a fence line perspective, we could say that we and the Farmer are inside the fence, while the other two groups, our customers, are on the outside."

The rest of the team crowds around the boards now, voicing their agreement. Even the Jackass nods in the back.

"All right!" the Owl sounds. "So we have *us* as *internal stakeholders*, and *them* as *external stakeholders*. This is a commonly used classification, and it will help us to keep the right focus on the right stakeholders."

"What do you mean by 'the right focus' and 'the right stakeholders'?" questions the Dog.

"What do I mean, indeed," the Owl returns. At this he swoops down to the wall opposite the group of animals and points to a new carving, one of the Woodpecker's works that the team has not yet noticed.

"This is something that I asked the Woodpecker to complete last night following our meeting," the Owl continues. "This is a modified *PICK chart*, and it will be of great help to us as we continue with our stakeholder analysis."

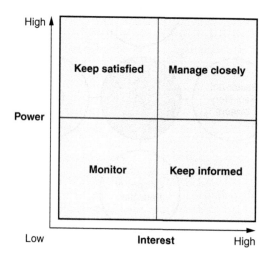

"How do we continue?" asks the Sheep.

"By having another discussion, this time about the interest and power levels of each stakeholder," the Owl replies. "We must ask two questions concerning the success of Lean Acres for each stakeholder:

1. How much interest do they have in our survival?

2. How much influence or power do they have to make our success a reality?

Now, if a stakeholder has a low level of interest and a low power rating, we know that we only need to monitor them. Just keep an eye on them so we are not caught totally unawares if they increase in either criterion. That stakeholder would be placed somewhere in the lower-left square. If a stakeholder has a high level of interest but a low power rating, we will need to keep them informed. They might not have a lot of 'push' at the higher levels, but they can be very helpful with the details of our effort. They are concerned, and communicating with them will maintain their level of interest. These would fall in the lower-right square. Some stakeholders will have a lot of power but less interest. These are groups that we have to keep satisfied. Their lives would not change dramatically if this farm were to shut down, but they do have the power to keep us around. We are talking about the upper-left square now. Finally, we have our stakeholders with a great deal of both power and interest. These folks play a big role in supporting this farm, and they depend heavily on its products for their own livelihoods. This does not mean that they can not live without us. However, if Lean Acres disappeared, they would have a hard time. This group is designated within the upper-right square."

The Rooster poses a question. "How do we know which square to put each of our stakeholders in?"

"For that," the Owl responds, "we are going to rely on your collective expertise as a group. Just as our previous discussions produced a SWOT analysis, this next conversation will yield our stakeholder analysis. The assessment of power and interest levels is a subjective pursuit because we do not have objective data to use. Instead, we will rely on each of you as subject matter experts to exchange and hone ideas into responses that the majority can agree on. Let us begin close to home. Where do you think the Farmer should be placed on the PICK chart?"

The animals look over the chart for a few silent moments, and the Pig speaks.

"I think that the Farmer is obvious," the Pig starts. "He has a high level of interest, and probably the most power overall."

Several of the other animals voice their agreement.

"Are you saying that the Farmer should be located in the upper-right section of the chart?" asks the Owl.

"At the very upper corner of that section," the Pig responds. "No one has more power over us, or more interest in our survival as a farm."

"I am glad you mentioned that, Pig," interjects the Owl. "No one has more interest in the farm's survival than the Farmer, and no one has more power over the animals. These are interesting observations. I will remind you though, that the 'power' levels indicated on the PICK chart are defined as 'the ability to influence the survival of the farm.' That being said, what do you think?"

"I think that the Farmer goes in the upper-right corner of the chart," insists the Pig. "He could sell the farm at any time to the Boo-chair." A ruffle of feathers and shuffling of hooves flares.

"I don't agree," interjects the Horse. All eyes focus on him.

"On which aspect, the power or the interest levels?" asks the Owl.

"On either," responds the Horse. "The Farmer is interested in the survival of the farm, but he will not get cut if he sells. In fact, he'll probably get a good deal of the green paper he likes so much. I think that he is interested in keeping the farm, but not as much as we are. And I think that he does have a high amount of power and can affect our success or failure, but I think that the busy-nesses in Perfection have more. They provide him with the most green paper and buy the majority of our products."

"I agree with the Horse," calls the Rooster. Other animals voice their approval.

"Pig," the Owl inquires, "What do you say? Can we place the Farmer in the center of the upper-right square?"

"That will be fine for now. I want to see how this thing plays out," the Pig answers.

The Woodpecker sends sawdust flying into the air.

"Very good," continues the Owl. "Since we touched on the busy-nesses in Perfection, the rester-unts and fact-stories, let us tackle them next."

It is the Sheep that begins. "It's like the Horse said. The busy-nesses will ultimately decide whether we stay or go. They send the Farmer the most green paper because they use most of our products."

"But I don't think they have as much interest in our survival," interjects the Cow. "We can't supply them with as much product as they want. That's why they're buying wool and milk and everything else from the other new farms at the market. If we were to be cut, they have other options. It would not be easy for them to make the switch, but they would survive."

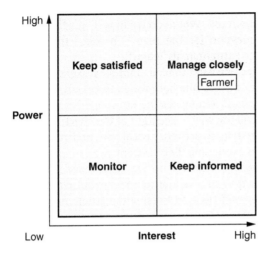

"Does anyone else have anything to add?" the Owl requests. There is no response other than silent nodding.

The Owl presses forward. "As a team, then, we agree that the busy-nesses have more power than the Farmer, but less interest. Is this correct?"

Every member of the group agrees in one form or another as the Owl scans the room, careful to make eye contact with each animal, and giving sufficient time for any protest.

The Woodpecker goes to work.

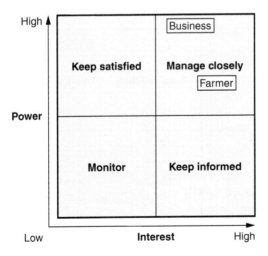

"What about us?! Where do we fit in?!" It's the Chicken.

"Great question for the team, Chicken," the Owl answers. "What about you, the Farm Animals Team?"

"Well, I for one can't think of another stakeholder with as much interest," says the Cat. "No one here wants to get cut."

"I agree, Cat," announces the Rooster. "Our interest is at the highest level, or, um, all the way to the right of the chart!"

The other animals are more vocal now, and in nine different conversations they are expressing their consent.

"But how much power do we really have?" questions the Dog. "I mean, we want to survive and to do well, but what amount of power do we truly possess?" He is addressing the group, not the Owl, and the Owl is pleased.

"We can make improvements, but we have considerably less power than the Farmer," adds the Pig. "We can try our best, but ultimately the decision is his."

"But we aren't powerless," the Horse speaks up. "I think that we fall somewhere in the upper-right corner of the lower-right square on the chart. We are definitely the most concerned, or interested, and we have some power. We will execute the improvement efforts and do our best, but we are doing all of this to please the Farmer and the busy-nesses. They have the most power."

The group concurs, and the Woodpecker etches the animals into the chart.

"You are all doing a great job," the Owl states, "and we have one more group to address. Let us talk about the human citizens of Perfection.

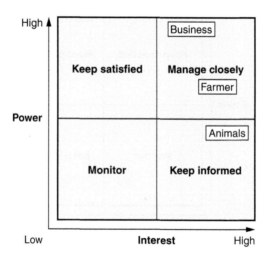

Consider them as a group of individuals who purchase your products at the market and from the busy-nesses. Think about them each in their own home, and what power and interest they might have in our survival."

"Well," the Bull begins, "they use our products. In doing this, they provide the Farmer with green paper. Not a great deal as individuals, but as a group they fall in at a close second to the busy-nesses."

"You're spot on, Bull," announces the Rooster. "Considering power, I would place them somewhere between the Farmer and the busy-nesses. However, I don't think that their interest level is that high."

"Why is that?" the Owl inquires.

The Rooster goes on. "Most of the humans don't buy incredibly large quantities of our products, and from what I've observed at the farm market, they don't have much trouble getting what they need from another farm when we run out. In fact, some of them have stopped using our goods and go only to the new farms at the stand now. I guess that the best way to say it is that they are flexible, and will use whoever can provide what they need. I would say that their interest is mild to low, somewhere in the left side of the PICK chart."

"Not too far left," argues the Cat, "because most like our products and come to us first at the stand. They like what we can provide most of the time. Maybe place them just a little left of center."

"What we have so far are recommendations to locate the humans between the Farmer and the busy-nesses on the vertical axis, and just left of center on the horizontal axis. Any disagreement?" asks the Owl.

The barn is silent, and the animals are nodding at each other, pleased with their product and their progress thus far.

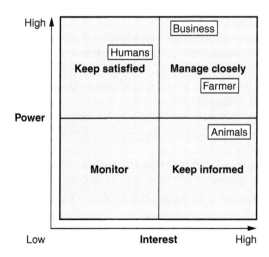

The Woodpecker adds the final stakeholder to the chart, and the animals gather even closer to study the results.

"How do we know if this is right?" the Pig inquires.

"We do not," the Owl addresses the team. The animals look shocked. "This stakeholder analysis will serve as a living, guiding document throughout our effort, and it is based solely on your experiences and subjective opinions. It may change over time, but it gives us a starting point from what we know now. We will need to manage the busy-nesses and the Farmer very closely, being constantly aware of their requirements and our ability to fulfill them. We will also need to keep the humans satisfied, and possibly work to raise their interest in our survival. Finally, as we move forward we will keep the farm animals informed of all plans, progress, and results. After all, the animals will be the ones working to improve Lean Acres. Now, I have a question for you. Of the stakeholders listed on our chart, who are your *customers*? Before you answer, go ahead and take a break and discuss this with your fellow animals. The Rooster is signaling that it is lunchtime. I will see you in an hour."

Customers

The sun is high in the sky now, beaming through the cotton clouds down onto Lean Acres Farm. Each of the designated animals from the improvement team makes their way back to the red barn where the Owl is waiting. They are talking with each other about their lunchtime discussions as they gather in front of the stakeholder PICK chart. There are revelations and revolutions concerning customer identification. Some are in agreement and some are not. There is an intense flapping of feathers, and the Owl is before them.

"I trust that everyone had a nice lunch," the Owl begins, "and that you all had time to consider the question of *customers*."

It is the Chicken who speaks. "I posed the question to the Hen House, and we know who it is! It's the Farmer! We produce eggs because he tells us to! He's the customer!"

"Right on!" bellows the Jackass as he looks around the group. "We work for him. He is our one and only and most important customer, hooves down!"

"I don't agree with that," the Cat interjects. "The busy-nesses buy our products, and several of the pens are in consensus that they are our customers. The Farmer is in charge, but he doesn't give himself green paper for our goods."

As more animals join the unwieldy conversation, the Owl interrupts. "Perhaps it would be valuable to define the term *customer*, and then to decide who fits that description."

The amalgamated conversations quiet down, and the team members are looking and nodding to the Owl and each other.

The Owl proceeds. "We defined stakeholders as a broad group of people or animals, basically anyone who cares about Lean Acres. Customers should be a more specific subset of stakeholders. While we do have *internal* customers, or stakeholders that we do things for within the farm, we need to focus on our *external* customers in this exercise. These are stakeholders who do not work with us. They do not live here on Lean Acres. This group is made up of whoever actually takes our products from the market. They give the Farmer the green paper for our goods. Make sense?"

"Well then," the Horse starts, "I think that with this definition, it's pretty easy to identify our customers. It's the humans and the busy-nesses, right?"

"I agree with you, Horse," says the Dog. "They come to the market and trade the green paper for our eggs, wool, milk, and corn. They must be our customers."

As understanding moves through the team, agreement abounds, and all eyes are back on the Owl.

"So, it sounds like the humans and the busy-nesses are the customers that we will focus on. Which group is the most important?" the Owl inquires.

"According to our stakeholder assessment, the busy-nesses have the most power and interest," says the Bull.

"Very good!" the Owl responds. "The busy-nesses are our primary customers, but the individual humans are not far behind. We will focus on both groups pressing forward, but always remember who your most important customers are, and do what you can to bring other customers up to or beyond that level. Now, what do these customers want?"

The Voices

"What do you mean, Owl?" the Cat asks. "The busy-nesses and the humans want wool, eggs, milk, and corn. That's all that we make here at Lean Acres." The other animals on the team mumble concerned agreement.

"You are right, Cat," responds the Owl, "I should have been more clear. What characteristics of your products are most important to them? What about your eggs do they want more of, and what do they want less of?

How much of your product will they purchase? This information is referred to as the *voice of the customer*. There are other voices that express concerns as well."

The Owl scratches shapes into the dirt with his claws. "The voice of the customer (VOC) defines cost, quality, or time targets for us to achieve. The *voice of the process* (VOP) tells us what we can currently deliver, and the *voice of the workforce* (VOW), or *animals* (VOA), details what the *doers* in our organization need to get the job done. From the top, the *voice of the busy-ness* (VOB), or the *voice of the farm* (VOF), directs specific strategic actions that will fulfill the requirements of the processes and the animals in order to satisfy our customers. Right now we are seeking the sound of the voice of your customers. What exactly are they calling for?"

"They just want more eggs!" exclaims the Chicken. "More! More! More! We can hardly keep up with the demand!"

"It's the same with all of our goods," the Bull adds. "The people at the stand want more and more, but we can't give it to them. That's why the new farms are springing up."

"Yeah—we're not getting enough corn to market!" sounds the Cow.

"And our wool is always short!" grunts the Pig.

"Do we ever have enough milk for the people?" asks the Horse.

The barn is buzzing now with rampant conversations. The Owl watches patiently as the animals come to a chaotic consensus. The volume fades as the Dog begins to speak.

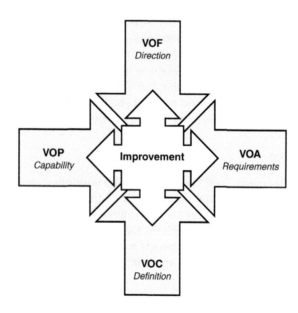

"We need to get more products out, Owl. That's what the customers want, and that's how we will stop animals from being cut from Lean Acres."

The other animals step forward in agreement, and the Owl asks a question.

"Are you sure?"

"What do you mean, 'are we sure'?" the Jackass belts. "We've all been to the market, and we've watched as our tables emptied and the people went to the new farm tables. They want more of our stuff! We've seen it!"

"I understand," the Owl replies. "But to be sure, have any people ever told you what they wanted, or are you basing your opinion on perception through observation?"

"In general, the people don't talk to us. Just the Farmer and maybe a kid here and there. How could we know exactly what it is that they want?" asks the Dog.

"Exactly," responds the Owl. "How could you know? I am not arguing that the people do not want more of your products. If you are stocking out at the market each week, then clearly their demand is outpacing your supply. But, it is critical that you understand that offering more of your goods in and of itself will lead to failure over time. *More*—the quantity or volume—is not enough to please customers. We must also consider the quality of the products that we offer. Quality is defined by the characteristics of our products that customers want more or less of. The customers have quite a bit to say about that, but you need to know how to listen."

"But they just trade the green paper with the Farmer and leave. The farm stand is really busy. We can't distinguish one conversation from the next in that place," the Cow asserts.

"I understand," says the Owl. "Sometimes we can survey the customers where they actually use our goods, at home or in the fact-stories or rester-unts. By surveying them, we can learn a great deal."

"Well, that's all well and good," starts the Pig, "but we don't have the means to conduct a survey."

"This is an area where I can apply my services," the Owl responds. "I have an integrated survey network that has been established in every human dwelling in Perfection. The members of this network are constantly exposed to the voices of the customers, and they have acute listening skills. Allow me to introduce you to my friends, the Mice."

As the Owl looks to a section of the barn floor on his left, the animals become aware of a presence. There are three mice standing upright on their hind legs in a row next to the crate. They have a slightly eerie aura, as if they have been there the entire day. In fact, none of the animals are certain that they weren't. The Mice remain immobile and looking at the Owl, void of any expression save for the occasional but slight twitch of the whisker or the bandaged, severed tail.

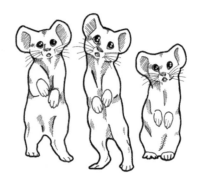

"The Mice hear especially well, thanks in part to their large ears. They have heard the humans in their homes and at their busy-nesses. You can ask them any questions you like, and they will answer with your customers' opinions. Go ahead, try it out," encourages the Owl.

"Um," begins the Horse. "What do you think about our eggs?"

The Mice shift their focus from the Owl to the Horse, and all three respond in unison:

We like these eggs,

They're something to tout.

At this, the Chicken and the Rooster puff up with pride.

They're fresh and delicious,

But they're always running out.

The Jackass opens his mouth to speak when the Mice continue with their three voices as one:

And the shells, they're all broken,

Each one covered in cracks.

If this continues,

We'll go to Shelley's Shack.

The animals are stunned.

"Cracks in the eggs?!" the Chicken exclaims. "That happens when they pile up! I knew that they weren't being gathered fast enough! What are we going to do?!"

"Relax, Chicken. We will get to that later," assures the Owl. "For now, we simply need to listen to the customer."

"What about the wool?" the Bull inquires.

The Mice shift their collective focus to the Bull.

"Cloud Nine" wool from Lean Acres is fluffy and nice,

But the flat stuff we get ain't worth the price.

The Sheep is shocked.

Sometimes the wool is matted down and flat,

You have to know we don't like that.

We've been considering stuff from a different barn.

Cumulous Hills wool might make better yarn.

We'll continue with Lean Acres as we have in the past,

If you give us more fluffy wool, and you give it to us fast.

The Mice trail off together after the last sentence, retaining their ocular lock with the Bull.

"Surely the customers love our milk," the Cow cries out. "It is good for their bones and teeth, and delicious . . ." The Mice interrupt.

The milk from Lean Acres used to be all we would drink,

But lately, well, frankly, the quality stinks.

Sometimes it's too sweet, and sometimes it's too sour,

And this changes often, maybe by the hour.

Now, Milky Ways Farm has joined in the race.

The stuff they make has a good, consistent taste.

But we get other goods from Lean Acres as well,

And switching suppliers might hurt like hell.

We will do it, however, we will make the move

If the milk from Lean Acres doesn't improve.

The Cow is flabbergasted. Embarrassment surrenders to full shame as she hangs her head low.

"I've known something was wrong. What are we going to do?" she utters.

"Easy now, Cow," the Owl intervenes. "Yes, there is bad news in that the taste of the milk is not as consistent as it used to be. But, there is good news too."

"What could you possibly derive as 'good news' from that report?" asks the Cow.

"The report itself is good news," answers the Owl. "The customer wants your product, and you are capable of producing what they want or they would not have become fans in the first place, right?"

"Well, I suppose that's correct," says the Cow.

The Owl responds, "Of course that is right. All we need to do is understand and deliver what the customer wants. We are at risk of losing the farm because we did not know what we did not know. But now—now we know what we did not know, and are working to understand the latter. Is that not encouraging in and of itself?"

Each member of the team looks at the others, nodding seriously and sharing glances of understanding.

The Dog speaks. "Alright, Mice, you've told us a great deal so far. What about our core product. What about the corn?"

The Mice look to the Dog and collectively chatter:

Oh, the corn from Lean Acres! That wonderful stuff!

Unfortunately, at the market, there just isn't enough.

When a load arrives, our hopes are foiled

Because a bunch of the corn is crushed and spoiled.

So we buy from Lean Acres and from Cornelius's Crops,

But this won't last long, and soon we will stop.

Although we've been with Lean Acres for years,

We'll go somewhere else to buy our ears.

"More corn?!" the Pig and the Horse shout together.

"How can we possibly pull more carts in a day?" asks the Horse. "And who has time to worry about the spoilage?"

"We'll get to that, Horse, if that is in fact the answer we require," responds the Owl. "Right now we are simply listening to our customers. The Woodpecker has been busy during this exchange, and if you would be so kind, please gather around the front of the crate and see what he has captured."

The animals had completely ignored the Woodpecker's activity as they were passionately engaged in the conversation. They all look at the diagram now as they gather around the crate, making a quick study of each element and its related characteristic.

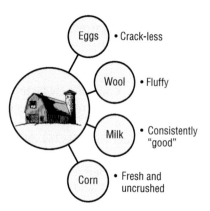

Eggs • Crack-less

Wool • Fluffy

Milk • Consistently "good"

Corn • Fresh and uncrushed

After a few moments, the Owl asks a question. "What do you see?"

"I see that we were wrong in most cases," answers the Pig.

"What do you mean? Please elaborate, Pig," the Owl requests.

"We assumed that the humans and the busy-nesses, our customers, just wanted more of our products. We never knew that there was anything that they didn't like about them," states the Pig.

"Yeah, I agree," the Bull chimes in. "It looks like they do want more corn, but all of our other goods need to improve in one way or another."

"Actually, they want us to improve our products in very specific ways," retorts the Cat. "The Woodpecker captured each characteristic that needs work for us, so this picture will help us as we move forward, right?"

"You are absolutely correct," answers the Owl. "We know why we need to improve, and what will happen if we do not. We know who our stakeholders are and how to treat each group. We know who our customers are and what they want from us. We know that we have competition, who they are, and what each provides. Next, we will need to discuss what we are supposed to do, in both the present and the future, and how we will survive the Boo-chair."

Step 2: Aim

Mission

"How do we come up with a mission statement?" inquires the Cow. "It sounds complicated."

"It can be," responds the Owl, "but I have a few tools that should help us along. Let us take a look at the products we have developed here in the barn."

The Owl gives the animals a few minutes to peer at the pictures pecked into the planks. Some are discussing the rationale behind the results, and others talking about content. Several are looking over the carvings silently, taking it all in from a cumulative perspective.

"Now, let us keep these products in front of us. We might need to reference them as we go through this next piece," the Owl says.

"What's the next piece?" It is the Dog, and the Owl notices that his tail is wagging slightly side to side.

The Owl continues. "The next piece is 'why.' Why does Lean Acres exist? What is its purpose?"

"The farm exists because the Farmer wants it to," bellows the Bull.

"That certainly is a part of it, Bull. Who else wants Lean Acres to exist?" the Owl requests.

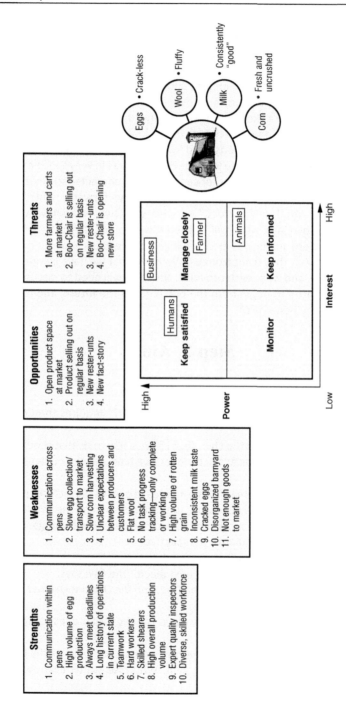

Strengths

1. Communication within pens
2. High volume of egg production
3. Always meet deadlines
4. Long history of operations in current state
5. Teamwork
6. Hard workers
7. Skilled shearers
8. High overall production volume
9. Expert quality inspectors
10. Diverse, skilled workforce

Weaknesses

1. Communication across pens
2. Slow egg collection/ transport to market
3. Slow corn harvesting
4. Unclear expectations between producers and customers
5. Flat wool
6. No task progress tracking—only complete or working
7. High volume of rotten grain
8. Inconsistent milk taste
9. Cracked eggs
10. Disorganized barnyard
11. Not enough goods to market

Opportunities

1. Open product space at market
2. Product selling out on regular basis
3. New rester-unts
4. New fact-story

Threats

1. More farmers and carts at market
2. Boo-Chair is selling out on regular basis
3. New rester-unts
4. Boo-Chair is opening new store

Eggs • Crack-less

Wool • Fluffy

Milk • Consistently "good"

Corn • Fresh and uncrushed

Power

High

Low

Interest

High

	Keep satisfied	Manage closely
Humans / Business		Farmer
	Monitor	**Keep informed**
		Animals

The Cat answers. "Well, according to our stakeholder PICK chart, the busy-nesses and the people want Lean Acres to exist."

"Why is that?" asks the Owl.

"Because they need our eggs, corn, wool, and milk?" the Sheep hesitantly mutters.

"I agree with the Sheep," barks the Dog. The Sheep is happy, but slightly embarrassed. "Our mission is to provide eggs, wool, corn, and milk to the people and the busy-nesses."

The Horse and other animals agree, and erupt in conversation over their newly attained clarity.

"This is an excellent start," the Owl calls. "However, we don't have our mission statement yet."

"What do you mean?! The Dog just said it!" cries the Chicken. "It's perfect!"

"It is an excellent start, but mission statements must be tested in order to be true," the Owl states. "A mission must be focused on your busy-ness domain, tied to your responsibilities to your customers and stakeholders, specific concerning your strategic advantage, inspiring and meaningful to the animals here on Lean Acres, and most of all, short and sweet, easy to understand. Do we have that with our latest version?"

"I don't think so," the Rooster comments. "How do we make sure that our mission statement is all of those things that you mentioned?"

"Very carefully and deliberately," the Owl responds. "What is your busy-ness domain?"

"The state of Perfection," says the Horse, of course. The others agree.

"So then," continues the Owl, "your mission is to provide eggs, wool, corn, and milk to the people and the busy-nesses in the state of Perfection?"

"So far," answers the Cat, "but you posed a few more questions that we need to answer. What was that about our responsibilities to our customers?"

"Indeed," replies the Owl. "What do you owe your customers?"

"That's easy!" shouts the Jackass. "Eggs, milk, wool, corn . . . just like we said before."

"This is true," states the Owl, "but only to a certain degree."

The Jackass frowns, but leans forward out of curiosity.

"What did the customer tell us that they want from us?" the Owl asks. "What did we discover when we explored the voice of the customer?"

"I see what you mean," the Cow speaks up. "The people and the busy-nesses, they don't just want our products, they want our products in a certain way. They want eggs, but they want them without cracks. They want our wool, but it has to be fluffier. They also want more corn than we are giving them now, and even though it hurts me to say it, they want sweeter milk."

"Now you are getting it," exclaims the Owl.

"So," the Dog begins, "our mission statement is to provide crack-less eggs, fluffy wool, abundant unspoiled corn, and consistently sweet milk to the people and the busy-nesses in the state of Perfection?"

"We are on our way," answers the Owl. "What about your strategic advantage here at Lean Acres? What can you offer your customers that your competitors can not?"

"Each one of them offers a product that we provide. That's why they're our competition!" the Pig snorts with some frustration.

"Yes, but none of them offer all of the products that we provide," replies the Horse. "Each of our competitors can't provide the range of products that we offer. And I remember that some customers really liked being able to get everything that they need from one table at the market instead of traveling from one to the next."

"What does that do to our mission?!" asks the Chicken.

"Well, I suppose that our mission is 'to provide a one-stop shop for crack-less eggs, fluffy wool, abundant unspoiled corn, and consistently sweet milk to the people and the busy-nesses in the state of Perfection,'" responds the Rooster.

"Is that it? Are we done?" asks the Bull.

"Not yet," the Owl says. "We need to inspire with this message, and to make it short and sweet. Does anyone have any ideas?"

The animals grow silent as beaks, snouts, and lips mouth voiceless words, deconstructing and reconstructing the mission statement in their minds. It is the Pig that steps forward.

"How about this?" he opens. "'At Lean Acres Farm, our mission is to provide a one-stop shop for high-quality products to the people and the busy-nesses in the state of Perfection.'"

"Very nice," meows the Cat. "Short and sweet."

The other animals join in the congratulations, and the Owl calls for their attention.

"This is a very good mission statement," the Owl states, "but is it inspiring?"

The animals settle down and consider this latest query carefully. After some time, the Pig speaks.

"Not yet it isn't. It tells us what we do, but it doesn't emphasize the importance of our work."

There is silence for a moment, and the Sheep whispers something from the back of the group.

"What was that?" asks the Owl. "Who has something to share?"

The animals look around, and the Sheep slowly steps forward with flushed cheeks.

"Well, with a few subtle changes, I think we can get there. We haven't included our interests in the mission yet, and we are stakeholders. What if we add the word *animals*, change the word *provide* to *serve*, call attention to the fact that we are the only one that can provide all of the products, and state what our products do for the people and the busy-nesses?"

"What would that look like, Sheep?" the Owl inquires. "Can you put that together for us?"

"Well, okay. It might sound something like: 'At Lean Acres Farm, our mission is to serve as the one-stop shop for high-quality products, supporting healthy animals, people, and busy-nesses in the state of Perfection.' That's just my idea." The Sheep finishes, and there is silence in the barn. Heads begin to nod and mouths twist upward into smiles.

"I think we've got it!" cries the Chicken. There is an eruption of agreeable excitement, and as it settles, all eyes look to the Owl.

"This sounds great," he states. "Let us put it to the test. This statement is focused on your busy-ness domain, or where and what you provide. It is tied directly to your responsibilities to your customers. It is specific to your strategic advantage, it is short and concise, and judging by your reaction as a group, I would say that it is inspirational. Can we hear it once again, please, so that the Woodpecker can capture your results? All together, if you please."

The animals respond in unison, "At Lean Acres Farm, our mission is to serve as the one-stop shop for high-quality products, supporting healthy animals, people, and busy-nesses in the state of Perfection."

"Simple and meaningful. Fantastic work," comments the Owl. "Please, take a break and let us meet back in here in fifteen minutes. We still have work to do. Congratulations on developing a great mission statement."

The animals exit into the sunshine, excited and smiling. Each goes to their own pen for a snack and a drink, with plans to share the mission with their fellow animals. The Woodpecker is outside of the barn above the main doors, engraving the new mission statement.

Core Competencies

As the animals return to the crate in the middle of the barn, they share the discussions that they held with their friends and coworkers. After some time, they notice that the Owl is missing.

"Where could he be?" says the Horse.

Each member of the group surveys the dark corners of the barn, straining their necks to peer up into the rafters and around into the stalls. There is no sign of the Owl.

"I am here." The Owl's voice resonates across the wooden beams from behind them. He is standing on the ground at the open barn door.

"Come with me, please. For this next part, we need to take a walk. Horse, would you mind grabbing the SWOT analysis and bringing it with us?"

The animals return into the sunlight and follow the Owl around the perimeter of the pens. He is walking slowly, observing the other animals as they go about their daily chores. Finally, he turns.

"What are our core competencies here at Lean Acres?" asks the Owl.

"What in the heck are core competencies?" the Bull inquires.

"Core competencies are those actions or traits that we focus on in order to provide value and results to our customers," responds the Owl. "We will try to keep it to the three most important, in order to remain concise. Consider the *strengths* we discussed in our SWOT analysis, and what it might take to overcome some of our *weaknesses*. Horse, please set the planks down right there. Thank you very much for your help. Now, the question is this: What will we need to focus on in order to achieve our mission?"

"We'll need to focus on the customer, that's for sure," grunts the Pig.

"Outstanding," the Owl proclaims. "So we have a recommendation for 'customer focus' as a core competency. Any comments on this?"

"I agree with the Pig that we will need to focus on the customer, but I believe that it will have to go deeper than that," answers the Cat. "We need to be loyal to the customer, to put them first . . . I guess the word that I am looking for is *commitment*. We need to exhibit customer commitment if we are to be successful here on the farm."

The group of animals is nodding, almost in unison, but certainly in consensus.

"So we have 'customer commitment' as our first core competency?" queries the Owl.

The animals all agree.

"Show me 'customer commitment'!" the Owl shouts toward the barn. The Woodpecker flies up to the exterior wall and begins working. As the wood chips fall to the grass, the Owl continues.

"What else is core to our success? What else will we need to focus on?" the Owl asks.

"We'll need to be great at our jobs!" shouts the Chicken. "We listed a lot of that stuff in our *strengths*, and some quality issues in our *weaknesses*!"

"The Farmer always uses the word *operations* when he refers to the work we do. Would 'operational excellence' be an appropriate core competency for Lean Acres?" asks the Dog.

"If you are trying to summarize what the Chicken said, then yes," answers the Owl.

"Well then, that could be our second core competency. What do you say?" inquires the Dog as he faces his fellow team members.

The Cow, the Horse, the Cat, and the Rooster voice their approval, while the others nod.

"Mr. Woodpecker," calls the Owl. "Please include 'operational excellence.' Thank you."

And the splinters fly.

"At this point," the Owl starts, "we have two of three core competencies listed for Lean Acres. Considering your mission, we will need to demonstrate 'customer commitment' and 'operational excellence' in order to be successful. What else will be required? Look around you, study the environment, and take your time."

The animals look over the barnyard. Their fellow farm-mates are working hard, putting in a great deal of effort to get through the day. The sun is warm, but a cool breeze is blowing, and the Farmer has stepped out onto his porch with a glass of lemonade. Then the Bull sees it. His horns hum with understanding.

"I think I have something," he says while his eyes are fixated on the barnyard. "I'm not sure, but it might just be . . ."

"What! What!" screams the Chicken, on the edge of an imaginary stroke.

The animals erupt into a furry and feathery frenzy of fury, and then the Bull speaks.

"Teamwork," he says. All fall silent. "We need to leverage our teamwork, and improve it, if we are going to achieve our mission. We can be absolutely committed to our customers, and we can perform every operation here on the farm with excellence, but it will take 'effective and efficient teamwork' in order to hold it all together."

"I agree with the Bull," the Horse declares. "They kind of build on each other, don't they? 'Effective and efficient teamwork' will enable 'operational excellence,' which is defined by and focused on 'customer commitment.' Right?"

"I think that you have something there, Horse," the Owl responds. "Let us put it to a vote. Please close your eyes and raise your wing, hoof, or paw as appropriate. Who believes that the core competencies at Lean Acres are 'customer commitment,' 'operational excellence,' and 'effective and efficient teamwork'? That these are the actions or traits that we need to focus on in order to provide value and results to our customers?"

Every paw, hoof, and wing is in the air.

"The ayes have it!" exclaims the Owl. "Now, let us get to work on discovering your values."

The Woodpecker continues his work.

Values

"What do you mean by *discovering* our values?" the Pig snorts. "We live by our values every day . . . don't we?"

The Owl responds, "You most likely do, Pig. When I say *discover* your values, I simply mean capturing or defining what the animals believe in on Lean Acres, what is important to the farm, and what the common expectations are for every individual in the organization. These values tend to serve as guides when it comes to making important decisions. Now, we are going to handle this with a different approach. First, we will brainstorm a list of seven values. There are no wrong answers during this exercise. We will then take that list out into the farm and ask each individual animal to select the top three values that are exhibited on Lean Acres from day to day. When you are all finished, we will return to this spot and analyze our findings. How does that sound?"

Once again, the animals murmur agreement.

"Well, who would like to start us off?" hoots the Owl.

"Flexibility!" shouts the Chicken. "We have to be flexible here on the farm!"

"Yes, but we must maintain our structure. Each pen has primary responsibilities," adds the Bull.

"I've noticed that a lot of the animals around here are enthusiastic about their work," the Rooster crows.

"And some animals demonstrate great determination, working against all odds to get the job done," adds the Horse.

"We do have great connections here, both to each other and to the farm itself," comments the Sheep.

"And we could not maintain close ties without a high level of integrity," sounds the Cow.

The animals voice their concurrence and the conversation tapers off.

"It sounds like we have our list, and it has been captured on the barn. Now, each of you needs to go back to his or her respective pens and ask each animal to identify the top three values on this list. Some of you will be working together, of course. When you have gathered inputs from every animal, go and see the Woodpecker and give him your results. He will help us to interpret them." The Owl has spoken.

With a swift downward thrust of his wings, the Owl is in the air and heading toward the Woodpecker. The animals go into the barnyard to complete their assigned task.

An hour passes before the animals begin to return, gathering around the Woodpecker and sharing their findings. When the last animal, the Sheep, steps away from the barn, the results are clear. Several of the animals don expressions of surprise.

"This is exactly why we term this exercise *discovering* values. Typically, each member of an organization has solid grounding in what they interpret to be values that are critical to the group as a whole. Once these opinions are brought together, however, the collective belief structure comes to light. As we can see from your findings and Woodpecker's chart, the top three values for Lean Acres are *determination, flexibility,* and *connection.* Does anyone disagree?" The Owl looks to each member of the group.

"I do as an individual," states the Pig, "but not for the farm. I can see how these three values summarize the key aspects of our culture."

"They appear to support our core competencies as well, with a direct correlation between 'effective and efficient teamwork' and 'connection.' Is this considered normal?" the Cat asks.

"Normal? No. But good? Yes," the Owl responds. "Too often, organizations develop strategies that lack support in their roots. The fact that your values support your core competencies, which in turn support your mission, is an indication of an integrated structure in your base strategy. We will need to carry this forward as we look to tomorrow and develop the heart of our strategy and the trunk of our Strate-Tree, our vision."

Flexibility	X	X	X	X	X	X	X	X	X	X	X	X		
Structure	X	X	X	X	X									
Freedom	X	X	X											
Enthusiasm	X	X	X	X	X	X								
Determination	X	X	X	X	X	X	X	X	X	X	X	X	X	
Connection	X	X	X	X	X	X	X	X	X	X	X	X		
Integrity	X	X	X	X	X	X	X	X						

Vision and Goals

"Where are we going with this, Owl?" the Jackass bellows, slightly annoyed.

"Our vision explains where we are going," says the Owl. "Each of you needs to consider what our customers want, what our strengths and weaknesses are, what opportunities and threats we face, what values we believe in, what core competencies we demonstrate, and what our mission is. Take all of that in, consider every aspect, and then tell us all where we are going as Lean Acres Farm. Ideally, what does our future look like?"

The animals fall silent in thought, some looking out across the pens, some into the fields, and others at the different statements and analyses captured by the Woodpecker.

"Shouldn't we aim to be the best?" inquires the Bull.

"That all depends on what you mean when you say 'the best,'" answers the Owl. "What does 'the best' mean to you?"

"Technically, we are the best now," interjects the Cat. "At the market we serve around half of all the people, or customers. The other farms provide for the rest. So we deliver about 50 percent of all the products in Perfection while the others capture approximately 17 percent each."

"Thank you, Cat," the Owl responds. "So, at 50 percent of the *market share*, or the portion of the market that you provide for, you are technically the best. However, as we learned in our SWOT analysis, your competition is closing in fast. With a vision statement, you want to set a *stretch goal*—a high-level achievement that will be difficult but not impossible to reach—or a series of such goals. You will also need to make that goal a number or percentage, something that you can measure and verify. You should also include how long you will have to achieve the goal, and where you will be competing. A good way to remember the requirements of a goal is that it should be SMARTER. This stands for *specific, measurable, aligned, realistic, time-oriented, evaluated,* and *reviewed*. For establishing goals, we will focus on the SMART attributes. As we manage the goals, they will be SMARTER."

"How about this?" the Horse offers. "In the next year, we will serve 75 percent of the market."

"That is a good start," replies the Owl. "Does anyone have any comments?"

"I do," sounds the Rooster. "I think that it will take longer than a year to achieve that increased share of the market customers, and I also think that 75 percent is not a high enough target. Let's aim for 100 percent!"

The Chicken nearly explodes. "100 percent! All of the customers! That's impossible! We've already lost some due to the issues that we are facing, and we won't get them back! Be reasonable here! We'll never hit that!"

"Settle down, Chicken. You're having a *molt*-down!" exclaims the Pig. "What about something in the middle. Say we aim for 90 percent of the market share. That still allows for some customers that we have lost for good, but keeps our sights set high."

The Chicken settles as much as she can, and agrees along with the rest of the team.

"How long will it take to make this vision a reality?" asks the Owl. "Is one year enough time?"

"Aggressively, we might be able to pull it off in three years," voices the Dog. "That would give us just enough time and trips to the market to assess our progress and change our practices as necessary. It will be tight, but we just might be able to do it."

The Dog looks across the group from face to face. Everyone agrees, and he continues. "So, maybe our vision is this: In three years, we will serve 90 percent of the market."

The animals like what they hear, and the Owl speaks.

"This is going well. A vision should be specific, so make sure that you include *where* this will be done."

"You mean in Perfection?" the Cow asks.

"Absolutely," answers the Owl.

"Alright," the Horse steps forward. "How about this? In three years, Lean Acres Farm will capture 90 percent of the total market share in the state of Perfection."

"I like it," says the Bull, "but I'm concerned that we have forgotten something, one of our key threats. Our reasoning behind all of this is to prevent any more *cuts* on our farm. No more animals to the Boo-chair. How do we incorporate that into our vision?"

"Through *phasing*," the Owl answers. "For some organizations, a simple vision statement and goal set, with a singular timeline for execution, is appropriate. Others require a phased vision, one that occurs over time, addressing immediate needs and progressing toward a *big, hairy, audacious goal*, or a 'BHAG.' One hundred percent of the market share is a good example of a BHAG. Does anyone want to try putting all of this together?"

"I will," the Cow responds. "Okay, let me see. From now on, zero animals will be cut. In three years, Lean Acres Farm will capture 90 percent of the total market share in the state of Perfection. In five years, we will capture 100 percent of the market share."

"That sounds good, Cow," barks the Dog. "Maybe we can make it more concise. Tell me what you think of this: 'Zero animals will be cut on Lean Acres. In three years, we will capture 90 percent of the total market share in the state of Perfection. In five years, we will be the sole provider.'"

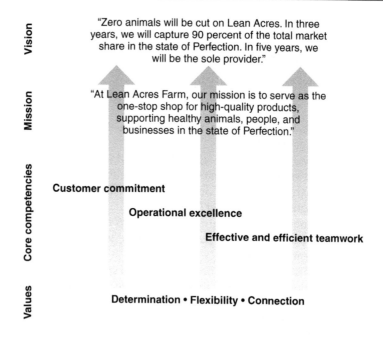

Vision
"Zero animals will be cut on Lean Acres. In three years, we will capture 90 percent of the total market share in the state of Perfection. In five years, we will be the sole provider."

Mission
"At Lean Acres Farm, our mission is to serve as the one-stop shop for high-quality products, supporting healthy animals, people, and businesses in the state of Perfection."

Core competencies
Customer commitment

Operational excellence

Effective and efficient teamwork

Values
Determination • Flexibility • Connection

"It's aggressive! It's inspiring! We can do it! I like it! I like it a lot!" belts out the Chicken. The other members of the team voice their approval as well.

"Outstanding," reports the Owl, "simply outstanding. We have values that support core competencies that drive our mission and enable our vision and goals. To top it off, our goals are *specific, measurable, aligned* to our vision, *realistic,* and *time-oriented.* Go home and rest for the night. Tomorrow, meet me in the barn and we will work on growing some branches."

The animals are smiling and talking as they depart, excited about the progress that they have made thus far, and anticipating the challenge ahead. The Owl meets with the Woodpecker as he finishes jotting the vision at the apex of the barn face, and then retires for a quick nap before his evening meal.

Step 3: Alignment

As the sun crests the horizon, Lean Acres springs to life at the call of the Rooster. The pigs shuffle off to the Hen House, and the sheep graze in lush green fields. The F.A.T. representatives are moving into the barn as a group, sharing thoughts and listening to ideas. The Owl is perched squarely on the crate, and he smiles as they enter.

"Good morning!" he calls to the group. Surprisingly, most of them repeat the greeting with equal enthusiasm.

"Today we will finish developing our strategic plan, or growing our Strate-Tree, as I like to say. We will be developing goals, objectives, targets, and initiatives, and leaving with a solid communication plan. Are you ready to get started?"

"Let's do this!" shouts the Cow. The other animals laugh in agreement, and demonstrate motivation each in their own way.

Objectives and Targets

"Now that we have developed our vision and goals, we need to figure out exactly what it will take to achieve them. To do this, we will consider our present situation and look forward to our vision. It is the gap in between that we need to cover with specific objectives—stepping-stones, if you will—guiding us out of the present and into the future of Lean Acres. This gap analysis will result in a path, and that path is the 'how' of our strategy. So the question is: How will you ensure that no animals are sent to the Boo-chair, and that we capture 90 and eventually 100 percent of the market share at the farm market?"

"Should we follow the *voice of the customer*?" asks the Pig.

"That is a great idea," returns the Owl. "What has the customer told us that we need to do?"

"According to the Mice, or the voice of the customer, we need to produce eggs with fewer cracks, fluffy wool, milk with a consistent good taste, and corn that isn't spoiled or crushed," the Horse replies. "And since we are always running out of corn, milk, eggs, and wool at the market, I suppose that we need to make more all around."

The Owl responds, "I will caution you against simply increasing production, Horse, and here's why. No matter how much we actually make, the only products that truly count are those that make it to the market. A focus on producing more in and of itself can actually hurt a farm like this. We need to keep all of our targets centered on the idea that we need to get more corn, eggs, and wool to and eventually sold at the farm market."

"But we've always measured what we've produced," grunts the Pig. "That's how we know how hard everyone is working!"

The team members chime in collectively, and the Owl pauses until the conversations lull to a manageable din. When the time is right, he speaks.

"I understand your concerns, and we will need to make another fundamental change here on Lean Acres Farm. Historically, when you have measured, you probably have been measuring activity. This has included carts harvested, eggs gathered, milk 'milked,' and wool sheared."

"It's usually worse than that. We just can't seem to measure what we do," the Sheep adds. "We do chores different ways depending on the animal in charge and the situation, and we've never been able to get a clear picture of our operations."

"The problem that you are having is not uncommon," continues the Owl. "The measures you are attempting to wrangle are effort- or task-based, with an internal focus, and they are blind to and independent of the customers and the farm as a whole. We have captured the *voice of the customer* and analyzed it in our discussions with the Mice. We also have heard the *voice of the farm*, or the *voice of the busy-ness*, as the humans say, and Lean Acres clearly needs to get more green paper from the customers in order to survive. Believe it or not, there is another voice that could come into play here, and that is the *voice of the workforce*. The animals on the farm team might want you to focus on issues that they face as well, but we will get to that later. Right now, in developing our strategy and growing our Strate-Tree we need to align with two of the voices—our customers and our farm—and we need to measure the results. The customer doesn't necessarily want you to work harder; they just want the end result of your labors. And, if you can do this by working smarter, you can pass some of the rewards, some of the savings, on to them, delighting them beyond their expectations. With more excited customers, Lean Acres will then acquire more and more green paper, and the Farmer will not have to cut any animals. We will listen to and apply these voices. We will improve your performance results and increase customer loyalty, both of which support your vision."

"So, let me get this straight," the Dog speaks. "I think I understand. It's not enough that we work to make products here. We need to make sure that enough of the goods make it to the market, that they are in the condition that the customer expects, and what we really care about is that these products are sold."

"Spot on," comments the Owl.

"Then we have been doing things wrong here," sighs the Dog. "What you say makes too much sense. Would an objective that is results-oriented sound anything like this: Increase egg sales?"

"Yes, Dog, you have got it," replies the Owl. "Now, how much do you want to increase the number of eggs? What do you sell now?"

The Cat perks up and reports, "We move anywhere between ten and twenty dozen eggs to the market each day. We produce more, but they all don't make it to the stand."

"Can we double that, Rooster?" the Dog asks.

The Rooster confers with the Chicken and the Cat, and after some heated squawking and meowing, the Rooster emerges.

"If you mean forty dozen each day, it will be close, but I think we can handle that."

"Then, the objective becomes 'Increase egg sales to 3360 per week,' right, Owl?" asks the Dog.

"Absolutely right," the Owl answers.

"How are we suddenly going to double egg sales?" the Jackass cries out. "We can't even get enough to the market now!"

"The 'how' concerning the objectives will be answered as we develop the initiatives, Jackass," states the Owl. "We will get to that as soon as our objectives and targets are set. Now, what about another objective? What about the wool?"

"They want it to be fluffier," sounds the Sheep.

"How much fluffier?" asks the Owl.

"We're not entirely clear on that, Owl," the Bull responds. "What we do know is that our product is ending up at the market as flat as a board. We also use too many pigs to run the process. We have four in there now, but we really need to get it down to two. We need the others to help with the feeding process that spans across all of the pens. We're selling out our wool at the market, but according to the Mice, our customers are starting to go to Cumulous Hills. Can we aim for providing fluffy wool versus the current flat wool? Is that measurable?"

"Yes and no," answers the Owl. "To increase from flat to fluffed could be considered the same as increasing from zero to one. This is an infinity percent increase. We could consider our aim to provide this quality characteristic as a satisfier for our customers. They are buying all of our wool, as flat as it may be, but they prefer to have it in a fluffy state. And now you will need to do it with fewer pigs in the shack. What is your proposal?"

"What about 'Increase wool sales'?!" asks the Chicken.

"We need to say by how much," interjects the Pig. "If we do dedicate time and energy to improving the shearing process, how much could we really get out?"

"I'm not sure," says the Horse. "We just don't have the capacity for quantity *and* quality."

"If you did," starts the Owl, "what do you think you could do? What should we aim for?"

"Well," the Cat answers, "I believe we deliver twenty bags each day, but most of that is flat wool. Making fluffier wool and more of it with less help? That's a tall order. I guess in keeping with our first objective, I would vote that we aim to double that."

"Forty bags per day?" questions the Pig. "280 bags each week?"

"You must be crazy," brays the Jackass.

"I'm not crazy," the Cat responds, "but I am setting an aggressive target. Is it completely out of our range?"

"I don't think that it is," responds the Sheep. "If we are going to take a look at our shearing process, we might be able to find room for improvement."

"I agree," the Dog announces. "Don't be afraid to push the boundaries here, folks. If we shoot for numbers just beyond our reach and fall short, we will still have improved."

"Okay then. Let's go for 280 bags per week. But let's really go for it," the Rooster crows.

"What is your second objective, then?" asks the Owl.

It is the Sheep that answers. "'Increase wool sales,' and our target is 280 bags per week."

The animals are getting excited. Most of the energy is very positive. Some doubt remains in the barn, but it is becoming a healthy counter that tests assumptions and validates targets. They continue the exercise developing objectives, and before long the last splinter has left the Woodpecker's beak on its way to the hay below. He flies across the barn and begins working in another area.

"Take a look at what we have." The Owl directs the animals' attention to the four objectives carved into the wood. "Test these in your minds. Are they *specific* to our farm, and to the core work that we perform? Are they *measurable*? Are they *aligned* to our strategy? Are they *realistic*? Are they *time-oriented*?"

The animals stare at the objectives while their minds work over the criteria.

"I believe that the answer is yes, Owl." The Cow nods as she offers her opinion. The others voice their approval, and even more important, their understanding. "I am concerned, though. We're trying to estimate what we can do and how much we think the customer wants, but we only have our anecdotes, and the Mice are gone, or at least I think they are."

"What an outstanding observation, Cow," returns the Owl, "and I am glad to hear that you are concerned. The ideal situation for growing the Strate-Tree would entail sufficient time and effort for research and analysis. However, in our dire situation, we are basing our targets on your experience and expertise. But these are only preliminary measures. As we dive

| Increase egg sales (3360/week) | Increase wool sales (280 bags/week) | Increase milk sales (500 gallons/week) | Increase corn sales (350 carts/week) |

deeper into each strategic objective and engage in improvement efforts, each discipline that we use will require that we measure our performance and constantly pulse our customers for measurable requirements. With that information in hand, we will be able to tend to the Strate-Tree, update existing targets, and establish new ones as well. This will increase your overall agility here on Lean Acres—the flexibility with which you can respond to your customers' needs."

"You mean that the Strate-Tree can change once we're done with it?" asks the Bull.

"Actually," the Owl asserts, "you will never be done with it. The Strate-Tree is a dynamic, living thing. If it is to survive, and Lean Acres as well, it will have to adapt to its environment. Consider it to be a hypothesis that is constantly being tested. New branches will grow, the old will be pruned, and all the while the strength of your organization will improve."

"*How* are we going to do all of this? I mean, hey, this is great conversation and all, and I enjoy a good fantasy a much as the next animal. But I just don't see how we are going to get all of this done," the Jackass states.

"Let us talk about that now," answers the Owl. "Let us talk about *how* and *who*."

Step 4: Assignment

Ownership and Accountability

"Come with me, please." The Owl motions for the animals to follow him to a set of planks off to the left of the crate. The planks have lines and names etched into them, but there are also a number of empty squares.

"This," says the Owl, "is what the humans call a RACI chart."

"A *racing* chart?!" squawks the Chicken.

"No, no. A *RACI* chart," the Owl assures the Chicken. "RACI stands for *responsible, accountable, consulted*, and *informed*. It will help us to discuss, understand, and capture the different roles that each animal will play in the accomplishment of our four objectives. Now, when we say that someone is *responsible*, this is the animal who will get the work done. In the performance improvement vernacular, we call this individual the *sponsor*. This animal should own the process that is being affected by the improvement effort and be able to make any required changes. Whoever is *accountable* for an objective is the animal who is answerable in the end for any success or failure. The *responsible* animal reports to the accountable one, who is also called a *champion*. *Champions* ensure the discipline, diligence, and ultimately the success of the deployment by developing and enforcing policies and demonstrating active interest

	Dog	Bull	Rooster	Cat	Chicken	Horse	Pig	Sheep	Cow	Jackass
Increase egg sales (3360/week)										
Increase wool sales (280 bags/week)										
Increase milk sales (500 gallons/week)										
Increase corn sales (350 carts/week)										

and participation. Several sponsors can report to a single champion, but there should only be one of each role for any particular effort. Those who are *consulted* are typically subject matter experts, and they usually provide information as requested prior to a final decision being made. They provide 'sanity checks,' and make sure that the objective action groups have the input that they need to generate feasible solutions. We have discussions, or two-way communication with these folks. Finally, there are those who need to be *informed*. The *informed* are those who will need to be told what happened after a solution or an improvement is implemented, because they will be affected by it, or they will need to take specific action in order to support it. This is one-way communication, typically in the form of a report. Now, you might notice that the Farmer is not listed on our matrix. He is what we call an *executive*. *Executives* support, monitor, and direct change, but are not active participants in the tactical implementation. That is our job here in the barnyard. We need to discuss each of your roles in accomplishing the four strategic objectives. May I suggest that we take them in order, one at a time, and progress from animal to animal as listed on the chart?"

"That sounds good, Owl," says the Dog. "Initially, I was going to state that I would be accountable for each of the objectives, but that might be too much, even for a Dog. I recommend that the Bull and I alternate accountability across the four objectives, and I will start it off by taking the first."

The Bull nods in his direction from across the barn.

"And by the definitions you provided, that would make me the responsible party," the Rooster states. "I run the Hen House, and I should be the one to make sure that the work gets done, right?"

"I could not agree more, Rooster," offers the Owl.

The Rooster continues, "I would also like to suggest that I consult with the Cat and the Pig. The Cat is our technical expert, and the Pigs gather and transport all of the eggs. What do you guys think?"

"I agree," the Cat concurs.

"So do I," says the Pig, "but I also think that I should be informed in the end, being as we do all of the work in the Hen House."

The Rooster's chest flares, and the Chicken's eyes grow wide. The Pig takes immediate notice and adds, "What I meant to say is, we carry all of the precious cargo. That's all."

Pig punishment by poultry has been averted. For now.

"Please take a look at what the Woodpecker has detailed, and provide any additional comments or corrections as necessary," the Owl proposes to the team. No further information is offered. After several silent moments, the Owl moves on.

"Very well. We have established accountability and ownership for our first objective. What about the second—increasing wool sales?"

"I believe that I will be accountable for that objective," the Bull responds.

"And I will be responsible," the Pig chimes in. "As the Rooster runs the Hen House, we pigs manage the entire shearing operation. I'll take this objective on, unless of course the sheep disagree."

The Sheep speaks softly, but firmly. "No problem there. That would leave us with the *consulted* role, I suppose. And maybe the *informed* role as well."

The other team members agree, and the Jackass speaks up.

"I think that I might fit that role as well," he offers. "While the pigs are shearing, I am packing and moving the bags out to the carts. I might have some experience to share, and I will definitely need to know about any changes that are made, in order to do my job properly. I might be stubborn, but I'm definitely a hard worker."

The Jackass receives confirmation from his teammates, and for the first time dares to smell hope in the air.

"Let us see what we have here," suggests the Owl. "Any issues or concerns?"

The team is actively engaged now, and to his surprise and delight, the animals continue the exercise until the RACI chart is complete.

"I think we've got it, Owl," the Dog remarks. "How did we do?"

"We can answer your question with a standard analysis of the results," the Owl returns. "Look up and down each single column and tell me what you see. Are there too many R's or A's in any one column? Are there any columns with no empty spaces? Are the roles detailed in each column appropriate for the individual assigned? What do you see?"

"I see a pretty even spread," the Horse remarks. "Sure, the Bull has two accountability roles and one responsibility role, but that's normal. He's a frontline supervisor. I think that the other assignments fit the individuals as well."

The Bull nods with determination and pride.

"I agree with the Horse," the Cow adds. "We can do this, we should do this, moreover, we need to do this."

"This is terrific work," the Owl commends. "It looks like the Dog and the Bull will serve as our *champions*. They are certainly at the appropriate level on the farm. The Rooster, the Pig, the Horse, and the Bull will be our *sponsors*. The Bull is wearing different hats for different efforts, and in small organizations that is to be expected. Now let us talk about what *getting to this* will entail."

	Dog	Bull	Rooster	Cat	Chicken	Horse	Pig	Sheep	Cow	Jackass
Increase egg sales (3360/week)	A		R	C	I		C/I			
Increase wool sales (280 bags/week)		A					R	C/I		C/I
Increase milk sales (500 gallons/week)	A	R		C					C/I	
Increase corn sales (350 carts/week)		A				R	I			C/I

Initiatives

"This is a simple exercise, more of a conversation, that we will engage in to break the objectives down into the next-larger pieces. I have witnessed human beings overcomplicating this pursuit to a frustrating and eventually fruitless level, and I want to make certain that we do not fall into that trap. That being said, think about the two to three actions or steps that we will need to accomplish in order to achieve each of our objectives."

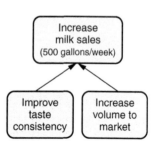

"What do you mean, Owl?" asks the Cow.

"Well, Cow," the Owl responds, "what will it take for Lean Acres to increase their egg sales and hit the 3360 eggs per week target?"

"I think it's pretty obvious," the Cow contends. "First we need to eliminate the cracks in the eggs, and then we need to get more over to the market, right?"

The other animals agree with the Cow and then look to the Owl.

"That is it!" the Owl exclaims. "It does not have to be harder than that. Now, the follow-on *how*, or how we will accomplish each of these two initiatives, will be decided after further evaluation of the situation and additional study of available methodologies like lean, Six Sigma, and a couple of others. But for now, these are outstanding strategic initiatives. What do we need to do for the others?"

"Some of the corn is spoiling before I can get it all to the market, so I can never get enough there," the Horse says. "So, if we are going to increase sales, we need to increase the volume and stop the spoilage."

"Let's face it," the Cat interrupts, "we need to get more of all of our products to the market in order to increase sales. It would be great to sell more milk, but we will need to focus on the taste factor first. If we get more to the customer in its current state, we will only accelerate our loss and our trip to the Boo-chair. I believe that all of our initiatives will have to be balanced for each objective, providing improved quality and increased quantity, if we are going to achieve our vision. Looking over our work thus far, I would say that we are inherently doing this."

"Well said, Cat," the Owl comments, "and on target as usual. Who would like to tackle the final objective?"

"I would," the Sheep calls. "Besides, this last bit is my bag."

The joke is not lost on the crowd. Laughter ripples across the group, and as it settles, the Sheep continues.

"At the start of this exercise I was confused, and I probably would have come forward with something like 'increase fluffiness.' But in this case

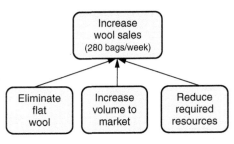

I would offer that besides an initiative directed at increasing the amount of wool that we are delivering to market, we should establish an initiative to eliminate the flat wool, and another to free up some workers. If we figure out how to do this and hit our 280 bags per week target, we should be working our way toward our vision. What do you guys think?"

"You know what I think?" begins the Jackass. "I think, well, I think you nailed it, Sheep."

Jaws drop around the barn, and the Owl smiles.

"Next," replies the Owl, "we spread the word. Come with me."

Step 5: Awareness

The Owl leads the animals outside. The farm is brimming with life, and the sky couldn't be more blue.

"What do you see?" the Owl asks.

"I see the farm," replies the Horse.

"And all of the animals!" adds the Chicken.

"And what do each of them see every day, what really stands out here on Lean Acres?" the Owl returns.

"Each other?" answers the Cow.

"No, Cow, it's the barn," the Bull adds. "This barn was the first structure built here by the Farmer. It's the biggest building we've got."

"Right," says the Owl. "The animals used to look at the barn every day, but from now on, they will see this . . ."

The Owl turns the corner and faces the broad side of the barn, the side that faces all of the pens and the Farmer's house. The red, painted wood is covered with detailed carvings. The image runs the height and width of the wall, and the words flow clearly across it. It is the Strate-Tree

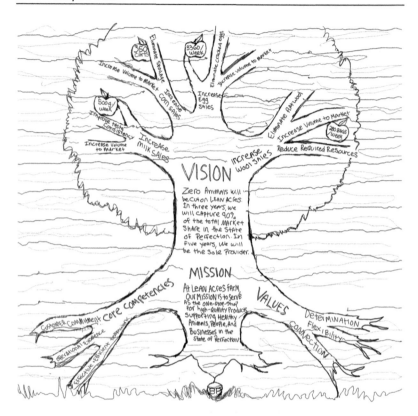

in its most current form, with all of the groups' inputs and creations integrated from its roots to its branches. Every animal stares, seeing a piece of themselves in the picture, and the future of Lean Acres in its details.

"Go and talk with your fellow animals," the Owl says. "Gather their opinions and thoughts, and share the rationale behind the Strate-Tree's structure, growth, and purpose. Make sure that you are actively listening to their words, and be prepared to answer their call for WIIFMs."

"What is a WIIFM?" asks the Dog.

"It stands for 'What's in it for me,' Dog," the Owl responds. "In order to gain the other animals' buy-in, it will be critical for us to apply the strategy from their perspective. The Strate-Tree, our strategy, can not belong to our group alone. If it is to thrive, it must belong to every individual in the entire organization. When it is owned, it will be integrated. When it is integrated, there will be commitment. When the animals are all committed, it will be successful."

"How do we start?" the Rooster inquires.

"Go out there and start conversations," the Owl answers. "Focus on the individual you are sharing with, and focus on the broad side of the barn. Let the Strate-Tree guide your conversation from the soil to its leaves. Let each animal know that the strategy belongs to them and to Lean Acres, and that it is dependent on them for victory, and they are dependent on it for survival. I will meet you in the barn tomorrow morning. The real work starts at sunrise."

With that, the Owl turns and takes to the air. He soars over the fields and into the bordering woods, disappearing in shadow. The animals spread out across the barnyard, and before long, all eyes and discussions are on the barn.

Rest/Reflect/Relate (R³)

1. What is your organization's strategy? How do you know? Is it communicated through an official document or plan? If not, do communications (verbal, electronic, publications, and so on) from your leadership present common themes or areas of emphasis? For example, a newsletter from the vice president of operations may repeatedly review safety statistics and delivery ratings, a potential indicator of strategic focus areas.

2. What are your mission, core competencies, values, and vision? How often are they updated? Who created them? Are they relevant? What inputs are used to review them?

3. What does your organization's strategy mean to you? What is the WIIFM from your perspective?

Chapter 5

Born in a Barn

Another flaw in the human character is that everybody wants to build and nobody wants to do maintenance.

—Kurt Vonnegut Jr.

I trust that you have enjoyed the journey thus far. The animals have completed the first five steps of the 7A approach (*assessment, aim, alignment, assignment,* and *awareness*) and will soon realize that the poor condition of their working environment—the barnyard—presents obstacles to performance improvement. The Owl is about to engage them in the *academics* phase of the 7A approach, and teach them the principles of 7S (*sort, straighten, shine, standardize, sustain, safety,* and *security*) and *visual management.* The animals will take this new knowledge and use it in the barnyard in the *action* phase, setting the stage for the application of lean, Six Sigma, the theory of constraints, and business process reengineering within their four key production areas. Get comfortable. Sit back and observe with me.

Dawn breaks on a new day. The Rooster announces the morning as the sun crests the trees that border the farm. Each animal pen scurries into consciousness, and while all mouths are engaged in their meals all eyes and thoughts are focused on the large words and drawings that cover the barn. As soon as the Rooster issues his last call, he purposefully struts across the yard to catch up with his farm-mates as they approach the barn door.

As the animal team forms a herd in the barn, the Owl descends from the rafters.

"Good morning to you all!" he shouts as he lands on the crate. "How was your evening?"

"We were just discussing that, Owl," the Dog replies. "Our fellow farm-mates were excited about our new strategy, and the Strate-Tree provided an excellent reference point for our conversations."

"Yes!" clucks the Chicken. "The girls were enthusiastic about a plan to eliminate cuts and cracks!"

"And the ladies in the cow pen were thankful for the attention to the quality of our milk," adds the Cow.

The Bull snorts once and then speaks. "This is all well and good, and I agree that the farm was wound up last night, but there was some negative feedback as well. I roamed from pen to pen and discovered a recurring theme."

The rest of the team nods, recognizing the issue each in their own mind before the Bull continues.

"What was the feedback?" the Owl asks.

"What about us?" the Pig responds. "We addressed our customer needs and those of our farm, but we did not address the needs of the animals here on the farm, beyond survival. Don't get me wrong," he continues, "survival is our number one goal, but in order to achieve that, we might need to handle a few things in the barnyard first."

"And what are these things?" the Owl encourages the team.

"The barnyard is a wreck!" brays the Jackass.

"I agree," the Horse whinnies. "We have old and new baskets, bags, and cart parts piled together here and there, and bales of hay—which, by the way, we don't even harvest anymore—stacked to the sky."

"And there are the corn carts," adds the Sheep. "They're parked all over the place and never in the same place twice."

"If I may," the Cat begins, "we also experience gridlock on a regular basis. The Horse and the Jackass pull the corn carts through the pen aisles differently from week to week. There have been some real close calls

where we have almost lost some of our smaller fellow workers, including me."

"I nearly molted when I almost got buried in bags last week!" the Chicken screams.

"We only operate that way because of the bags and baskets that the pigs leave around the yard! They're always somewhere new and they're always falling over," the Horse interjects.

"What are we supposed to do?" grunts the Pig. "We're working overtime and then some. If you were in our hooves . . ."

The Owl hoots over the group. "Fellow animals and teammates, believe it or not, this is all good news."

"I think that you might have spun your head around one too many times, Owl," the Jackass says.

"Not at all, Jackass," continues the Owl, "but thank you for your concern. This is good news because we have now heard the voice of the workforce and can incorporate it into the deployment of our strategic plan. This is a good example of how some initiatives in our plan are strategic—from the top down—driven by the customer and the farm, and some are tactical—from the bottom up—driven by the workforce. Our Strate-Tree will grow a new branch for the right reason. We can focus on workforce safety, and even aim for zero injuries and zero near-misses as preliminary targets. After all, no one wants to get hurt. There are specific methodologies or approaches precisely intended for this type of situation. We will begin with 7S and continue through establishing a visual workplace. Are you ready?"

The animals take their places around the crate, and the Owl begins.

Step 6: Academics

7S and the Visual Barnyard

"Whenever you encounter a situation that involves an environment, like your barnyard, that inhibits progress or evokes safety hazards, you can rely on the 7S approach to see you through," the Owl reports.

"What is the 7S approach?" the Sheep asks.

"Quite simply," the Owl responds, "it stands for five continuous actions and two focus points. The actions are: (1) *sort*, (2) *set in order*, (3) *shine*, (4) *standardize*, and (5) *sustain the discipline*. The two focus points are *safety* and *security*. In essence, we will sort through the material and equipment in the barnyard, separating the good from the bad. We will mark the undesirable stuff with a stripe of red paint, consolidate it all in an area, and then dispose of it. Next, we will take all of the remaining equipment and put each grouping of items in a place in an orderly fashion. We will also mark and label the place for each item or group of items to let others know exactly where they should be placed. Then we will clean the barnyard, including all of the items that we have determined are good."

"So this is like a spring cleaning?" the Cow inquires.

"Absolutely not," replies the Owl. "We will need to standardize our efforts so that they can be repeated on a regular basis. This is a workplace maintenance and improvement methodology, and we will need to come up with a way to make certain that this becomes an expected practice in the culture here on Lean Acres. Many different groups use inspections and a checklist to do just that. Not only will the barnyard be clean and organized, but it will also be *safe* and *secure*."

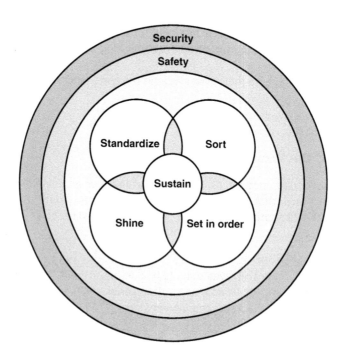

"How will cleaning up make us safe and secure?" the Cat asks.

"Quite simply, by uncovering potential problems," answers the Owl.

"I get it! I get it!" the Chicken declares. "If we keep the floor clean in the Hen House, we might be able to find those weasel holes! They keep stealing our eggs!"

"And I guess if we organize the equipment and mark paths for the carts, we could make the barnyard a safer place to live," adds the Bull.

"Exactly. By sustaining the first five S's, we can achieve two key overarching objectives for any workplace, those being safety and security. We can also become more visual here on the farm. *Visual management* is often integrated with the 7S approach to reinforce the discipline. We can use visual signals and controls to manage the traffic and organize your equipment. In a visual workplace, we use simple visual indicators to help animals know whether they are using the desired standard condition or if they are deviating from it," asserts the Owl.

"Are you ready to get started?"

"Yes," sounds the Pig, "but how do we begin?"

"By 'rolling up our sleeves' as the humans say, and getting to work. Let us go outside."

Step 7: Action

The animals leave the barn and step into the blinding sunlight. As they recover their vision, and thanks to their most recent instruction, they perceive the barnyard in a new way. Following their discussions concerning the issues around the property, some are having trouble seeing the yard through the "mess" altogether.

"What should we fix first?" the Owl asks.

"Well," begins the Dog, "we sure heard a lot about the egg baskets and the wool bags. And from here, I can see them all over, around every pen. Can we start with those?"

"Let us do it," the Owl responds.

Busted Baskets and Bags

"First, I will need each of you to step forward and dip your tails into this." The Owl steps aside and reveals an old bucket of red paint.

"You want us to do *what*?!" the Chicken cries.

"Settle down, Chicken," the Owl answers. "You will be going down into the yard and inspecting every egg basket and wool bag that you find there. When you come across a basket with a hole in it or a broken handle, or a bag that is torn, you will need to mark that item with a red stripe. This will indicate that the bag or basket is unfit for use and that it should be disposed of. This is part of the 7S methodology and is called a *red tag* program. Do you understand?"

"Yes!" the Chicken blurts, "But my feathers . . ."

"Don't worry," the Bull asserts, "that paint will come off in the pond." The Chicken relaxes . . . a little bit . . . for now.

One by one the animals step forward and plunge their tails—fur and feathers—into the open pail and then proceed into the barnyard to conduct their inspection. Two hours pass before their task is complete, and the Owl meets with them in the barnyard.

"How did we do?" the Owl asks.

"Well, we finished," the Sheep responds through hushed huffs.

The Cat responds as well. "I noticed that a lot of baskets and bags I looked through were broken in one way or another. And then on my way over here to meet the team, I saw red stripes everywhere. Do we really have this many 'bad' items on the farm?"

"Apparently we do," the Dog replies. "It is very obvious to me now."

The other team members crane their necks to look around the yard and are somewhat surprised by the red bombardment before them. The scene is reminiscent of a woven war with wounded warriors from two armies—baskets and bags—lying scattered across the battlefield. A long moment passes before the Pig speaks.

"What do we do now?"

"Now," starts the Owl, "we complete the sort phase by removing the items with red stripes. We need to gather the baskets and bags that are marked and move them to an isolated area where they can be disposed of."

"All right, let's get moving," calls the Dog. "Horse, you and the Jackass can each pull a cart. Pig and Cow, you can help gather the marked items. When you've got them all, go ahead and stack them by the big silver cans outside of the Farmer's house. There are some men that come by in a truck that makes a terrible noise. They empty out the cans and grab anything near them and throw it in the back."

"What about the rest of us?" asks the Rooster.

"We will need to set everything in order," replies the Owl. "A helpful phrase to remember concerning the 7S approach is this, 'A place for everything and everything in its place.' So, we don't want to simply put all of the good items back where they were. We will need to designate the best place for baskets and the best place for bags, and then place them there in an orderly fashion. Does that make sense?"

"Too much sense," says the Bull. "Why haven't we done this before?"

"You've probably performed individual S's throughout your entire life," the Owl answers. "How many times have any one of us straightened up an area, cleaned a floor, or thrown away unwanted 'stuff'? The difference with the 7S approach is that the core elements work together in a perpetual cycle. It provides a disciplined program that helps to ensure success."

"I'm starting to understand and see the value in this idea," the Dog comments.

"Good," responds the Owl. "While the Horse, Bull, Pig, Jackass, and Cow are collecting and relocating our 'red tag' baskets and bags, we should talk about best location ideas for the remaining items."

"Okay, I have an idea," sounds the Rooster. "Let's put all of the bags behind the Shearing Shack and all of the baskets behind the Hen House. That way we can have each group in the right place, and they will be out of our way. No more tripping over baskets or snagging claws on burlap."

"That is an interesting idea, Rooster," the Owl replies. "Does anyone else think that the rear of each of the respective buildings is the best place for the baskets and bags?"

"I agree," begins the Cat "that they should be stored in a safe area, but it might make gathering eggs and wool difficult if the equipment is located at the rear of each building. Neither has a back door, so the pigs would have to do a lot of work just to get any baskets or bags that they might need. I think that the time that it could take would eventually add up, and delays could hurt our progress toward our strategic goals."

"I have an idea," the Sheep mutters.

"Let us hear it, Sheep," encourages the Owl.

"What if we stacked the baskets and bags on both sides of the opening into the Hen House and the Shearing Shack? They would be accessible *and* out of the way."

"I like it," the Rooster says, "but how will we keep animals from treading on or tripping over them?"

The Sheep continues. "I think that the Owl told us a little about something called a *visual workplace*. We could clearly mark the areas for the baskets and bags on the ground and even make signs identifying and reserving that space." The Sheep finishes and looks toward its front hooves as they scratch at the dirt.

"This sounds like a plan," the Dog inserts. "Owl, are we moving in the right direction?"

"You may have already arrived," the Owl replies.

"Let's get to it, team!" barks the Dog.

The Rooster, the Dog, the Sheep, the Cat, and the Chicken scamper excitedly into the barnyard and begin stacking bags and baskets in their appropriate areas, forming one column of items on either side of the building doors. When they have completed the gathering and setting, the Dog runs into the barn. There is what sounds like a brief tussle, and he emerges with several smaller wooden planks in his mouth. With a full mouth and without a word he returns to his teammates. The Cat and the Dog work with the planks to form a square at the base of each stack, and the Sheep begins to tamp the planks down with her strong rear legs. The Rooster and the Chicken are working with the Woodpecker, who is tapping something into the front left side of the Hen House, just above the tower of baskets. They move to the right side and then on to the Shearing Shack. The Cat is busy inspecting each stack of equipment, ensuring that they are straight and, more importantly, safe. The Horse, the Cow, the Bull, the Pig, and the Jackass return from their task and rally with their farm-mates. The Owl sees that they are all smiling. Before long, the Dog howls for the Owl to join them. He is in front of the Shearing Shack in seconds.

"What do you think?" asks the Rooster.

The Owl observes the front of the shack. The bags are piled neatly on each side of the door. There are wooden planks on the ground forming a box around the base of each column. The Woodpecker has carved "Wool Bags" on the front of the building above each stack, and also on the front plank of each foundational box. The Owl walks with the team to the Hen House and, after looking at the results in detail, he speaks.

"What I *know* is that you have completed the first two steps of the 7S methodology for this portion of the barnyard. You have sorted the good from the bad, isolated the broken equipment for disposal, designated space for the items you need, and carefully set them in their respective places. You now have a location for the baskets and bags, and their proximity will support your egg-gathering and wool-shearing processes. You

have also effectively removed tripping hazards, making this area much safer. Great work, and more importantly, great results."

"How do we move on to shining, standardizing, and sustaining?" the Pig asks.

"We will get to that soon, Pig," the Owl responds. "First, let us complete the first two steps, sorting and setting in order. I believe someone pointed out that we have a problem with the corn carts and their associated spare parts?"

Sloppy Spare Parts

"Of course we do!" the Jackass replies, exasperated. "Look around all over the ground. There are parts everywhere! I thought we had a problem before, but getting the bags and baskets off the ground only revealed that there were more parts underneath them."

The other animals look concerned, some even intimidated by the seemingly insurmountable task at hand.

The Owl responds. "I have a good friend, the Flamingo, and he has a wonderful expression for moments like this: 'How do you eat an elephant?'"

Some of the animals look confused. Others appear to be offended by the thought.

The Owl continues. "The answer is this: one bite at a time. Just as you tackled the issue of the baskets and bags using the 7S approach, performing one step at a time, you will do the same for the corn cart parts. First, we need to sort through the pieces, separating the 'good' from the 'bad.' Then we will move the bad parts to the disposal area and organize the remaining 'good' parts in a careful and deliberate way. We will need to get our tails dirty again with red paint, but before that we need to know what makes a corn cart part 'bad.' Horse? Can you help us with this?"

"Of course," says the Horse. "If the collar is cracked or the axle warped, they need to go. Also, if any spokes are missing from a wheel, it should be thrown away as well."

"So now we know what we need to do," the Bull states. "We need to go through the barnyard and inspect each item according to the criteria from the Horse. What next? We can't just stack these parts like the baskets and the bags; they're not shaped for that. And I don't think that a box on the ground will hold these parts in. What are we going to do?"

"Take it 'one bite at a time,'" returns the Owl. "After you have completed the first step, sorting, the Woodpecker and I will introduce a new tool, the *shadow board*. But do not worry about that now. First things first. We need to sort out the spare parts."

The animals divide back into two teams, some with fresh red tails, inspecting the items scattered across the barnyard, and some pulling carts to collect the pieces that have been tagged with red stripes. Axles wobble and roll, spokes are counted, and collars are held up to the sun. Defects are found and parts are marked. The 'bad' ones are relocated to a pile of broken baskets and torn bags near the Farmer's silver cans. Before too long, carts are empty, the red stripes have abandoned the yard, and the animals are meeting with the Owl around a surprisingly small number of spare corn cart parts.

"So now," the Owl starts, "what do we have here?"

"These are all of the parts that passed inspection," reports the Cat. "And there aren't many."

Some of the animals look concerned. The Horse does not.

"We have three corn carts on the farm," says the Horse. "We try to keep two wheels, one axle, and one collar on hand for each of them. It looks like we just might have enough here to cover that."

Relief ripples across the ranks.

"But," the Pig interjects, "how are we going to organize and store these parts? And where are we going to keep them?"

"I can help with the first question," answers the Owl. "Allow me to introduce you to an old friend of mine. He has a face that you will learn to love. Meet the *shadow board*."

The Owl directs their attention to a large wooden board leaning against the Milking Parlour. It has been engraved by the Woodpecker with two large circles, each with the word "Wheel" engraved above. An oval is placed in the upper middle section, and it has been labeled "Collar." At the base, a long, thin rectangle runs the width of the board with the word

"Axle" in the center. The round shapes have wooden pegs protruding from the top center, and the rectangle has three wooden pegs evenly spaced across its bottom border. And yes, it does look somewhat like a face.

"That's a shadow board?" asks the Cow. "What does he, I mean it, do exactly?"

"A shadow board, like the plank squares around each group of baskets and bags, serves as a medium for visual control. The words that are pecked into the wood of the Hen House, the Shearing Shack, and this board are visual signals. They grab your attention and relay information. Visual controls are a little bit stronger. The squares around the stacks of bags and baskets, combined with the labels and the shapes on the shadow board, indicate where certain items are to be parked. Humans use these all of the time. I am always fascinated by the way thin yellow lines on dark ground force them to position their cars in a certain way. Where was I? Oh yes, the shadow board. The shadow board offers a higher level of visual management and control for several reasons. The first is that the shapes accompanying each peg indicate the place for each spare part. The second is that when positioned properly, the board will be elevated off of the ground and visible from almost anywhere in the barnyard. This will allow anyone and everyone to see if a part is missing or if a piece has been placed in the wrong area. If a wheel is hanging from an axle peg, for example, it will be fairly obvious to all, and should be corrected immediately."

"Why didn't we use a shadow board for the bags and baskets?" inquires the Sheep.

"Because some items do not lend themselves to hanging storage," replies the Owl. "And, shadow boards are typically used for a small quantity of like items. If you were keeping ten spare wheels for each cart, I would not recommend this tool. Do not ever attempt to align your storage requirements to a specific tool. Instead, align the tool to your requirements."

The animals nod in understanding.

"So, where are we going to put these shadow boards?" asks the Jackass.

"I am hoping that you can tell me," the Owl answers. "Just as the baskets and bags were placed where they needed to be for the most efficient and effective use, we need to do the same with these spare corn cart parts. Where are the corn carts supposed to be located?"

Crazy Corn Carts

"Typically, when we finish hauling," the Horse responds "the Bull, the Jackass, and me, we each go our separate ways with the empty carts in tow.

Whenever we get unhitched, the carts are pretty much all over the place. It's a real pain when we start up the next day because we end up starting in different places and cutting between the pens to get to the cornfield. It would be great if we could all park our carts right outside the barn, next to the fields, but we don't ever seem to get there."

"That would make sense, Horse. We pass alongside the barn on our way back from the market. Why don't we park the carts there?" asks the Bull. "We could mark the place for each cart on the ground, just like we did with the baskets and bags."

"And we could place the spare parts shadow boards at the head of each space! That would be easy enough to see! Everyone can see the barn from anywhere in the yard!" voices the Chicken.

"They would also be consolidated with the carts," adds the Cat.

"That takes care of the corn cart issues then," announces the Dog.

"Almost," the Sheep responds.

"What do you mean?" asks the Dog. "The corn carts and the corn cart spare parts have a place designated that is near where they are used. What else is there?"

"There is the issue of the cart traffic through the pen areas," answers the Sheep.

"But there won't be any anymore, right Horse?" questions the Cow.

"I'd like to say yes, but that wouldn't be true," the Horse remarks. "Although traffic through the pens will be significantly reduced, we might need to use those routes every now and then. When the ground is soft, for example, the carts sink in the soft soil near the barn. We'll still use the pen paths as alternates. I don't know how to fix that."

"Yeah," the Pig joins in. "We can't just put boxes around those paths when we need to use them."

"You could do that," the Owl remarks, "but it would not be very practical, or helpful. But there is another way. While we can use visual management techniques to control static inventory like the baskets and bags, we can also use it to control the flow of mobile equipment, like the corn carts."

"How in the world can we do that?!" asks the Chicken. "Those carts are big and fast and scary! Half of the time they can't even see us when they're moving those things through here! They've even come close to running over each other!"

The other animals agree, and side conversations erupt throughout the group.

The Jackass's voice rises above the others. "The corn carts are heavy, and we have to keep moving to get the corn to market. I'd like to see a Chicken give it a whirl!"

"If I may," the Owl interjects, "I would like to attempt to summarize the issues that you have addressed. I might even be able to make a few recommendations as well."

The chatting devolves to silence, and each team member looks to the Owl.

"From what I have heard so far, I believe that you are saying that there are safety issues involving the corn carts. These issues include potential dangerous speeds and traffic flow. Is this correct?"

"I think so," the Bull answers. The rest of the team seems to agree.

"If that is the case, we can continue to make this a visual barnyard using more signals and controls," replies the Owl.

"Remind me, Owl," requests the Cow, "what is a visual signal versus a visual control?"

The Owl continues. "That is a great question, Cow. Remember that a visual signal relays information and grabs your attention, whereas a visual control requires adherence."

"So," the Sheep joins the conversation, "if we want the carts to slow down to a walk as they move through the pens, we could put up a sign, or a control, that says just that?"

"Yes indeed," the Owl responds.

"I think I get it too," the Horse says. "If we want to keep from running one cart into another, we could also put up controls that direct the flow of traffic, like a sign that requires that we only travel through the pens one way, from the fields toward the barn. Maybe a sign that stops us before we enter the pens. That would give us a moment to survey the situation before proceeding through."

"That would be pretty helpful," asserts the Bull. "It can take a long time and a great deal of effort to back those carts out of the pen paths when we meet in the middle."

"Would it make sense to post warning signs?" the Cat asks. "Something along the lines of 'Small Animals at Work'? Just as a reminder?"

"Yes it would," states the Owl. "Great solutions! Do you believe that this is a step in the right direction?"

The animals look to each other and join in blended conversations. After several minutes pass, the Dog steps forward.

"These traffic signals and controls will make Lean Acres a safer place to work and live. If we could borrow the Woodpecker again, we'd like to get to work setting up the parking spaces, shadow boards, and traffic signs for the corn carts."

"That sounds like a good plan, Dog," the Owl answers. "What do you say, Woodpecker?"

Before the question is finished, the Woodpecker lands on the Dog's shoulder.

"Have at it!" encourages the Owl. "Please meet me by the Hen House when you are done, and we will continue our journey by shining, standardizing, and sustaining the barnyard."

The animals hold a brief discussion, split into teams, and continue to transform their world.

Making the Yard Work

In a remarkably short amount of time the group has gathered in front of the Hen House, and the Owl stands before them. They are tired but happy, and the Owl is pleased with the progress that they have made on Lean Acres Farm and within themselves.

"Thus far," the Owl begins, "we have worked diligently with the equipment here on Lean Acres, sorting it and setting it in order, and we have applied various tools making the barnyard a more visual workplace. Now we need to *shine*. Rather, Lean Acres needs to shine. We have already done some of this by clearing the open areas of baskets, bags, and corn cart spare parts. And we have standardized these solutions with visual signals and controls. It is time to go inside, into the buildings where a good portion of your work is performed. There we will decide what to clean and how to clean it, and also how often we should do it. Then, the Woodpecker can help us capture these rules or standard practices somewhere highly visible for reference and inspection purposes. Let us start with the Hen House. Rooster, would you mind asking the ladies if we might have a few minutes alone with their quarters?"

"No problem," the Rooster replies. He enters the Hen House, and with a few clucks every chicken exits the facility in single file with heads held high. Some look at the animal team with curiosity, a few with disdain, but most are smiling and glad to feel the sun on their feathers. Almost every one of them pauses for a moment in the yard, obviously surprised by its new and improved state. As the last lady leaves, the Owl steps toward the door.

"Now," he begins, "we can not all fit in the Hen House at once. I propose that we select a representative to inspect the building while we observe from the doorway."

"It's our house, so the Chicken or I should go in, right?" the Rooster inquires.

"Not necessarily," responds the Owl. "Sometimes it is more beneficial for an outsider to inspect an area. They could have a more critical eye and are typically not attached to any conditions of or rationale for the current state. It is completely at your discretion."

"I like that idea," says the Cow. "I wouldn't mind a new set of eyes on the Milking Parlour."

"Let's try it," voices the Pig. "And if we are looking to learn from a detailed perspective, the Cat is our animal."

No one disagrees.

"Alright then," the Cat meows, "if there aren't any objections."

After a long silence, the Cat walks through the door, and the other animals gather around, peering inside the dark and dusty house. The Cat walks nimbly through the spilled straw on the floor, smelling, looking, and feeling. He climbs each tier and inspects every nest. The Cat returns to the floor with a graceful leap and rejoins the group.

"What did you find?!" calls the Chicken. She is anxious beyond expectation.

"Two things," the Cat reports. "The first is that you do have a weasel problem. I caught their scent on the floor, but I can't figure out how they are getting in because straw from the nests is covering the floor."

"We can fix that," the Rooster decrees. "When we shine the Hen House, we'll make sure that we remove all of the straw from the floor and keep it that way. We have to plug those weasel holes. They steal our eggs and knock others over on their way out. That's part of the whole cracking problem."

"Excellent," the Owl says. "What is the second issue, Cat?"

"The second issue could be contributing to the weasel problem as well," the Cat replies. "It appears that some of the chickens are bringing food into their nests. The rotting smell is pungent, and that might be drawing those interlopers, the weasels, into the Hen House as well."

The Rooster responds. "We can handle that as well. If we start with those two focus areas, I think we could see a dramatic improvement in our quarters. They won't just be clean, they will be secure as well. Thank you, Cat."

"My pleasure," returns the Cat, and he rejoins the team outside of the building.

"What do we do now, Owl?" the Horse asks.

"We will need to divide into four teams, one for each work area here on the farm. Each group can repeat the process that we just observed in the other three buildings. Inspect the area, identify cleaning requirements, and then put them into practice. The Woodpecker will assist you by capturing the required cleaning actions on a wall of your choosing. Just make certain that it is readily visible to anyone who enters the facility. These cleaning, or shine, lists will serve as the standard for our efforts moving forward and help us to sustain a 7S environment. Are you ready?"

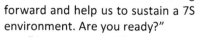

"Come on, team!" presses the Bull. "Let's knock this out!"

The Dog partitions the excited animals into four teams, and they depart to their assigned areas. The Rooster, the Chicken, and the Dog stay behind to work on the Hen House, sweeping out straw and picking food bits from the nests. The Woodpecker has carved text into the wall facing the door that reads:

Rules for a Safe and Secure Weasel-Free Home

1. Keep the floor clear of straw.

2. Keep food out of your nests.

The floor is clean now, and the Rooster removes the last piece of corn from a nest. The Dog fills every weasel hole with tightly packed clay. This is not a new Hen House, but it sure looks like one. The same is true for the entire farm.

The Dog, the Rooster, and the Chicken meet with the other animals outside. They reunite one group at a time until all ten members have gathered in the fading light of day. Several animals are sharing stories with one another, recounting specific actions undertaken and discoveries encountered while shining and standardizing their workplaces.

"Before we retire for the evening, we have one more phase to discuss," announces the Owl.

The conversations quiet, and the group looks to the Owl.

"After all of your hard work," the Owl continues, "we need to make certain that Lean Acres does not regress into its previous state. We will need to sustain the results that you achieved."

"Yes," says the Pig. "This has been a rewarding day, no doubt, but I don't want to go through this again. Ever. How do we make sure it stays this way?"

"I think that inspection might be the answer," the Cat responds. "Just as my brothers and sisters and I inspect the milk and the eggs, we could inspect the farm to ensure that the standards that we have developed here today are being followed."

"But we need you and your siblings working on the milk and the eggs, Cat," the Dog inserts.

"I agree," comments the Rooster. "And keeping Lean Acres in order should be everyone's job!"

"What about a rotating inspection plan?" the Sheep asks quietly. "We could take turns performing the inspections. As long as we stick to the standards that are etched in every building, box, and shadow board, we will all be looking from the same vantage point. That could keep everyone engaged, and maybe even more aware of any of their own shortcomings in adhering to the standards."

"This is a good idea," the Dog asserts. "If we're all involved, then we all have something at stake."

"What about the results?" questions the Cow. "How will we communicate the inspection findings to everyone? Shouldn't we do that?"

"Yes, you should," the Owl replies. "Some organizations report the results of their inspections by work area. That can create tension between functional teams. For Lean Acres, I recommend that you group your scores by each of the seven S's. That removes the sense of competition and encourages collaboration and cooperation."

"And how exactly are we going to make the results visible to everyone?" the Jackass presses. "We're not going to carve another tree into the barn, are we?"

"No, we will not do that," the Owl responds.

"Well then," the Jackass continues, "what solution are you going to weave for us?"

"I am not going to weave any solution for you," returns the Owl.

The Jackass smiles with pride and disdain at each member of the team. He is happy with himself. That is, at least, until the Owl speaks.

"The Spider is," the Owl states. "I have worked with her sisters in the past, one in particular on another farm, and they are wonderfully gifted. Her innate ability to craft words, numbers, and shapes from her threads will be incredibly useful. Does anyone know where she is?"

"She and the Pig are always hanging out together," the Horse neighs.

"I'll get her," the Pig volunteers. He dashes off to the barn and returns in minutes. At first the animals believe that he is alone, but as he closes in on the group everyone notices the passenger on his snout. It is the Spider, and she greets them warmly.

"Hello, my friends," she offers. "And Owl, I have heard great things about you from my family. Your reputation precedes you. The Pig has informed me that you may be in need of my assistance. How can I help?"

"If I could have a minute of your time, Miss Spider, I will explain," the Owl requests.

The Spider casts a line and swings over to the Owl. He leans toward her, and the two converse. Hardly a moment passes before she nimbly ascends a nearby post. At the top she is met by rafters, and the Spider commences an acrobatic display, every move traced by a thin line of webbing. Concentric shapes surround each other, and lines intersect and connect the entire image. Numbers fall at different levels, and soon familiar words take their place around the edges. The web is large enough to see from across the barnyard. When it is complete, the Spider descends on her own silk and settles gently to the ground near the Owl.

The animal team members gather close to the Owl as he begins to explain.

"This is called, believe it or not, a *spider chart*. The support lines that run from the center of the web out to the edges designate the different categories that we are tracking. In our case we have seven, one for each of the S's in our 7S program. The rings of the web that radiate outward

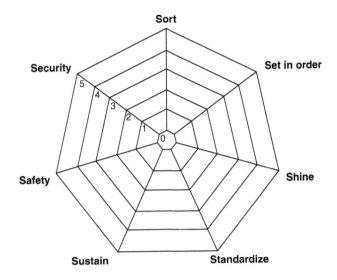

from the center indicate the score for each category. We will use a scoring system that ranges from zero to five, with a score of five being the best."

The Bull interrupts. "I think I understand the setup, Owl. After each inspection, we'll record the scores for each category, and the spider chart will display the results for all to see. But how are we going to indicate the scores for each category?"

"If I may," the Spider requests, "by using whatever is hanging around. Please observe." The animals notice that several flies have been caught in the web during their brief conversation. The Spider repositions them carefully and then joins each fly to the next with an especially thick silky strand. She skirts off to the nearest wooden beam and smiles a fanged grin at the team.

"An excellent solution," commends the Owl, "and an outstanding example. Based on the Spider's work, not only can you readily observe the score for each of the S's, but you can also assess where the most improvement is needed."

"Do you mean *shine*?" the Cow asks. "It looks like this is telling us that we're weak in that activity. Would we look for any place in the web where the thicker strands are pinched in toward the center, toward zero?"

"Right you are," confirms the Owl. "The spider chart is a versatile and exacting visual management tool that reveals overall program status and specific problem areas."

"We can use this to monitor and improve the barnyard *and* the 7S program," the Dog suggests. "*Continuous* improvement."

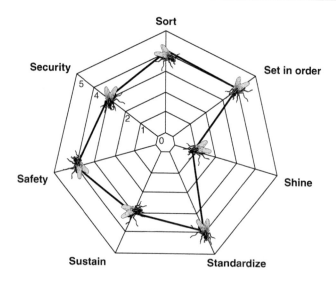

"And that," the Owl adds, "is how you achieve sustainment. My advice is that you go for it. You have integrated visual management with the 7S approach, and realized benefits including safety and security. You have a plan to sustain this improved state, and the farm truly is a better place because of your efforts and ideas. You have set the stage for achieving your customer and busy-ness goals by answering the concerns of your workforce. Look around. This is what progress looks like. Dusk is upon us now, and I am sure that you are all ready for some food and some rest. Please meet me in the barn at dawn, and have a wonderful night."

The Owl peers into the sky and bounds upward with mighty strokes. Before long, he joins the coming night and disappears into the black. The animals disband slowly, holding on to conversations about the day's activities and the amazing transformation on the farm. Soon, the barnyard is quiet, the pens are still, and the tree frogs sing everyone to sleep.

Rest/Reflect/Relate (R³)

1. Are there safety or security issues in your workplace that could be linked to the lack of a standardized and sustained approach to housekeeping?

2. If you were to engage in a 7S effort at your workplace, what areas would you target, and in what order? Why?

3. If you were to engage in a 7S effort at your home, what areas would you target, and in what order? Why?

4. How does the condition of the environment in which you work affect your ability to deliver products and/or services to your customers? Consider both pros and cons.

Chapter 6

A Lean Diet

Waste is worse than loss.

—Thomas A. Edison

The animals sleep soundly. The work on Lean Acres is taking its toll on each member of the team. Even the most diligent fall prey to the tight clutches of restful slumber.

"Come on. Let's get going." A burst of breath and hushed words nearly knock the Rooster from his perch. His dream of sunbathing hens is abruptly ended, and he stares up into the face of the Horse.

"What are you doing?" the Rooster utters angrily as he rubs the light crust from his eyes. "Nobody wakes me up!" he blares through a whisper. "That's my job!"

"I know, I know," the Horse responds with repentance. "I'm just excited. I think we're going to work on the first branch of the Strate-Tree today. You know, the corn harvesting. I just can't sleep anymore. Could you possibly crow a little early today?"

The Rooster is clearly offended at this, but his frustration gives way to understanding. On this morning and only this morning, the animals at Lean Acres awaken to the stars of a predawn sky.

As the team gathers in the barn, the Owl and the Woodpecker review new images that have been carved into an interior wall. There are shapes that are barely discernable in the shadows, and the Farm Animals Team members can't make sense of it. Not yet. The Owl turns and greets the group.

"Good morning, team. This is the first of our four final days together. I have been summoned by the Council, and must return to my fellow owls for a conference."

The animals are stunned. Jaws and beaks hang open.

"How are we going to fix all of our problems in four days?!" the Chicken cries. "We're doomed!!"

"Doomed?" asks the Owl. "I think not. Did you know how to 7S the barnyard last week?"

"No, not at all," the Pig responds.

"Do you understand the 7S methodology now?" the Owl continues.

"Well, of course we do. You explained the approach and then we put it into practice," the Cow comments.

"And we will do the same for each of the branches on our Strate-Tree," the Owl assures. "In order for performance improvement to become a reality on Lean Acres, you have to own it. I will always be available to support you in the future through advice, coaching, and mentorship, but your future does not and should not hinge on me. This is your farm. It is your future. I will teach you the tools. You must master them, own them, and apply them."

The sun crests the horizon, and orange morning light pours into the barn. The shadowed shapes on the wall are revealed as boxes and arrows, and the animals move closer to study the details of their design.

"What is all of this?" the Pig questions.

"This," replies the Owl, "is our next step forward. Let us take a look at that first branch of the Strate-Tree and improve your corn sales. Horse, you are responsible for this process according to the RACI chart. Bull, you are accountable for the results. You both have excellent visibility on the current state of operations. What can you tell us about delivering the corn to the market?"

"Basically," the Horse says, "the Jackass begins the process by gathering and staging fifteen carts worth of corn at a time near the barn. He goes back and forth all day long for about ten hours, about 150 trips altogether. The pigs and a few of the other animals pick the corn and fill the carts. Anyway, after we stage all of the corn in a big pile, the pigs and sheep push it all forward to the next step."

"Why do you push fifteen carts forward at a time?" asks the Owl. "Why not ten or five or even one?"

"Because that's about as much corn as we can handle at a time," shouts the Pig from the back of the group.

"And besides," the Sheep offers, "this is how we've always done it."

"Thank you for your responses," the Owl replies. "Please continue, Horse."

"Alright," the Horse says. "During the next step some of the chickens help the pigs shuck the corn, removing all of the leaves. They're pretty dang quick, and we do this because the humans at the market like to see the kernels. Then some more pigs and sheep push it forward again. Actually, they push the corn along throughout most of the process. Next, the cats inspect it all, one piece at a time. A big problem is that the corn at the bottom of our stockpile tends to get crushed and spoil under the pressure of all that weight and from the lack of air. Some also gets messed up as it's pushed along the ground from one process step to another. We end up losing about a third of what we haul in from the fields. We put the good corn off to one side, and the stuff that's ruined off to the other. Then we load the damaged corn back up into the carts and roll them off to the compost mound."

"I am sorry to interrupt again," leads the Owl, "but you did say that approximately one-third of the corn you process ends up on the compost heap, correct?"

It is the Bull who answers. "Yes. But again, that's why we keep the Jackass staging the corn throughout the day—to make up for our losses."

"Got it," the Owl responds. "Please continue."

"No problem," comments the Horse. "When we've completed the disposal runs, the pigs load the carts back up with the good corn, and then the Bull and I start making trips to the market. There are thirty large containers there in the Lean Acres section, and each can hold just about a cartload. The market's only open from nine to five, so we have to start harvesting at seven in the morning. There's just not enough sunlight to work in before then, and after five, well, there's just no point. Even with starting two hours before they open, we still get the corn there well after nine o'clock, and you can forget about filling all of the containers in any given day. After our first load's delivered, we don't get back to the market but every two hours."

"Why is that?" the Owl inquires.

"Because it takes us two hours to load the carts!" the Jackass bellows. "After the inspection and disposal runs, the ears are left scattered all over the ground!"

"This really hurts," the Horse continues, "because when the people see the bare containers, they assume that we are sold out and buy their corn elsewhere. By 'elsewhere' I mean the Cornelius's Crops stand. Those guys never run out. Sometimes they sell up to forty containers of corn a day. Forty containers! I bet that we could sell fifty containers, but we only get thirty carts in each day on average, and our first load doesn't even get there until around noon. That's what the Rooster says. And of those thirty loads, we only sell about twenty, 'cause the third batch of ten carts doesn't arrive until the last hour, right before closing time. All too often we have to get rid of the last load because no one's there to buy it. Then we come back here and stop the harvesting process midstream, right about closing time for the market."

"What happens at that point?" asks the Owl.

"Then we take all of the corn that has piled up between each activity and take it to the compost pile. It stinks, but this is how we've always done it. We've tried tweaking it in the past, but nothing's come of it yet. I just can't think of a better way to do it," the Horse finishes.

"You have not thought of a better way to do it *yet*," responds the Owl.

"What are you saying, Owl?" inquires the Bull. "That we can 7S this process?"

Several team members look encouraged by this.

"Not at all, Bull. The 7S approach is environmentally-focused and can not be applied to processes," the Owl answers. "However, I do know of another methodology that could help. After listening to the Horse, and based on your experiences, would you say that a term like *waste* might describe some of the activities involved in corn harvesting? Is there a lack of flow, or continuous movement of the corn from the fields to the market? Are you pushing the product forward as fast as you can, applying maximum effort and resources, and still falling behind?"

"I think you're right on target," the Bull says.

"I agree," adds the Rooster. "We just can't meet our customers' needs."

"You can not meet them *now*," the Owl interjects. "Let me tell you about the *lean* methodology."

Step 6: Academics

"The lean methodology," the Jackass bellows. "I think that we've heard about that before here on Lean Acres! Every time an animal gets 'cut' we become a little leaner. It hasn't worked out too well for us so far!"

"If that is your idea of lean, then of course it has not worked to improve your situation," responds the Owl. "The lean methodology that I am referring to is not about animal reductions; it is about waste reduction. The *lean* that I am familiar with promotes farm growth, not downsizing. This is the lean that you have all been waiting for. There are four basic steps, or principles to follow. Each of these contributes to one enduring goal."

"That sounds simple enough," the Cow says. "What are the steps?"

The other team members are interested, and they gather closer to the Owl as he begins.

"The four steps consist of *customer value*, *value stream*, *flow,* and *pull*. These contribute individually, sequentially, and collectively to the goal of

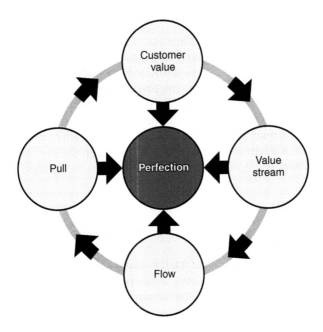

achieving *perfection* in what we do. We will never achieve perfection, but if we constantly strive for it, we will continuously improve."

Customer Value

"The first step involves the identification of customer value. This is very similar to the exercise we went through with the Mice while we grew our Strate-Tree. When applying lean, we need to know what the customer wants—including product characteristics like sweetness or fluffiness—how much of it they want, how quickly they want it, and so on."

"So we already have that answer, right?" asks the Rooster. "When we developed our strategic goals and objectives, we discovered that the people and the busy-nesses want more corn from Lean Acres."

"But they didn't say anything about the crunchiness or the taste of the corn," the Cat asserts. "Is it okay to focus on volume alone?"

"It sure is," the Owl responds. "Customer value evolves over time, changing as certain needs, like volume, are met. Other requirements will arise in time, and by listening to the voice of the customer you will be able to respond or adapt proactively, and that will improve your organization as a whole. *Customer value* is the base of any lean operation. Building upon anything else is the first step toward failure. Remember, without customers, there wouldn't be a farm."

"So, we know what the customer wants," says the Bull. "What do we do with that?"

"We need to compare it to the *voice of the farm*," the Owl responds. "In the strategic planning process, we heard the voice of the farm asking us to reduce spoilage. Apparently, the spoiled corn creates extra work around here, and it reduces the total volume that we can send on to the market. If we focus on reducing spoilage, or *scrap*, and increasing the amount of corn that we deliver to the market, is there a conflict?"

"No, I don't think so," the Dog answers. "So, now what do we do?"

"We follow whatever carries that value through the process. This is the second step, and it's called *value stream*," responds the Owl.

Value Stream

"A *value stream*? Is that anything like the stream that winds through our western fields?" the Cow asks.

"Yes," answers the Owl. "In fact, it is exactly like that stream."

For those that have eyebrows, they rise in surprised interest. For those that don't, the expressions are similar enough.

"Allow me to explain," continues the Owl. "Imagine a leaf in the stream, riding the currents from the spring in the woods all the way to the pond beyond the Farmer's house. That stream is like our corn harvesting process. We want to know where it starts and ends. We also want to know where and how it flows, and what happens to the leaf along the way. Does it get caught up behind other leaves? Are there rocks in the way? Does the stream become too narrow or too shallow? Once we have this information, we can track our product, similarly to the leaf, as it rides the currents of the linked set of activities from the field to the market. We will use symbols like boxes and arrows to map out our own value stream, and we will analyze the complete picture, looking for activities that slow or limit our production capabilities and capacities. In the lean methodology, we call problem areas *waste*. Waste is anything that does not add to or diminishes the value that the customer is looking for."

"How will we know what is waste and what isn't?" questions the Pig. "We've always harvested this way and we've never seen anything wrong with it. How are we going to suddenly see this waste if we have never noticed it before?"

"Good question," the Owl replies. "We will need to look over our value stream from a new perspective. There are nine general categories of waste that we can use as a reference throughout this effort. An easy way to remember them is to think about the *DOOMED PIT* that they will drag you into. The Woodpecker was kind enough to carve them into the wall over here." The Owl motions to his right, and the animals notice the list of words hewn into the boards of the barn.

Defects
Overproduction
Overprocessing
Motion
Excess inventory
Delay
Poor communication
Injury
Transportation

"What in the heck does all of that mean?" asks the Pig.

"Well," starts the Owl, "*defects* describes anything that we produce or deliver that is not in tune with the voice of the customer. This could be sour milk, cracked eggs, or flat wool. It could also mean a late delivery of corn. Basically, a defect describes something about what we offer that the customer doesn't like."

"What about *overproduction*?" ventures the Cow. "How could making a bunch of stuff be a bad thing?"

"We need to produce and deliver only what the customer needs, when they want it. If that is a large quantity, then great. But, if you harvest too much product, there is a potential that some will not be sold or used, so that portion that you brought in from the fields 'just in case' would be discarded, the effort of harvesting it would have occurred in vain, and it would take extra work just to get rid of it. More is only better if it is what the customer wants. Do you understand?"

"I do now," replies the Cow. "I just never thought of it that way."

"Most animals and people do not," assures the Owl. "There are only a few farms in the world that embrace the search for these nine wastes, and that constant search for and elimination of these wastes makes them the best at what they do."

"Please tell us more, Owl," requests the Dog.

"Where were we?" the Owl ponders. "Ah yes, *overprocessing*. This means doing more to a product or offering more in a service than is required by the customer. For example, if you were to stack each ear of corn neatly on top of one another in the back of the cart, you would be engaged in overprocessing. It might make the cart of corn more aesthetically pleasing, but the questions must be asked: 'Does the customer care about this?' and 'Would the customer be willing to pay for the extra time and effort that it takes to do this?' If the answer is no to one or both of these inquiries, then you can consider the activity to be a form of overprocessing."

"But sometimes presentation is important," the Cat interjects.

"It is not a form of waste if you can prove that the activities that you are engaging in are selling more products. But you must be able to identify a definite relationship between the work you are doing and the benefit of your labor. For every minute that you spend organizing and arranging products at the market, you need to know how much more green paper you are getting. Otherwise, you are operating on a guess, and that is a dangerous place to be."

"How can *motion* be a form of waste?" the Horse asks. "We have to move!"

"Yes, you do," the Owl replies. "But sometimes, bending and reaching and turning can be a real pain in the neck, literally. This is the motion that is considered to be waste. We try to eliminate these unnecessary movements by rearranging work areas so that they are more user-friendly. The humans call this *ergonomics*, a fancy word for whatever it takes to stop your back from hurting."

"What about moving the carts across the fields?" the Sheep asks. "Is that a form of motion?"

"Actually," responds the Owl, "only movements from a fixed point are considered to be motion. Movements from one point to another are called *transportation*, but we'll get to that soon. Let us continue exploring the DOOMED PIT. I believe that we have arrived at *excess inventory*."

"Like the corn loads that end up by the barn?" the Rooster inquires.

"That is exactly right, Rooster," comments the Owl. "Excess inventory basically means *extra stuff*. The corn piled by the barn, the cart parts littered across the barnyard along with the baskets and bags, maybe even surplus eggs. We all have to constantly remind ourselves that we want to have the right amount of the right product to the right customer at the right time. This is called *just-in-time* operations. Too often, however, we find ourselves working in a *just-in-case* environment, where extra stuff is set to the side, just in case somebody needs it. Excess inventory is especially dangerous because it can hide other problems, like defects, and even cause some, like motion, delays, transportation, and injury. You all saw some of that when we engaged the 7S program in the barnyard."

"I still can't believe that we found all of those parts!" the Chicken exclaims.

"And how much time are we going to save walking straight through the barnyard instead of tiptoeing around those baskets and bags?" adds the Rooster.

"Precisely," the Owl says. "Those delays that you have experienced are also a form of waste. Anytime that you have to wait for something or you are slowed in your progress, you are experiencing a delay."

"Can one area or one step in the process have more than one waste?" asks the Bull.

"Sure it can," answers the Owl. "Did you have a specific example?"

"Well, I keep thinking about the way we harvest the corn, and that big pile that we form by the barn. It seems to me that we are creating a delay with excess inventory and that we are overprocessing each ear by handling it twice, and also incorporating more motion."

"You are right," the Owl responds. "It is actually pretty rare to discover an isolated form of waste as you work your way through the value stream. You must be ever vigilant and always watchful. Where there is one, there are likely to be others. Now let me tell you about the *PIT*."

The animals look to the Owl with fascination and the initial understanding. They are grasping the concept of lean, and are eager to learn more.

"The *P* stands for *poor communication*. When we assume that we know what the customer wants or what the rules around the barnyard are, we are participating in poor communication. The same is true when we hold on to information that our fellow workers might need, or keep the best way to do a chore to ourselves. This form of waste is an individual effort that affects the entire team. We all need to be aware of what it is that we need to know and how our knowledge can positively impact others."

"We certainly could work on our communication across the pens," the Pig says.

"And within them," the Cow adds. "This is helping me tremendously, Owl. I see more and more waste as you go on. What does the *I* stand for?"

"The *I* stands for *injury*," begins the Owl. "Any time that an animal is hurt on Lean Acres, the entire farm suffers. It increases the workload of each animal and lowers morale. Injury can come about from various other wastes, including excess inventory, poor communication, and motion."

"That seems simple enough," the Dog speaks. "What about the *T*?"

"The *T* brings us to the end of our list, and it stands for *transportation*. Whereas motion is limited to stationary movement, transportation entails traveling between two points over a distance. For example, hauling the corn carts from the field to the barn."

"But again, Owl, we have to move the carts," the Jackass interjects. "How can we get from the fields to the market without some form of transportation?"

"It is very rare to eliminate transportation altogether, Jackass," answers the Owl, "but you might be able to significantly reduce the distance that you are traveling through route optimization, for example. If you must transport goods, you will want to ensure that you are doing it in the most effective and efficient manner possible. You will never eliminate every type of waste from your operations, but you can constantly and consistently reduce its occurrence and its impact over time. That is the real goal. Elimination is simply the ideal that we strive for—climbing out of the DOOMED PIT."

The group is murmuring amongst themselves, and the Owl catches bits and pieces of conversations targeting problem areas around the farm and identifying the waste within.

The Bull raises his voice above the din. "Where do we go from here?"

Flow

"I am glad that you asked," the Owl replies. "In the third step, *flow*, we will need to look for these types of waste in the corn harvesting value stream and develop creative ways to mitigate or eliminate their sources. We want our product to flow from the fields to the market without any hesitation and without any hindrance. This brings us to our final step, *pull*."

Pull

"Let us consider the stream on Lean Acres. If it rains, and the stream flows too quickly with an ample supply of water, what happens?" inquires the Owl.

"The pond overflows," responds the Cow.

"And is that a good thing?" the Owl asks.

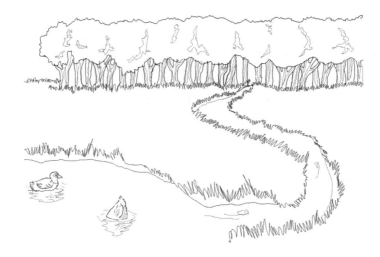

"No," continues the Cow. "When the pond floods, some of the best grass in the meadow dies. The flies and mosquitoes come out too."

"So there are problems when the stream *pushes* too much water into the pond. Do you all agree?" inquires the Owl.

The entire team is nodding.

"What happens when there is rain? How do the stream and the pond work together to avoid oversaturation, to keep from flooding the meadow?" asks the Owl.

The Dog answers. "The Farmer says that the pond and the spring have an agreement of sorts. He says that the pond collects water for the meadow, and that the water seeps into the soil to feed the grass. Not too much and not too fast, but just enough when it's needed. He says that the grass pulls the water out of the ground, the ground pulls the water out of the pond, the pond pulls its water from the stream, and the stream, well, it pulls its water from the spring. Everything moves at an even rate, just a sip at a time and when it's needed. I don't know if he's right, but I've always liked the sound of it."

"I like the sound of that too, Dog," the Owl replies. "In fact, that is a wonderful demonstration of the *pull* concept, and our corn harvesting value stream should perform in the same fashion. We need to look for opportunities to embrace a pull system in delivering the corn to market. If we allow the customer demand to pull the corn as needed, from the loading point rippling back all the way to the fields, we should be able to establish a process that fills every customer's need and eliminates spoilage and overharvesting. The basic premise is that you work on one and only one flow unit, or one cart in your case, and do not start another until either the customer or the activity in front of you pulls that cart forward. *Pull* is the fourth and final step in a lean iteration, but always remember that this is *continuous* performance improvement. There is no end. Once the process has been improved, it is time to reassess customer value, to listen to the voice of the customer, and then to move through the steps again, taking your capabilities to the next level."

"Let's go! Let's go!" shouts the Chicken. "When can we start already?!"

"Right now," the Owl responds.

Step 7: Action

Current State

"We now know what value is to our customers and to our farm," continues the Owl.

"Yeah, we need to get more corn to the market for our customers," begins the Cat, "and we want to have less spoil along the way."

Every animal agrees.

"And how do we measure units of corn?" asks the Owl.

"By the cartload, of course," responds the Horse.

"By the cartload it is, Horse," returns the Owl. "Thank you for your help. So, the flow unit, or the thing that we will need to track through the harvesting process from start to finish, is the cartload of corn. This is the *thing* that carries value, or corn, from the fields to the market. Does anyone disagree?"

"No, you've got it right," offers the Bull.

"Well then," continues the Owl, "let us take a look at how we deliver this value by creating our own value stream map. Just as the stream flows from the spring to the pond in the meadow, we will map the journey of our carts of corn from the fields to the market. However, in our map we will start at the finish, and finish at the start. Let us just get right to it. The Woodpecker will capture our discussion along the way. So, where does your process finish?"

"Definitely at the market, Owl. That's where the people buy our corn," the Cat responds.

"And how much corn do the people want from Lean Acres?" the Owl asks.

"Our Strate-Tree calls for fifty containers worth each day," offers the Horse.

"What would they do with fifty containers of corn?" the Jackass whines. "We can't even get thirty containers sold! Most of the time we only get green paper for twenty of them."

Sixty containers are what you'll make.

Sixty containers are what we'll take.

A synchronized set of slightly dissonant voices responds from under hoof and claw.

When we go to the market, we will make one stop.

We want all of our goods from the same shop.

Corn from Lean Acres is the best stuff,

But most of the time there isn't enough.

Bring in more, go tell the Horse.

And you will be our only source.

The Mice stare upward through their glazed black eyes at the team members. Each member of the group is stunned by the number of containers, and by the entrance of the Mice. A few wonder if they had been there all along. Some venture for a second glance, but the Mice are gone.

"But our Strate-Tree only calls for fifty containers," starts the Horse. "Which target should we work toward?"

"Remember that we should always treat our strategy as a hypothesis, Horse," the Owl explains. "The Strate-Tree is alive, and it can and will adapt to its environment. Between planning and action, changes will occur. This is why it is essential to continuously pulse the customer and listen to their voice. In this case, we could modify the appropriate apple, increasing our target by ten carts per day."

"That's 420 carts per week," says the Rooster.

"Can we get that much corn to market?" the Cow asks.

"We'll have to, or we'll miss the chance to get more green paper," the Dog reminds the team. "If that happens, we lose and the Boo-chair wins."

Every team member concedes to the modified goal, and the Woodpecker alters the numbers within the fruit on the Strate-Tree.

"So," continues the Owl, "we know where your value stream ends, and a few other important pieces of information. We know that you have ten hours of sunlight available for work, and we know that your customers want sixty containers of corn each day. That is enough to calculate something that the humans call *takt time*."

"Tack time?" questions the Pig.

"No, *takt* time," the Owl answers. "There is a *t* on the end. *Takt* time tells us how quickly we need to harvest corn in order to keep up with customer demand, assuming that that demand is constant. There are ten hours, or six hundred minutes of daylight available, and your customers want sixty loads of corn. With the information that we have, it looks like you will need to deliver one cart to the market every ten minutes."

"Every ten minutes!!" the Chicken molts.

"How in the world are we going to do that?" the Rooster crows. "We'll need more animals, and . . ."

"Rooster, please," the Dog asserts. "The Owl is taking us through the value stream process. We'll get there."

"We will," affirms the Owl. "Remember, Rooster, we are discussing the *what* right now and will get to the *how* soon enough. Let us see what we have so far on the barn wall, courtesy of the Woodpecker."

The animals gather around an etching that has been framed with a large square. The market has been drawn in the upper right-hand corner, along with information concerning demand, availability, and takt time.

"We will need to take a few more steps back in the process, one activity at a time, and all the way to the fields. Would anyone like to give it a try?" poses the Owl.

"I'll give it a whirl," says the Horse. "Right before we deliver the corn to the market, I guess we ship it from the farm."

"How many carts do you send to the market each day?" inquires the Owl.

"We get ten out on each of the three runs. But I guess we can only really count two because the third never gets there on time," the Horse responds.

"We can count each of the thirty carts," starts the Owl, "but we will account for the scrap, or the corn that does not get sold, in our map. And what happens before you ship the corn?" continues the Owl.

"We load the carts, ten at a time," answers the Horse.

"And we inspect the corn before that," the Pig offers.

"Hold on now," interrupts the Horse. "We do inspect the corn before we load it, but there's a step in between. After the inspection, we get rid of all of the bad corn so that we don't mix it in with our shipments to the market. We dump about five carts, so we only push about ten cartfuls of corn forward to be loaded."

"So you inspect the corn, then dispose of whatever has been determined to be bad product, and then you load the carts?" the Owl clarifies.

"I think you've got it," the Horse affirms. "The cats inspect the corn, separate the good from the bad, and all fifteen loads go on to the disposal step. And before the cats inspect the corn, we shuck it after we dump our loads in the staging area near the barn. Both of these activities move fifteen loads at a time as well. I think that that's about it."

Customer demand = 60 carts/day

Total available work time = 10 hrs/day

Takt time = 10 minutes/cart

Market

"We are almost there, but we need to follow the process back just a little farther," says the Owl. "Where do you bring the corn from?"

"We haul it in from the fields," offers the Bull.

"Thank you, Bull," replies the Owl. "And how do you measure what you've brought in from the fields?"

"What do you mean?" asks the Dog.

The Owl proceeds. "How do you know how much corn you have harvested in a day? Do you count each ear?"

"Heck no," responds the Horse. "We haul it in by the cartload."

"Excellent!" the Owl hoots. "And how many carts do you haul in from the fields each day?"

"The Jackass hauls in about one-hundred and fifty carts each day," the Horse answers. "He just keeps on bringing it in, and some of the animals push it forward. That wears me out just saying it."

"Hang in there, Horse," encourages the Owl. "I have one more question for you. How do you know when and how many carts to haul in from the fields?"

"That's an easy one," smiles the Horse. "The Dog tells us to harvest carts every day around seven o'clock. We know it's coming, so sometimes we even start before he gets there."

"And the Farmer tells me," interjects the Dog. "He looks at me after breakfast and says 'Alright, Dog, get them carts of corn off to the market for me. Make it happen.' I run over to the Horse and bark out the order, and the work begins."

"And we have arrived at the beginning. Thank you all for your contributions," the Owl beams. "Now please, gather around the value stream map that the Woodpecker has captured on the wall and take a look. So far, we should have captured the information flow and harvesting process as it is today in the current state."

Each team member approaches the fresh etching as the last splinters fall to the straw below. They walk through the process with their eyes, counting and recounting steps and activities that they have witnessed and participated in every day since birth. The animals nod to themselves and each other in confirmation, and the Horse speaks.

"I think this captures it, Owl. I'm just not sure how this value stream map is going to help."

"It will help," the Owl states, "once it has been completed. A value stream map is intended to capture and relate three things. The first is the process itself, or the steps that you are performing while harvesting the corn. The second is the information flow—understanding how orders are communicated, from whom and to whom. The third aspect is the material flow—how long does it take for each activity to be performed on a flow

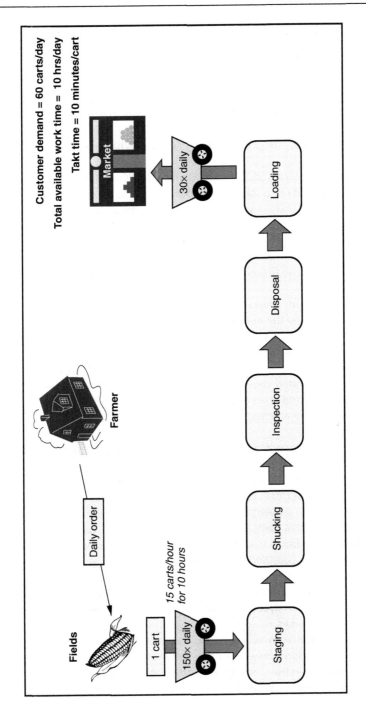

unit or batch of flow units, and how much material moves between process steps. You have described the first two wonderfully, and the Woodpecker caught every detail in the wood. Now we need to discuss different time and material measures.

"We can start with the activities that take place within the harvesting process and how long each takes from different perspectives, including cycle and batch times."

"Alright, Owl," begins the Bull, "I'll give. What are cycle times and batch times?"

"I am glad you asked, Bull," the Owl smiles. *"Cycle time* is the time that it takes an activity or a step within your process to complete the required work on a flow unit. In your case, this could mean how long it takes to stage or inspect one cart of corn."

"Would batch time be the amount of time that it takes one of the harvesting steps to complete the total carts that we push through one at a time? Like the fifteen that go through staging and inspection?" the Cow asks.

"Exactly right," responds the Owl. *"Batch time* is simply the cycle time multiplied by the number of flow units in each of your groupings, or batches, of product. At the staging and inspection phases of harvesting, you would multiply your cycle times by fifteen, whereas the cycle times for disposal and loading would be multiplied by five and ten, respectively, reflecting the batch reductions following inspection. Now, who knows how long each step takes in the corn harvesting value stream?"

"Well, I have an idea," starts the Horse, "but I'll bet that the Rooster knows for sure."

Chest feathers puff as the Rooster struts forward. "This would happen to be my specialty. How can I help?"

"This time, let us start from the beginning of the stream. How long does it take to perform each of the five steps listed on our value stream map? Before you answer, remember that we are looking for the cycle and batch times at this point. These are the times that it takes one cartload of corn and one batch to move through each process step respectively."

The Rooster considers the question carefully as he pores over the diagram etched into the wall. He calculates silently in the computer beneath his frock, his head tilting suddenly this way and that as data is called, sequenced, and analyzed. In moments he turns to the eager group and presents his findings.

"Staging the corn averages four minutes per load, or sixty minutes per batch. Shucking only takes two minutes, that is, thirty minutes for each batch. Inspection consumes approximately four minutes per cart and sixty minutes for each batch as well. We only dispose of five loads each

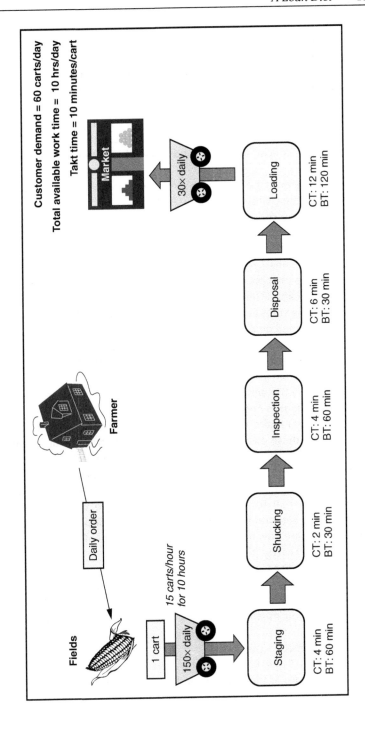

Customer demand = 60 carts/day
Total available work time = 10 hrs/day
Takt time = 10 minutes/cart

Fields

Daily order

Farmer

1 cart

150× daily

15 carts/hour
for 10 hours

Staging
CT: 4 min
BT: 60 min

Shucking
CT: 2 min
BT: 30 min

Inspection
CT: 4 min
BT: 60 min

Disposal
CT: 6 min
BT: 30 min

Loading
CT: 12 min
BT: 120 min

30× daily

Market

iteration, and at six minutes each, the batch time for that step is thirty minutes. And loading takes about twelve minutes per each of ten carts, or one-hundred and twenty minutes total. How does that strike you?"

The Horse and all of the other animals nod along the map as they review and test the numbers silently.

"If I may," the Sheep suggests, "I believe that you've got it. Nice work."

"Is everyone in agreement?" the Owl requests.

The animals concur, and the Woodpecker chisels the figures into the planks.

"Now let us examine your inventory levels and *work-in-progress*, or *WIP* for short," the Owl suggests.

"What do you mean by inventory levels?" the Cow inquires. "And what the heck is WIP?" By their looks, it appears that several other animals have the same question.

The Owl explains. "Your *inventory level* refers to the corn that is waiting between the process steps in the value stream. It seems to me that there is a significant difference in batch and cycle times between the disposal and loading steps in your process, and that corn might pile up as it is waiting to be loaded on carts bound for the market. Is this true?"

"Yes it is," answers the Pig. "Those mountains of corn are a little scary at times, the way that it keeps piling up. When we start working, it takes a while to get out from under its shadow."

"That's really the only spot where that happens," bleats the Sheep.

The other animals nod in concurrence.

"Good then. I heard you correctly," replies the Owl. "The corn that waits between these two activities in your value stream map is called inventory. This basically means that it is product that has not been sold and it is not currently being worked on. In a value stream map, inventory is represented by a triangle with the letter *I* inside of it, and it is placed between the activities where it accrues. Underneath the triangle, we annotate how much inventory is there. For example, between the disposal and loading activities, there are how many loads of corn at the end of the day?"

"About forty carts," the Rooster answers.

"Thank you," the Owl responds. "Now we need to discuss WIP. When you stop working at five o'clock each day, how many cartloads of corn remain at each station?"

"What do you mean, Owl?" asks the Horse. "Like stuff we're still working on?"

"Exactly," answers the Owl.

"On average," the Rooster begins, "we have approximately fifteen carts worth of corn at the shucking and inspection stations and ten carts worth at loading. That's forty loads altogether."

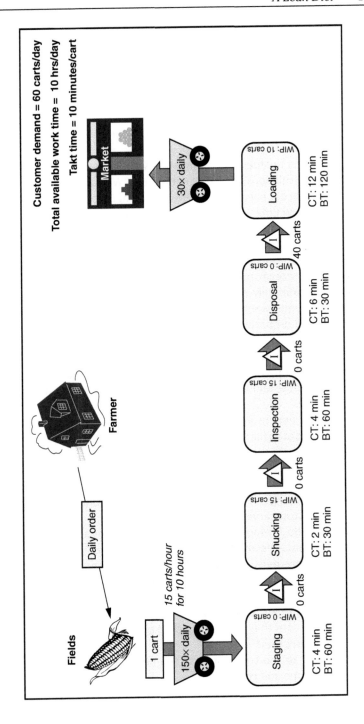

"To be certain, what happens to all of this corn, both the inventory and the WIP, at the end of the day?"

"We get rid of it, of course," the Jackass replies. "Can't just let that corn lay around. It'll spoil!"

"Thank you, Jackass," offers the Owl. "Let's take a look at what we have now."

As the animals peer at the revised image, the majority are stunned by the numbers posted before them.

"Now we can finalize our current state value stream map by capturing pertinent calculations," the Owl continues. "We can look at our WIP, which will include our inventory, our average completion rate, our process lead time, our flow time, total carts to market, carts sold, and scrap, both in-process and the total at the end of the day, including WIP and any corn that does not sell at the market."

The team settles in around the Owl, eager for their next lesson.

"Our value stream map indicates that when we are fully engaged there are approximately eighty cartloads of corn in the harvesting process. If the customer wants sixty carts each day, this means that we have roughly one-and-a-quarter days worth of inventory on hand. Does this seem like a problem to anyone?" questions the Owl.

"Not really," the Horse replies. "We need to keep that corn moving through our system. We're always trying to get that last load of corn to the market on time, and we need to be able to work with as much produce as possible."

"And what happens at the end of the day? More so, what happens if you are forced to stop harvesting in the middle of any given day?" inquires the Owl.

"At the end of each day, we gather up any corn piles from staging on forward and take them to the compost," comments the Bull. "However, as far as simply stopping midday, I have to defer to someone else."

"We never stop harvesting!" the Jackass argues.

"Oh yes we do," responds the Cow. "And it happens a lot in the spring. Whenever it rains, the mud becomes especially thick and slippery up by the barn where most of this work is done. It makes it impossible to move the corn, and the Farmer gets pretty upset when we pull carts through soft soil in the fields. It messes up the crops."

"Thank you, Cow," continues the Owl. "When this happens, what becomes of the corn that is already picked or processed? What happens to the work-in-progress?"

"We take it to the compost heap the next day," the Bull offers. "It wastes a lot of time and corn."

"Well then, I believe that we have captured a significant measure," says the Owl. "We can capture the amount of WIP from our current state value stream map in a summary box on the bottom right-hand side. What else should we include?"

"How often are we able to send a batch off to the market?" asks the Sheep.

"You are referencing the average completion rate," the Owl responds. "This is an assessment of the time that it will take every order following your first order to arrive at the market. In other words, if carts of corn continue to move through my process in batches or in single-piece flow, how often can I get them to my customers?"

"This sounds complicated," starts the Cow.

"It does not have to be," responds the Owl. "Just find the process step that has the longest cycle or batch time, and that is your average completion rate. You can only continuously produce as fast as the slowest step in your process. For example, the loading activity is the longest in your current value stream at 120 minutes. Therefore, after the first batch arrives at the market at noon, the next batch should arrive at two o'clock and the next at four o'clock. Unfortunately, as you know and as you can see here, any batches after the third batch never make it to market. So every batch that you do work on after the third contributes solely to waste. Simple enough?"

"I'm reluctant to admit it," begins the Bull, "but this is making sense. What if we have a special order, like a customer who wants silver queen corn versus yellow? How can we figure how long it takes for that order to get through our process?"

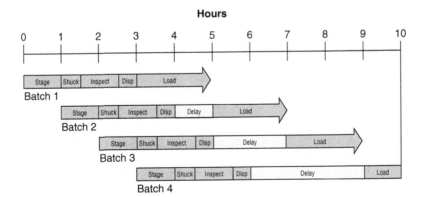

"Terrific question, Bull," answers the Owl. "You are referring to a measure that is called the *process lead time*. This accounts for the cycle time at each step and the WIP that is in front of the special order throughout the process. Assuming that we are using a *first-in first-out*, or *FIFO*, approach, we can apply a simple formula that is referred to as *Little's law*. This states that the process lead time is equal to the WIP divided by the average completion rate."

"We already have those numbers, right Owl?" the Chicken suggests.

"We do indeed," the Owl continues. "We currently have eighty carts of WIP, and our average completion rate is one batch of ten carts every 120 minutes, or one cart every twelve minutes. One divided by twelve is 0.08333, and eighty divided by that value is equal to 960 minutes. This tells us that if our process was in full swing and a special order came through, it would take us a little over one and a half days of production at six hundred minutes each day to get it to market."

"But our customers won't wait that long," expresses the Dog. "We have to do something about this."

"And we will," encourages the Owl.

"You know," starts the Cow, "I'd like to know how long it takes a batch of corn to make it through our process despite the WIP in its way. What does that look like?"

"Very good," the Owl replies. "The time that it takes to move one cart of corn through the harvesting process is called *flow time*. This is all of the time that it actually takes to do the work in every step of the value stream. This is also the time that it takes for your first cart of the day to arrive at the market. We can perform this calculation using either batch or single cart data, depending on the type of system you are using. In your current state, I believe that it is abundantly clear that you are batching your loads in groups of fifteen carts at a time. At the rates you are currently performing, your first cart is ready at the three hundred minute mark. Should it really take five hours to get a cartload of corn from the fields to the market? Just a question for you to consider. Are there any other requests?"

"How much corn are we losing in our current state, Owl?" the Sheep requests. "And the stuff that's lying in between steps, there's about forty loads in all, I think. Does that count?"

"It absolutely does," answers the Owl. "Capturing *scrap*, or the product that we dispose of for any reason, is an incredibly valuable metric to track across your value stream. Hauling in 150 loads each day and losing 130 is dramatic, to say the least. This number includes the eighty carts of WIP, the forty carts that are scrapped in the disposal step or 'in-process,' and the ten carts that do not sell at the market. By reporting these numbers on your map, it could help you to identify opportunities for improvement. What do you think of that?"

"If we're breaking our backs to bring that many cartloads to market every day and then busting them all over again just to throw more away, I'd like to fix that," says the Bull.

"And I believe that you mentioned annotating those carts that we do sell at the market each day," mentions the Cat.

"Absolutely correct," affirms the Owl. "And the last measure that I will recommend for this effort is the total number of carts that you can send to the market."

"We know that we send thirty carts off each day right now," the Jackass says. "What do we need a calculation for?"

"For assessing the *goodness* of future state value streams that you develop, Jackass," the Owl answers. "We will need to know if the improvement ideas that you generate are helping our cause and by how much. To arrive at this number, you will need to take the total time available, or six hundred minutes, and subtract the time that it takes to deliver the first cart to market. For the current state, that leaves us with three hundred minutes. Now we divide the time remaining, the three hundred minutes, by the average completion rate and drop any decimals. Three hundred divided by 120 is what, Rooster?"

"Two and a half," reports the Rooster. "I mean two, if we drop the decimal."

"Thanks again, Rooster," remarks the Owl. "So, accounting for any scrap as well, we can deliver the first batch of ten cartloads plus another two batches. We drop the decimal because in our case we can not deliver fractions of carts. This makes thirty cartloads of corn in all. The current state value stream that you have mapped here is only capable of delivering half of what the customer wants. Does this seem like a valuable metric to capture for review?"

"It does," the Bull sounds as the other animals voice their own agreement.

"Thank you, Bull. Woodpecker, if you would please do the honors," directs the Owl.

Woodchips fly, and the current state value stream map is completed. The team members nod toward each other and the fresh diagram on the barn wall. They understand where they are, and they are ready to improve.

"How do we get better?" the Horse requests.

"By engaging the principles of *lean* and looking for opportunities for improvement," responds the Owl. "What issues do you see on the current state value stream map? What steps add value to the corn, and

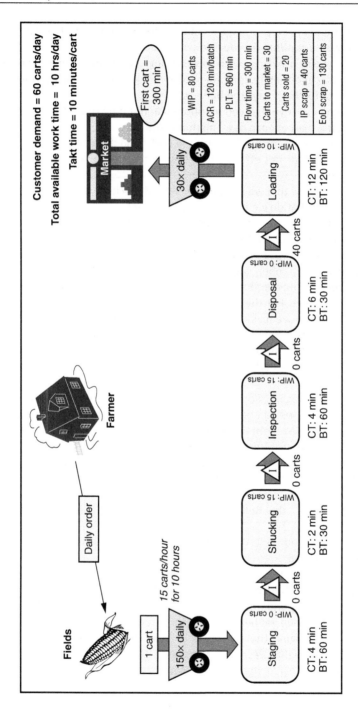

what steps do not? Where is flow interrupted or even halted? Where is the product pushed forward rather than pulled? Do you see any of the nine wastes? Let us have a conversation, and the Woodpecker will capture the highlights. Remember that the objectives of the lean methodology are decreased processing times, improved customer service, reduced inventory, and increased capacity. Let us talk about your ideas."

Lean Application

"If I may," the Cat begins, "I believe that we could count any spoiled corn as defects, and probably any that don't get delivered on time or sold as well. That's eighty-seven percent of our daily haul."

"Why do we lose so much corn?" the Sheep asks.

"The staging process is a piece of it," the Bull replies. "Piling the product up like that causes about a third of our problem."

"Well, why do we batch and stage the corn?!" the Chicken belts.

The Horse responds. "We've always done it that way. To accommodate for the spoilage, we bring in enough corn to accommodate the loss. And we've always tried to move the loads of corn through as a batch so that we can deliver it to the market all at once. Now that I say it, it sounds more like a form of waste, of overproduction."

"It seems to me that we have a few of the wastes in our harvesting system," says the Rooster. "We overproduce the corn because we have no communication from the market, and we receive pushed orders from the Farmer based on a guess. Because we overproduce the corn, it causes excess inventory, and we have to overprocess it with inspection, disposal, and then loading it back up again. It also causes delays between the

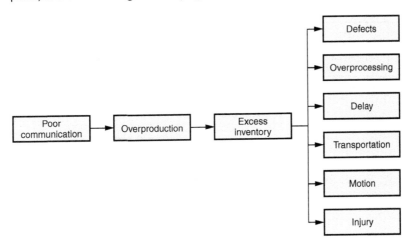

activities that we perform. It looks like we have thirty minutes worth of downtime between staging and shucking for each batch, and thirty minutes between inspection and disposal. That's sixty minutes for each batch lost every single day!"

"I have a question, Owl," the Cow states. "Could we stop batching our produce and send it to the market one cart at a time as needed? Would that help?"

"As a matter of fact, it would," comments the Owl.

A majority of the team looks shocked.

"Allow me to demonstrate and explain," he continues and begins to draw in the dirt with his claw. "The solution that you are referencing involves *one-piece flow* in a *pull* environment. That means that you harvest a cartload of corn when and only when a container is emptied at the market. As one is purchased, another is called, or *pulled* forward to the point of need. For you, that's the market."

"How in the world could that be better than the way we do it now?" questions the Pig.

"Let me show you," proceeds the Owl. As he speaks, he continues developing a diagram on the floor. "Imagine if we only pushed batches of five carts through a process with three steps, in which each activity had a cycle time of two minutes. Thus, batch time at each step would equal ten minutes. If we were to operate such a process, it would take thirty minutes to push one batch of five carts through, and the first piece—the first cart of the batch—would not be ready for twenty-two minutes and not delivered until the thirty-minute mark. Take a look for yourselves."

Each animal takes their time reviewing the diagram, questioning and then comprehending the basic tenets as espoused by the Owl.

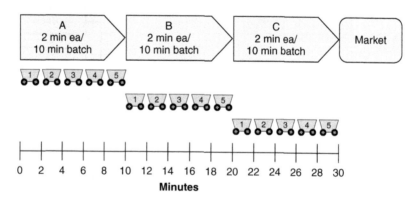

Flow time = 30 minutes for 5 carts
First piece out in 30 minutes

"Now," the Owl continues, "imagine that instead of pushing as much product forward as possible, we filled only one cart at a time and did not gather more corn until the next step in our process *pulled* that cart forward. This *pull* would be initiated at the end of our process, where the customer actually purchases our goods. As they take one, we make one. Thus, we incorporate the principles of one-piece flow and pull. On our current state value stream map, we indicate that we are pushing the corn forward with arrows between our activities. *Pull* is indicated by a circular arrow that starts with the next activity or customer and rounds through the previous activity. This is what said process would look like in an environment where the demand is constant. The curved arrows indicate the *pull* rather than the straight arrow *push*."

As the Owl stands aside, the team members bustle up and around the sketch in the dust.

"In a system based on flow and pull, we can treat all goods and services as perishable. Some call this a cradle-to-grave approach, but they are wrong. They dismiss the delicate nature of whatever they provide as it travels from source to destination, and that their goods do lose value over time. Always consider the products or services that you provide as constantly developing "from seed to sauce," as in apples. Every step in your process should add value, or nourish your goods, and the faster you can deliver them to your customers, the fresher and more valuable they will be. In the end, it all depends on your process flow, but these two principles can increase your speed and your volume."

"How do we do this?" asks the Horse. "How do we improve our process flow?"

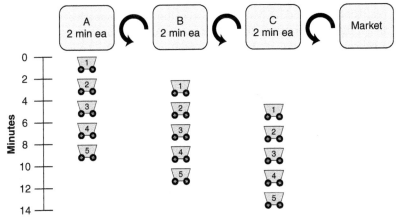

Flow time = 14 minutes for 5 carts
First piece out in 6 minutes

"We continue the conversation addressing the nine wastes and flow and pull. However, before you decide where to flow and when to pull, you will need to identify your process steps as either *value-added* or *non-value-added*, differentiating the effect that they have on your product. Some folks prefer to include a third category, *non-value-added but required*, but that is adding an excuse to the nomenclature. Adding the *but required* to the description just makes it easier to leave non-value-added work in place. The end goal is to eliminate any and all non-value-added work from your value stream and ensure that any time and effort spent on your corn increases its quality or its speed to market. Would anyone like to take a crack at defining the nature of the staging process?"

"I would say that it's non-value-added," the Horse offers. "The customer doesn't ask us to do this, and it certainly doesn't add any value to the corn. I think we all agree that staging the corn actually causes damage and slows down our flow."

"I agree!" shouts the Chicken. "But shucking, they care about that! Right?!"

"I believe that they do like that, Chicken," the Horse inserts. "As I'm dropping off loads at the market, I do catch glimpses of those humans just marveling over our corn."

"But we have to inspect the corn," the Cat insists. "The humans don't want crushed or spoiled corn. That has to be a value-added step."

"Hold on a second, Cat," interjects the Cow. "If staging is non-value-added and that is the cause of the damage that requires inspection, is inspection really value-added?"

The Owl replies. "Consider this: any activity with a *'re'* prefix is non-value-added, such as *re*package or *re*stock. This includes inspection, or *re*looking at a product. Value from a customer's perspective includes getting it right the first time from the source. You can not inspect quality into a process or a product. It has to be built in. It sounds like you've already thought through the root cause of the inspection, and preliminary findings have focused on the staging process. If a non-value-added activity causes the inspection, the inspection itself can be considered non-value-added as well, no matter how critical it might be to your current state of operations. Does that help?"

"It does. I'm not totally convinced, but I will consider it," the Cat responds.

"If inspection is non-value-added, then I guess that the same could be said about disposal," sounds the Pig. "We only dispose of corn because the inspection step tells us to, and we only inspect the corn because of the staging process. I think I'm getting this." His snout turns up at each corner as he smiles.

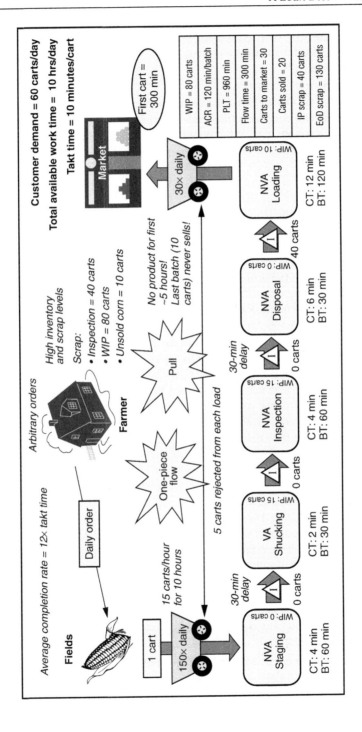

"In that case, then loading, or 're-loading,' is also non-value-added," the Dog barks. "We load the corn again at the end because we staged it in the beginning."

The team is in agreement.

"Well," the Owl begins, "thanks to the ongoing discussion, the Woodpecker has been able to capture some of your key concerns and main ideas in our value stream map. What do you say to implementing the lean principles and developing a future state map?"

Future State

"Let's get to it!" the Horse exclaims. "Can we work on the one-piece flow and the pull system first?"

"If that is what the team wants. Are there any issues with the suggested approach?" the Owl queries the group. There are no negative responses. "This means that the orders will originate from the market based on a signal to the loading stage. They will no longer come from the Farmer based on historical information and, frankly, a guess. In the end, even the most calculated forecast is still simply a guess. For your situation I recommend that you utilize your market containers for visual cues. An empty container is a call for a cart of corn. Carts will be harvested one at a time, complying with the one-piece flow paradigm. As the orders are pulled forward from the market, the carts will also be pulled forward from activity to activity throughout your value stream from the source in the fields. Animals at each step in the process will only conduct their actions when the last cartload of corn that they have completed processing is taken by the animals at the next step down the line, and again, this flows all the way to the market. Is this what you would like to see?"

"Yes!" several animals shout at once. Their excitement is palpable. The Cat does present caution.

"While reducing the corn levels at the staging phase will help to diminish our amounts of scrap, it won't eliminate them. All that rolling and shuffling on the ground takes its toll. We'll still most likely lose around ten carts total. I'm okay with the change as long as everyone understands the quality issues at hand."

The team members thoughtfully consider the Cat's comments and then agree one at a time. Once consensus is reached, the Owl continues.

"Rooster, please confer with the Woodpecker and adjust the numbers as appropriate."

The Rooster steps forward and the two go to work. Splinters and equations fly as the next phase of the value stream map evolves. In a few minutes, the image is prepared for review.

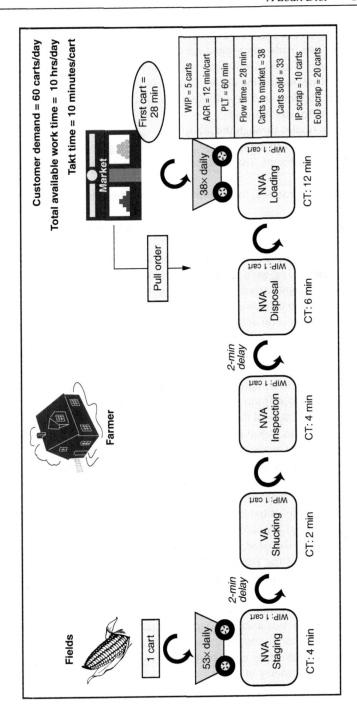

"What do you see?" asks the Owl.

"Well, we made some significant progress," the Pig contends. "If we do it this way it looks like we can get our first cart to the market a whole lot faster. How much time did we save there, Rooster?"

"Two hundred and seventy-two minutes, or about four and a half hours," the Rooster responds.

A gasp ripples through the group.

"And we cut our delays, too," continues the Pig, "by uh . . ."

"Fifty-six minutes. That's almost a whole hour, give or take," adds the Rooster.

"Our WIP dropped, too," inserts the Cow, "from eighty to five carts. Not bad."

"And we cut our scrap by 110 carts," the Cat chimes in. "This looks pretty good."

"But not good enough. Not yet," interjects the Dog. "If absolutely nothing goes wrong, we'll still fall short of the sixty-container mark. We're getting thirty-eight carts to the market, but five of 'em are arriving too late to sell. What else can we do?"

"You have several options here, Dog," the Owl answers. "At this point in the effort, you could look into each of the activities listed on the value stream map and attempt to increase the efficiency within. For example, you might choose to evaluate the disposal process, seeking ways to reduce the time it takes to complete this step. You can also move to eliminate the non-value-added steps in the process. This is the right thing to do, but it usually requires several iterations of removal in order to weed out all of the wasteful steps. Another option includes innovation. Everyone, please consider how you would move the corn through your process if you were the Farmer for a day, and recommend a new and different approach. Consider any means that will save time and effort."

After a few moments, the Sheep speaks. "What if we don't stage the corn anymore? What if we leave it on the cart and move it through the process that way? It would free up some of the pigs and other sheep, and would eliminate the need for loading at the end."

"What about the pigs and sheep?!" the Chicken bawks. "We're not talking about *cuts*, right?! We wouldn't send them to the Boo-chair, would we?!"

"That is not the intent at all," announces the Owl. "Lean is focused on waste reduction, not animal reduction. A core focus of this approach is growth, doing more with the animals and other resources that you have. Simple sustainment does not serve as a successful strategy. If your goal is to maintain your standing in a competitive environment, you will eventually be overrun by organizations that are expanding and penetrating new markets. With that in mind, what do you think of the Sheep's suggestion?"

"That sounds like it could work," the Horse replies. "Could we drop inspection and disposal as well?"

"Not yet," argues the Cat. "I get it. I understand now that inspection doesn't add any value to the corn from the customer's perspective. But as inspectors, we cats are extremely hesitant to trust in the quality of any product. I'm not saying that we couldn't get rid of the inspection process in the future, but I recommend that we take this gradually. Can we leave the inspection and disposal processes in our future state value stream map for now, but keep them labeled as non-value-added so we can target them on our next run at this?"

"This is an accepted practice in the lean methodology, Cat," says the Owl. "Lean does offer an iterative approach to performance improvement. It's entirely up to the discretion of your team."

"What do you guys think?" questions the Cat. "Can we see what this would look like—shucking, inspection, and disposal—piggybacking on the Sheep's innovative idea of carting the corn throughout the entire process? And I'm sorry, Pig. The phrase just fits."

"No problem," the Pig responds. "And I'm fine with your suggestion too."

"As am I," joins the Dog. "Does anyone object to the Cat's proposal?" There is no response.

"How about this," the Dog continues. "Everyone close your eyes."

The animals do so, and the Dog continues. "Raise a hoof, claw, or paw if you like the Cat's idea."

Within moments, each team member is standing on one less appendage.

"Very well," inserts the Owl. "Please open your eyes, and let us put the Rooster and the Woodpecker back to work."

The two birds meet near a clean section of barn wall and revise the map once more. As they complete their new draft and step back, all can see that there have been significant reductions, including the length of the value stream itself.

"Whoa," says the Horse. "And I thought that our last map was good. That looks amazing."

"And to capture all of the differences, I wonder if the Woodpecker and the Rooster wouldn't mind constructing a daily summary table for us including all of our key metrics. Those would be takt time, processing time, batch processing time, first cart to market, delays, WIP, scrap, and maybe even non-value-added steps. Could you two whip that up for us?"

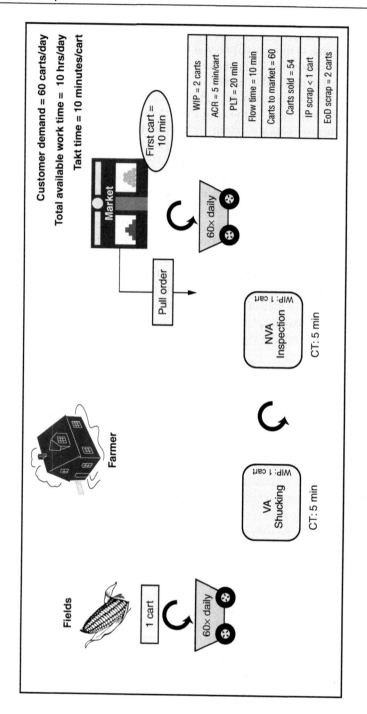

	Measure	Current state	Future state draft	Future state final
A	First cart to market	300 min	28 min	10 min
B	Takt time	1 cart/10 min	1 cart/10 min	1 cart/10 min
C	WIP	80 carts	5 carts	2 carts
D	ACR	120 min/batch	12 min/cart	5 min/cart
E	PLT (C/D)	960 min	60 min	10 min
F	Flow time	300 min	28 min	10 min
G	Carts to market	30 carts	38 carts	60 carts
H	Carts sold	20 carts	33 carts	54 carts
I	IP scrap	40 carts	10 carts	<1 cart
J	EoD scrap (C + I + [G – H])	130 carts	20 carts	2 carts
K	Delays	60 min	4 min	0 min

"No problem," the Rooster responds. As he dashes back and forth between the maps on the wall, the Woodpecker hones rows and columns into the planks. The numbers and letters continue to flesh out until a fresh product is complete, capturing the improvements that each successive value stream offers.

The animals are simultaneously stunned and motivated as their eyes travel from figure to figure. The improvements that they have realized through this exercise are significant, to say the least, and each knows that the solutions driving these results can be implemented. The problems that they face are homegrown, but so are the answers.

"What do you say?" asks the Owl.

"We're hitting takt time," begins the Horse, "and the progress that we have made in the other areas is remarkable."

"Concerning takt time," addresses the Owl, "please remember that working at takt time is a theoretical goal. In the real world, events occur that tend to modify our schedules. Ideally, you want to produce just a little faster than takt time to accommodate any variation, but that balance needs to be tested and adjusted over time. That being said, your results today are quite remarkable."

"I didn't think that this was possible, Owl. But now I'm a believer. We didn't need more animals or better carts, we just needed a lean value stream. What do you think, Jackass?" inquires the Pig.

"I think that this *could* work," the Jackass says, "but I'm still not sure whether it will or not. It will take a lot of coordination and effort to make these drawings a reality, so I'll save my celebration until I see the first cart get into the market in ten minutes."

"And that is healthy skepticism," comments the Owl, "and extremely appropriate. All of the work that you have completed today—it's an idea. An idea without action is nothing more than a dream. You will have to plan and implement your ideas, these solutions, with the same if not more robustness than you exhibited here today. Treat your future state value stream map as a hypothesis, because this is an iterative methodology. Put your solutions in place and test them, constantly and continuously gauging them against the voice of the customer, the branches of your Strate-Tree, and the needs of the farm and the animals within. The lean approach is a dynamic one, and it only fails when its practitioners become static. Do not sequester these tools and philosophies in a box, but make them a part of your every waking moment. Always look for value. Always despise waste. Do this, and Lean Acres will truly exhibit its namesake. It has been a very rewarding day, and a long one for all of us. Please, return to your pens and share the news of your accomplishments. Eat, rest, and enjoy your evening. I will meet with you at the Milking Parlour in the morning."

As the animals walk through the doors and into dusk, each engages in the first steps of their individual lean journeys, wondering how they might improve processes in their personal lives. The Owl thanks the Woodpecker once again for his services, and then joins with the shadows in the rafters above.

Rest/Reflect/Relate (R³)

1. Have you ever been involved in a lean effort in your current organization? What value stream did you focus on? What were the prominent forms of waste that you discovered in the process?

2. What (other) processes would you like to target? Which value streams provide the most beneficial products or services to your customers? What do you think the most obtrusive forms of waste are in these processes?

3. Do your own processes, at work or home, involve batch or one-piece flow processing? Why? What is the specific benefit to your practices, or are they simply "the way it has always been done"?

4. Have you ever applied the lean methodology in your personal life? If not, where could you apply it? Value streams could include working out, getting the kids off to school, or preparing to attend church.

Chapter 7

Skimming Six Sigma

Aim at perfection in everything, though in most things it is unattainable. However, they who aim at it, and persevere, will come much nearer to it than those whose laziness and despondency make them give it up as unattainable.

—Lord Chesterfield

The ladies are up and about early this morning. This has been an exciting week to say the least, and when their pen-mate, the Cow, returned last night, the news that she carried left them in utter anticipation. They can all see the Strate-Tree from anywhere in the barnyard, and everyone on Lean Acres knows that one of the branches focuses on increasing milk sales from three hundred to five hundred gallons per week. To do this, and as the smaller branches indicate, they are going to have to increase the volume of milk that they deliver to market and improve the sweetness of its taste. Actually, if they improve the sweetness factor, less milk will be dumped and more will make it to market. But they just don't know how they're going to do it. It is embarrassing to have that out in the open for all to see, but everyone knows that sour milk has been

an ongoing issue here on the farm. The cows know it and the cats definitely know it. The Strate-Tree just helps to capture the problem and to make it a priority for attack. So, the cows are awake and ready this morning. They are nervous but also excited. The animal team is coming to the Milking Parlour.

The Rooster's crow echoes between the buildings and across the fields as the sun peeks at the new day. He scurries down from his perch atop the Hen House and meets with the Chicken on the ground. They are joined by the Pig as they make their way between the pens, and not long after, the Sheep joins their ranks. The procession grows as the Horse finds his way and the Cat nimbly dismounts from the fence. The Jackass catches up as they approach the Milking Parlour, where the Dog and the Bull are waiting. The animals greet one another in the growing light, and the Dog looks out over the team.

"I'm guessing the Cow is inside. Has anyone seen the Owl this morning?" he asks.

"Last I saw of him he was in the barn talking with the Woodpecker, but that was last night," reports the Pig.

"Well I wonder . . ." the Horse begins before a loud, sharp, and rapid tapping noise explodes from the interior of the Milking Parlour.

"What in the world?!" yells the Chicken as the sound continues.

"It's got to be the Woodpecker," shouts the Cat. The noise halts for a moment and then proceeds to dominate the conversation.

"Let's get inside!" belts the Bull, and the team members cautiously make their way single file through the narrow gate.

As they round the corner they see the Cow standing apart from her sisters. She is facing the far wall, which is serving as the Woodpecker's newest canvas. Again there are images covering the surface, some of which the animals have not seen before. There are lines, both straight and curved. There are also letters and numbers, but these are in new combinations. The Woodpecker flits and pecks along the wall, crafting new images in the blink of an eye. As the slivers of wood crowd the air, it appears that the Cow is talking to herself, questioning, pausing, and then demonstrating some form of comprehension. The display is troubling to a few of the animals, and expected from the others. However, as they continue to move into the Parlour, they notice that the Owl is standing on a post to the Cow's right and engaging her in an active conversation. The Owl's large eyes catch the group members as they shuffle in through the straw, and at the raising of his right wing, the Woodpecker holds his work.

"Good morning to you all!" beams the Owl. "Welcome to another day bettering Lean Acres, bettering your lives, and last but certainly not least, bettering yourselves! What is on the agenda for this morning?"

The Dog replies. "Well, we're here in the Milking Parlour, so I'm hoping that we're going to do something, lean or whatever it takes, to make consistently sweet milk and get more of it to the market."

The animals are nodding and curious about the Owl's coming response.

"So let me get this straight," the Owl begins. "Somehow, somewhere in your milking process, and at some time, something is happening that makes the milk taste, well, let's just say, not as it should. Is that correct?"

"Unfortunately, yes," the Cow answers softly. "It wasn't always this way. The milk, I mean our milk, used to be the envy of all Perfection. It was the creamiest, most amazing stuff that you could imagine. Now, something's happened. The Cat says that we end up dumping about half of what we produce because of the taste, and sometimes the stuff that's too sweet or too sour actually makes it to the market. We're missing sales opportunities and losing customers at the same time. We still eat, drink, exercise, and milk the way we always have, but something's different. We just don't know what it is or how to fix it."

The Owl watches as her face fades from white and black to a stunning red. She is brave but embarrassed.

"Thank you for sharing that with us, Cow," the Owl consoles. "I do have good news for you this morning. There is a methodology that specifically addresses the quality of the outputs from a process. There is a way to fix this."

The Cow's visage transforms from shame to enthusiasm. "What is it?" she asks. "How?"

"Fortunately, the same answer is appropriate for both the *what* and the *how*," the Owl replies. "The answer is Six Sigma."

Step 6: Academics

"Six Sigma," continues the Owl, "is a name for a goal and a methodology."

The Sheep is curious. "What's the goal part of it?"

"The goal is to make things, like your milk, as good or as sweet as your customers want it to be. Nothing more and nothing less, but right on target. Cat, you have a scale that your brothers and sisters use to evaluate the flavor of the milk, correct?"

"We sure do," the Cat responds. "We use a scale that starts at zero and ends at ten. All cats are in tune with the scale, and we all interpret taste exactly the same. It's in our genes. A zero indicates very sour milk, whereas a ten means that the milk could not possibly get any sweeter. In fact, it's too sweet for the humans' taste buds. It overloads them. A nine is about as high as we can go if we want to keep them happy."

"Let us just say that your customers want their milk to be a seven, but they are willing to accept as low as a five and as high as a nine," starts the Owl, but he is cut off by the Jackass.

"I don't get it. Why in the world wouldn't a customer want their milk sweeter than a nine? That's ridiculous! If they could have milk rated at a ten every time, I'm sure they would love it!"

"Not necessarily," replies the Owl.

"What do you mean?" Now the Bull and a few others are interested.

"Producing milk that is consistently rated as a ten might cost too much, either in green paper or in the time it takes to produce it. It also might just be too sweet. Maybe a score at nine or below complements their cooking just so, or makes their cereal taste just right." The Owl pauses and looks at each team member.

The animals seem to understand, and they look to the Owl for further information.

"So, Six Sigma uses some number tools, or *statistics* as the humans call it, to center their results on the score that your customers want, and to reduce the variation around it. Let's say that you average a score of seven, and that is what the customers want. Every time that you produce milk that is not a seven, for example, that milk and its score have deviated from the central tendency, the seven. That deviation is the variation that I am referring to."

Precision and Accuracy

"I think that I understand," says the Dog. "The Farmer, he has a BB gun that he uses to, well, let's just say *take care of* any crows that come along. When there aren't any around, he likes to practice shooting at these circles that are drawn on paper. There's a small circle in the center, and a bigger circle around that, and then an even bigger circle around that one. When he shoots the BB gun, the little metal balls make holes in the paper. Is the variation that you're talking about kind of like the times that the Farmer aims at the center but hits around it?"

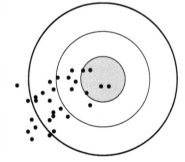

"Yes it is," the Owl answers. "Actually, it's just like that, and what a wonderful example. Allow me to take it a step further. Imagine that the middle of that center circle represented the milk score that your customers wanted, and that the Farmer fired thirty BBs into the paper. It might look something like this."

The Owl clears away straw and scratches out the circles in the dirt with his claws. He dots the image several times with a single talon, and then returns to the conversation.

"If the Farmer was in fact aiming for the center of this target, you can see that there is quite a bit of variation between each of his shots."

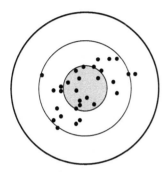

Each animal looks at the image and nods their head. The Cow speaks first.

"It doesn't look like he's a very good marksman," she offers.

"Exactly!" commends the Owl. "The Farmer's shots are spread out and not centered on the bull's-eye, if you'll excuse the expression, Bull. Six Sigma helps us to shift the average, or the middle of the shot grouping, over to the center of the target. By shifting the average, it might look more like this." A few more scratches in the dust and a second sketch is complete.

"It's definitely more accurate," says the Cow.

"But it's not very precise," adds the Cat. "The shots are really dispersed across the target." "And you are both right," inserts the Owl. "A wide spread, or *distribution*, of shots like that across the target indicates a lack of precision, and this is another area in which Six Sigma can help. We can reduce the variation, or the spread of the BB holes, putting more through the center of the target on a consistent basis. This is why Six Sigma is helpful as a complete practice. It does help us to improve our precision, thus reducing variation. But we also use the tools in this box to center the results of the process itself. Six Sigma focuses on reducing variation, thereby increasing precision, and shifting the mean, or the central tendency, until it is on target, thereby increasing accuracy as well. This will address quality and volume issues simultaneously without increasing production efforts. We will make more of our product just the way our customers want it. The fewer scores off-target, the less we dispose of and the more that makes it to market. With a little bit of work and some careful analysis, we can make the picture look like this." He drafts the soil once more, and the animals gather around to view the final image.

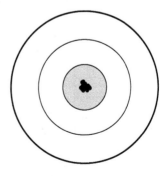

"Now, that would make the Farmer happy," the Dog sighs.

"If we could give the humans milk that tasted just as sweet as they want it every time, no one would even consider going to Milky Ways for their stuff. We'd be the toast of Perfection once again," regards the Cow.

Percentages versus Parts per Million Opportunities

"Did you say that Six Sigma also represented a number?" inquires the Horse.

"I did," the Owl begins, "and it does. Quite often when we perform work and produce a product or deliver a service, others talk about how well we have done through the application of percentages. You might hear phrases like 'fifty percent of the straw was saved after the storm' or 'we do it right ninety-five percent of the time.' You might even hear something about 'ninety-nine percent accuracy,' to build on our previous discussion."

"So what?" asks the Jackass. "Ninety-nine percent accuracy is a good thing, right?"

The team seems to agree with the Jackass, and they look to the Owl for clarification.

"It does sound good, doesn't it?" the Owl queries. "In fact, ninety-nine percent accuracy or ninety-nine percent on-time deliveries both sound great. However, percentages only paint a true picture if you're only considering one hundred occurrences. Ninety-nine percent sounds wonderful if you mean that you've only made one mistake. But how many goods do you only produce one hundred of on this farm?"

The group considers the question, and after some time the Bull responds, "Never. We make a lot more than a hundred of everything here."

"And that's why Six Sigma emphasizes a view of quality through the perspective of *defects per million opportunities* (DPMO)," asserts the Owl, "and as yield, or good products, increases, so does the *sigma level*. It looks like this." The Owl motions toward the leftmost side of the wall in the Milking Parlour. The animals move closer and look over the Woodpecker's work.

"How does ninety-nine percent, or four sigma, look to you now?" asks the Owl.

Sigma level	DPMO	Defects (%)	Yield	Yield (%)
1	691,462	69%	308,538	31
2	308,538	31%	691,462	69
3	66,807	6.7%	933,193	93.3
4	6,210	0.62%	993,790	99.38
5	233	0.023%	999,767	99.977
6	3.4	0.00034%	999,996.6	99.99966

"Does this mean that if we were to operate at a four sigma level, right around ninety-nine percent yield, for every million gallons of milk that we produced we would put out over six thousand gallons of bad stuff?" the Cow inquires.

"Yes, it does," replies the Owl.

"Well, I don't know about everyone else, but I don't like that one bit," exclaims the Horse. "That's not going to be good enough for the people of Perfection, and it won't save Lean Acres."

"But six thousand mistakes out of every million opportunities just doesn't sound that bad to me," states the Pig. "Help me to understand, Owl."

"Let me try to make this clearer through a practical example," returns the Owl. "I've spoken with the Dog about water consumption here on the farm. Each year you use about one million gallons of drinking water. Take a look at the table on the wall. If the State of Perfection Water Works were to consider ninety-nine percent quality levels to be acceptable, how many gallons of unsanitary water, or defects, would you be potentially exposed to each year?"

The Rooster reviews the numbers on the wall and in his head before he responds.

"Six thousand, two hundred and ten gallons," the Rooster reports.

"Oh my, that doesn't sound so good," says the Pig.

"Would you feel safe taking a drink if you knew that was their standard?" presses the Owl.

"Not at all," the Pig returns. "I get it, I get it. Wow!"

Each team member has a look of disgust on their face. Apparently, they understand too.

"Would you feel comfortable allowing your customers to drink milk that was produced at a four sigma level?" questions the Owl.

"No, not now," offers the Cow. "But we didn't know this before. Now that we understand the implications of masking our results with percentages, how can we control the quality of our outputs?"

"By controlling the quality of your inputs," the Owl answers.

Quality In = Quality Out

"Another key aspect of the Six Sigma methodology is this: the quality of the product that you produce is a function of the inputs that you use," the Owl continues. "In mathematical terms, we express this relationship like this." The Owl points to a few letters and symbols on the wall, just to the right of the sigma level table.

$$y = f(x)$$

"The *y* is the symbol for the outputs, or in this case the milk. The *f* represents the process by which the milk is made. I'm not talking about the milking process here, but the manufacturing piece that occurs within each Cow. And the *x* stands for the inputs, or the food that the cows eat, which is in turn converted into milk. If we were looking at this from a cause-and-effect standpoint, the *x* would be the cause and the *y* would be the effect. Does this make sense to you?"

"Sort of," the Rooster speaks, "but not completely. Are you saying that we can't control the quality of our outputs without controlling the quality of our inputs?"

"Close," the Owl responds, "but not entirely true. I am saying that you must *control* the quality of your inputs and *monitor* the quality of your outputs. As stated in the lean phase, it is impossible to inspect quality into a product or a service. It must be built in. You can't make the milk sweeter by inspecting it."

"All that we can do is separate the good from the bad," comments the Cat. "And even with all of our work, we don't catch all of it. We can't."

"Exactly," the Owl says. "Inspecting the milk is a reactive process. What you need is a proactive approach, and that is what Six Sigma offers. By controlling the quality of the inputs, or the feed, and monitoring the output, that is, your milk, you will be able to work toward a six sigma level of performance."

"Alright, Owl," inserts the Cow, "I think we're catching on. You made the lean approach easier for us by laying out the four steps that we needed to follow. Does the Six Sigma methodology have steps too?"

"It certainly does," replies the Owl. "Only, this time there are five phases in a Six Sigma project. They are: *define, measure, analyze, improve,* and *control*. This is also called *DMAIC*, or *da-may-ick*, for short."

"It sounds great," barks the Dog. "We're ready when you are."

"Then let us get started," says the Owl. "Here is a quick reference for you that provides an outline of the DMAIC approach." He points to an image hewn into the wooden wall.

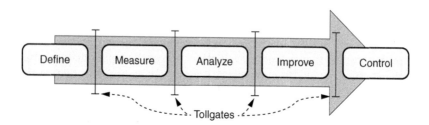

Step 7: Action

Setting the Course

"What do we do first?" asks the Horse.

The Owl moves toward the wall in the Milking Parlour and gestures toward an image with the words 'Six Sigma Project Charter' engraved above it. "We are now in the *define* phase of our project. First, we need to make sure that we all have a common understanding of the task at hand. To do this, we will address each item on the project charter one at a time. We will treat the charter as a draft for the first three phases of the DMAIC cycle, finalizing it only as we enter into the *improve* stage. How does that sound?"

"It sounds good," the Bull answers. "What do we put in the *Challenge* block?"

"We capture the problem statement here," replies the Owl. "This should include a few key points detailing our target in terms of what dissatisfaction our customers and our farm are experiencing, how much, and why. We will need to keep this as simple as possible, and we can fill in the details as we progress through the *analyze* phase. As before, the

Six Sigma Project Charter		
1. Challenge:	4. Impact:	
2. Scope:	5. Barriers:	6. Enablers:
3. Goal:	7. Team:	

Woodpecker will capture your comments during our discussion. Would anyone like to give this block a try?"

"I will," the Cat volunteers. "I'm pretty close to this one." The Cat stares at the charter template and begins mouthing silent words to herself. After several muted mental arguments she addresses the group. "Tell me what you think of this. 'We are producing five hundred gallons of milk every week. We are losing sales because fifty percent of our milk does not get delivered to the market due to poor quality. Some is too sour and some is too sweet. We are losing customers because some of this *bad* milk does make it to the market.' Is that simple enough?"

"I think that sounds good," remarks the Cow. "But it's so negative. Should we mention something about how we plan to use Six Sigma to fix the problem?"

"Not at all," inserts the Owl. "Remember, in this first piece of the charter, we are only addressing the problem as it affects our customers and our organization. We are not referencing solutions. Not yet."

"If that's the case, then I like it too," adds the Pig. The rest of the team agrees.

"What about the second block?" asks the Bull. "The one that says *Scope*? What do we put in there?"

"Simply stated," the Owl begins, "in this section we discuss the boundaries of the process that we are exploring, where it starts and where it ends, and what is *in* and what is *out* concerning the practice of milking. By this I mean what we can affect and what we can not affect due to physical or other restrictions."

The Cow speaks. "The feed is harvested from the fields. Sometimes it's grass and sometimes it's corn. We eat it, do our thing, and then the pigs and sheep are kind enough to relieve the pressure by milking us. The milk goes directly into jars, which the cats inspect. The good stuff goes on to the market. The sour milk gets dumped on the compost pile at the end of the day. I think that's it. What do you guys say?"

"You would know better than us, Cow," responds the Dog.

"Based on this information," begins the Cat, "I would argue that the harvesting and delivery processes are out of scope for us, but everything from feeding through inspection is in play."

"I also think that the milk-making process itself is out. I mean really, we can't change the internal activities that the cows use to turn the feed into milk," says the Bull.

"We can't change them, but we might be able to affect them by working on the inputs," the Sheep adds.

"And what would the goal of all that work be?" asks the Jackass.

"That's the next block!" the Chicken calls. "What is our goal?! How do we define that?!"

"With SMARTER measures," the Owl responds.

"We talked about this when we were developing our strategic goals" the Dog interjects. "SMARTER stands for *specific, measurable, aligned, realistic, time-oriented, evaluated,* and *reviewed.*"

"Oh yeah," the Horse recalls. "Could our project goal be the same as our strategic goal of increasing milk sales to five hundred gallons per week?"

"Overall, yes," the Owl answers, "but what will it take to get there?"

"I think that our objectives cover that," offers the Rooster. "We need to increase our weekly volume to five hundred gallons, and in order to do that we'd better focus on dumping less bad milk. We should focus on improving the quality of the milk."

"And right now we're averaging a seven on the ten-point scale," the Cat comments. "That's borderline sour from the customer's perspective."

We want eight.

That would be great.

The harmonic response echoes off the tin wall. The Mice have returned, completely unnoticed. They stand shoulder to shoulder on their hind legs atop a stall gate and stare at the team through glossy, black eyes. This disturbs the Cat more than anyone.

Lower than seven is too low, that's sour.

We'll dump it out in a milky shower.

And greater than nine is too high,

Milk like that we will not buy.

We like milk that scores an eight.

Give us that at a steady rate.

Three voices trail off as one, from squeaks to whispers to silence.

"So then," the Cat continues, looking cautiously toward the Mice as they stand fixed on the post, "could our goal be to improve the quality rating of our milk to an average score of eight, with zero gallons above nine or lower than seven, and deliver five hundred gallons of milk to the market each week?"

I think that we can, Cat," the Bull replies. "It's SMARTER alright. Does anyone disagree?"

All heads are moving right to left and left to right.

"And why should you do this?" the Owl asks.

"What do you mean, *why*?" questions the Cow.

"The next block of the charter is titled *Impact*," clarifies the Owl, "and you will need to express the benefit that this project will yield for Lean Acres. How does it align to your Strate-Tree?"

"If we do this right, it should satisfy one of our strategic goals, one of our main branches on our Strate-Tree," argues the Horse.

"That is correct, Horse. But what will that do for Lean Acres?" prods the Owl.

"It's only a piece of it," starts the Cow, "but it will help us to keep the farm and prevent any more of us from going to the Boo-chair."

"Now we are getting there," encourages the Owl. "Does anyone else have anything to add?"

"I do." It is the Cat. "If we apply the Six Sigma methodology appropriately, would this effort also free some of the extra inspectors that we have assigned to the Milking Parlour? We have other areas on the farm where we need them, and they might even find time to eat and sleep."

"If you apply it correctly, it could," the Owl responds.

"Then I vote that we include that information as well," contends the Cat.

"If there are no objections, we only have two more blocks to complete," announces the Owl. The Parlour is silent for a few moments, and he continues. "What are the barriers that could slow you down or stop your work improving the quality of the milk? Also, what might work in your favor? What are the potential enablers that might serve to overcome any barriers that you identify?"

"One barrier that comes to mind has to do with attitude. I'm not certain that the cats here in the Milking Parlour really feel that improving the quality of the milk is important," says the Dog. "I mean no offense, Cat, but these guys and gals have been running around this way for such a long time that I don't think they remember or can conceive of a better process or a better product."

"I agree with you, Dog," the Cat replies. "But we do have the Strate-Tree on the barn. We can all see it clearly from here, and I spoke about it at great lengths with them the night our team finished it. We can always refer my fellow cats to that image and to that ideal. Maybe that would provide them the direction and motivation that they need. After all, that is the purpose of the Strate-Tree, isn't it, Owl, to stimulate and guide conversations, understanding, and commitment?"

"Yes it is," answers the Owl. "It seems that we have our first pair of barrier and enabler. Are there others?"

"From all that we've learned, it seems to me that Six Sigma is heavily dependent on data," offers the Pig. "I don't think we have a lot of that around here."

"Each Cat is supposed to keep detailed records of their inspection findings," the Cat responds. "We don't use a Woodpecker, but we do keep tallies for each week's milk production on the trees behind the Milking Parlour. You didn't think that we scratched our claws on trees for fun, did you? We captured the data, the count of good and bad gallons of milk, for every week that has passed since the Milking Parlour was raised. I'll check with each of my brothers and sisters to ensure that absolute data integrity has been maintained."

"Very well," interjects the Owl. "Are there any other barriers or enablers that stand out?"

"Could this whole approach be a barrier to our project?" the Rooster inquires.

"What do you mean, Rooster?" asks the Bull.

"Well, we're all used to doing our chores our own way. For each job that we do, we created the *how* right here on Lean Acres. Now we're going to tell the cows and the cats about Six Sigma, and that wasn't invented here. They could resist the change, even if it is improvement, simply because it's not organic to our farm. You know?"

"I know what you mean, Rooster," replies the Sheep, "and I concur with you. Perhaps the Owl could give the cats a brief overview of Six Sigma, each of us could explain how it complements the Strate-Tree, and we could also discuss how that tree is going to save our home."

"Those are great ideas," assures the Owl, "and they could help to overcome the transformation barrier. The last block is an easy but essential one. This portion of the charter is reserved for the names of everyone who is serving on the project team. We use this space to identify the project sponsor as well. Just as the RACI chart we developed named the Horse as the sponsor of the corn-harvesting event, the Bull has been identified to lead this effort. Once the Woodpecker pecks the final piece, please peer at the presentation."

"Are we done?" asks the Jackass.

"With the charter, for now we are," returns the Owl. "Please remember that this is a living document, and consider this version to be a draft. We might make a few discoveries along our Six Sigma journey that change the charter—some as additions, some as deletions, and others as simple revisions. Your project has now been defined. With the Bull's approval, we will need to measure."

"I agree with you, Owl," says the Bull. "Let's get to it."

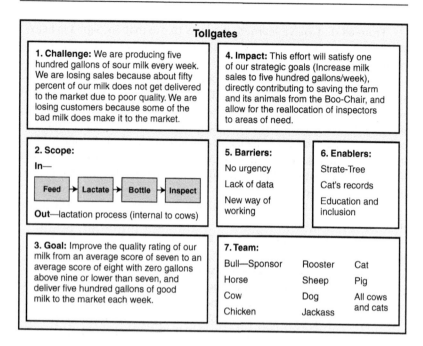

Tollgates

1. Challenge: We are producing five hundred gallons of sour milk every week. We are losing sales because about fifty percent of our milk does not get delivered to the market due to poor quality. We are losing customers because some of the bad milk does make it to the market.

4. Impact: This effort will satisfy one of our strategic goals (Increase milk sales to five hundred gallons/week), directly contributing to saving the farm and its animals from the Boo-Chair, and allow for the reallocation of inspectors to areas of need.

2. Scope:

In—

Feed → Lactate → Bottle → Inspect

Out—lactation process (internal to cows)

5. Barriers:

No urgency

Lack of data

New way of working

6. Enablers:

Strate-Tree

Cat's records

Education and inclusion

3. Goal: Improve the quality rating of our milk from an average score of seven to an average score of eight with zero gallons above nine or lower than seven, and deliver five hundred gallons of good milk to the market each week.

7. Team:

Bull—Sponsor	Rooster	Cat
Horse	Sheep	Pig
Cow	Dog	All cows and cats
Chicken	Jackass	

Confirming Confidence

"Alright," responds the Owl, "we need to get a solid picture of our current performance. To do that, let us take a look at the data that we have. Welcome to the *measure* phase."

"How are we going to do that?" asks the Pig.

"By consulting with your experts, the cats," the Owl answers. "I met with the Cat and her family last evening to prepare for this event and reviewed the vast amounts of information that they keep, and *vast* is an understatement. The scores for individual bottle inspections over the last two years are truly dizzying, but there is a solution. We have every quality score for every bottle, good or bad, for this time frame. This is the population of data, every single score. That's five hundred bottles each week, or fifty-two thousand scores altogether. Attempting to assemble that information for analysis could prove to be quite a challenge, but the Six Sigma methodology offers us an alternative called *confidence*. By applying random sampling and certain formulas, you can figure out exactly how many individual scores you would need to look at in order to assess the entire population with an acceptable degree of certainty, or confidence. For a population of this size, we needed to randomly select a sample composed of three hundred and eighty-one individual quality scores in order to achieve a *confidence interval* of plus or minus five percent and a *confidence level* of ninety-five percent. This group of scores that we select from the population is known as a *sample*. Ninety-five percent is the confidence level that many practitioners deem to be acceptable. This all means that if our findings reveal that fifty percent of the milk produced over the two-year period is sour, we can be ninety-five percent confident that forty-five to fifty-five percent of the individual scores from the entire population would be sour as well. It's basically a level of comfort that you can embrace in measuring a smaller piece of the whole. Does this make sense to you?"

"I don't completely get it," replies the Horse, "but the approach makes sense. What does our sample look like?"

Distributing Results

"Like this," the Owl says as he points his wing toward the back wall. Individual X's have been staked in varying heights forming a rough, rounded shape against a numerical foundation. A bell-shaped curve surrounds the structure like a bubble, and the animals don't know what to make of it.

"This is a *frequency distribution*," announces the Owl. "The numbers along the bottom represent a range of quality scores for each individual bottle of milk over the last two years. As we reviewed each individual score from the sample of three hundred and eighty-one, we placed an X over its value on the number line. If there was more than one score that matched that value, we simply stacked the X's on top of each other. By doing this, we can observe the number of times, or the *frequency*, that a particular value occurred within the sample that we collected. This is an exceedingly expedient and simple way to assess your performance, visually recognizing aspects such as average—ours is seven—and our range from four to ten, both at a glance. The curve drawn over the chart represents the actual values for the population, and the bell-like shape of ours indicates

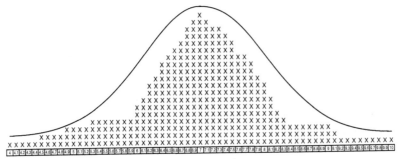

Sweetness scale

that the data in our sample are normally distributed. A normal distribution is defined by the central tendency and the spread."

"Normal distribution. That's good, right?" asks the Dog.

"Yes and no," the Owl replies. "It is good in that it means that the data from our samples are normally distributed, with most of the sample values remaining close to the average and fewer and fewer occurring as you move toward the extreme upper or lower scores. This allows us to predict our performance over time. If there were different peaks rising from different values across the chart, or a sharp bend to the left or the right, that could be indicative of other issues. If you don't have a nice bell curve, that does not mean that anything is wrong with your process, and there are ways to normalize the data for analysis purposes. However, it is our customer requirements—their upper and lower specification limits—that gauge our performance. Take a look at the frequency distribution against these parameters. I believe that people want their milk to have an average score of eight, with a low score of seven and a high score of nine."

"Woodpecker," calls the Owl, "could you please show us what this looks like against our current performance?"

The Woodpecker nods and scurries into action. The animals venture to see the additions, one at a time, and soon the entire team looks on with surprise.

"What do you see?" asks the Owl.

"I think I see that we really are losing half of our milk," answers the Cow. "It looks like the first BB gun example we discussed where the Farmer wasn't accurate or precise."

The Pig joins the conversation. "Even if we were hitting an average score of eight, which we're not, just look at how widely spread our results are. We would still have scores that are out of specification, well beyond the limits set by our customers."

A Measure of Milk

"How do we figure out just how wide our spread is, Owl? Is there a way to measure that?" the Rooster inquires.

"There are, in fact, four ways to assess this spread, or *distribution* as it is called," replies the Owl. "The first is called the *range*. The range is simply the value of the highest score minus the value of the lowest score. In this case of the milk, this would be ten minus four, which is equal to six. The frequency distribution chart that we are using makes this measure very easy to see and to assess."

"That seems easy enough," comments the Bull. "What are the other methods for measuring distribution?"

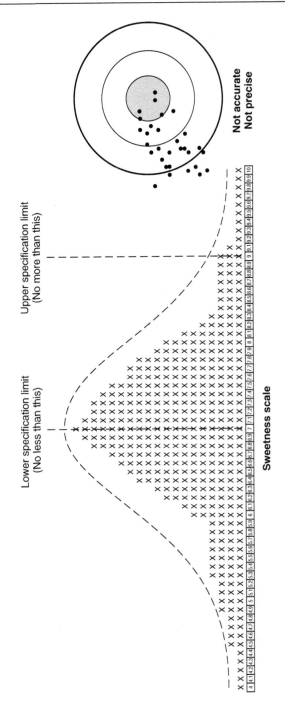

"The second option is called *deviation*," the Owl continues. "This is the distance between a single point of data, or a milk score, and the average. This lets us know just how far the score falls, or deviates, from the average. Obviously, minimal deviation is desired."

"Makes sense to me so far!" claims the Chicken. "What's next?!"

"The third and fourth options are more complicated," responds the Owl. "I'll explain the basics, but please understand that we could spend an entire day discussing the rationale behind and the application of these measures."

The animals are silent and attentive, ready and waiting.

"*Variance* is a way to assess the spread of our data, and it simply tells us how far all of our individual quality scores are from the average quality score as a whole. This gives us the total picture rather than the focused snapshots that deviation can portray. The problem with variance is that the results yielded from the equation always appear in units squared, and we do not measure or report things that way in the real world. You would never ask how the milking process is doing and expect an answer in the form of so many points squared. That would be confusing."

"Well, how should we do it then?" questions the Cat.

"The easiest way possible," responds the Owl. "If we want to understand the variation that is occurring in our process and report it in the same units that are collected for analysis, we can take the square root of the variance. This is called the *standard deviation*, and this is the most commonly used measurement to describe process spread. In fact, we call it the Six Sigma methodology because the goal is to have a capable process with six *sigmas*, or standard deviations, between the process average and the closest specification limit as determined by your customers."

Capturing Capability

"What are you talking about when you question whether or not our process is *capable*?" the Jackass interjects. "We're making milk, aren't we? And it looks like at least half of it is just as sweet as the customer wants it to be."

"When we talk about the capability of a process, Jackass, we consider two factors. They are width, or *precision*, and centering, or *accuracy*. Let us consider the gate to the Milking Parlour as an example," suggests the Owl. "When you entered this morning, were you able to come through all at once, side by side?"

"Of course not," the Jackass replies. "The gate's not wide enough for that. We had to walk in single file."

"Good," responds the Owl. "Consider the gateway, or the fence posts on either side of the opening, to be the specification limits established by the voice of the customer. Imagine that they are each prickled with splinters. Also, think about the width of the animals passing through as the width, or *dispersion*, of the process. If you and a few of your teammates were to attempt to enter the Parlour perfectly centered on the gate and shoulder to shoulder, what would happen?"

"We wouldn't get through," the Pig states. "Our group would be wider than the gate, and the folks on the outer edges would get splinters or just run into the posts!"

"Absolutely," the Owl offers. "You would be incapable of entering the Parlour, or to put it in process-speak, you would be incapable of meeting the specification limits established by your customers. Your procession would simply be too wide."

"That just makes too much sense," adds the Jackass. "Is that all there is to it?"

"No, there is also the aspect that includes centering the process," the Owl continues. "What if you could walk through, let us say, two at a time? How would you proceed?"

"Very carefully," the Sheep comments. "I would try to walk right down the center, keeping as much distance as possible between that wood and my wool. I would also tell my friends to follow right behind me in a single-file line."

"I'm sure you would," assures the Owl, "and that is the essence of understanding process capability. We need our process to operate in a targeted fashion, centered right on the average score in between the customer's specifications. And the *thinner* that our distribution is—the more room we leave in between our results and the customer requirements—the safer we will be."

"No splinters," sighs the Sheep.

"No splinters indeed," the Owl agrees. "This is key to the Six Sigma approach. We want to get all of our data points, the sample scores that represent our performance, to fall within the specification limits set by the voice of the customer."

"Well, how do we know if we're thin enough and centered?!" calls the Chicken.

"Thanks to our frequency distribution chart we can see that the spread, or the dispersion, of our scores would not fit neatly in between the parameters set by our customers even if we were averaging a quality rating of eight. We are running too wide. We can also see that our average is far from the center of both the upper and the lower specification limits.

As of now we are running wide and headlong into one of those splintery fence posts."

The animals consider their situation. Some look to the frequency distribution plot, some at the formulas scratched in the ground and etched into the wall.

"What can we do with this information? How can we improve?" The Bull steps forward. The faces of his team members reflect his concern.

"Now that we know more about our process," states the Owl, "we can determine our current sigma level, how many defects per million opportunities we are creating, and what our yield actually is. We can then use this information to complete the baseline activities and update our charter. Take a look at the table the Woodpecker carved earlier. This will provide a general sanity check concerning the accuracy of our calculations, the first of which will be *defects per million opportunities*, or *DPMO*. This is a simple one. How many opportunities are there to produce a defect in the sample that we generated?"

"I don't know," starts the Pig. "It looks like about half the milk we produce is sour, and we have, what was it? Oh yeah, 381 scores altogether. So, like around 190 opportunities?"

The Horse disagrees. "Not our defect count, Pig. He asked about opportunities to produce defects. I think we all agree that a gallon of milk outside of the customer specifications is a defect. It's either good or it's bad. If there are 381 quality scores in our sample, I'd say that every one of them presents an equal opportunity for a defect to occur."

"And you would be correct," adds the Owl. "If your product can be evaluated in a binomial manner, either it is good or it is bad, then each one that you make is an opportunity for a defect. Now, how many defects were actually produced? What does our sample show?"

"One hundred eighty-five," quotes the Rooster. All eyes turn to him as the animals stare in amazement.

Sigma level	DPMO	Defects (%)	Yield	Yield (%)
1	691,462	69%	308,538	31
2	308,538	31%	691,462	69
3	66,807	6.7%	933,193	93.3
4	6,210	0.62%	993,790	99.38
5	233	0.023%	999,767	99.977
6	3.4	0.00034%	999,996.6	99.99966

"I counted them when we first got here," the Rooster claims. "What? I like numbers!"

"Alright," the Owl says. "Thank you, Rooster. Now that we have these two figures, we can calculate the DPMO for the milking process. We divide the number of defects, in our case 185, by the total number of opportunities, or 381. This gives us 0.4856, which we then multiply by 1,000,000 and we get 485,564. This means that for every million gallons of milk you produce, 485,564 of them get dumped on the compost pile. It is not quite half, as we originally estimated, but it is darn close. Our *yield* is calculated by subtracting 0.4856 from one and multiplying the difference by 100 percent. For this process, our yield is 51.44 percent. As far as a sigma level, based on my knowledge of the appropriate calculations and tables, we are sitting on a score of about 1.54 sigma. How does all this sound, Cow?"

"It sounds like we're wasting a lot of energy, time, and ultimately milk," reports the Cow. "No wonder Milky Ways has been outpacing us at the market. How in the world are we going to compete? What are we going to do?!"

"We're going to improve, Cow," barks the Dog. "We have a strategy in place, and we are moving in the right direction. Just look at the barnyard, it's spotless. And the harvesting process? We are going to see some big gains with our corn. We're here now, in your area, in your world. We'll work together and we'll make it better."

"How?" the Cow questions quietly.

"First," announces the Owl, "we are going to update our charter with the knowledge that we have gained from our measurement activities. Woodpecker, if you please."

The Woodpecker performs an aerial display over the face of the existing draft charter. With a series of taps here and there, the information in the *Challenge* and *Goal* blocks is clarified with specific terms.

"How now, Cow?" asks the Owl.

---

1. Challenge: We are producing five hundred gallons of sour milk every week. Our current critical measures include:

DPMO: 485,564 • Yield: 51.44% • Sigma level: 1.54

We are losing sales because about fifty percent of our milk does not get delivered to the market due to poor quality. We are losing customers because some of the bad milk does make it to the market.

3. Goal: Improve the quality rating of our milk from an average score of seven to an average score of eight with zero gallons above nine or lower than seven, and deliver five hundred gallons of good milk to the market each week. Critical measure targets include:

DPMO: 3.4 • Yield: 99.99966% • Sigma level 6

"I think we've clarified the problem and our desired end state. I just don't understand how we are going to get there," responds the Cow.

"Before we can answer to the *how*, we will address the *why*," the Owl leads. "Let us discover *why* the milk is sour with root cause analysis."

Digging Up Roots

"My head is still spinning from the variation and the curve and the capability and the thing with the stuff. I don't know how much more I can take!"

The rest of the team looks fatigued as well. It has been a very busy day, and noon has only just arrived. The Owl swoops down to face them at ground level.

"Performance excellence requires diligence and discipline," he begins. "Just like Six Sigma teaches us, what you get out of it depends on what you put into it. I know that some of the equations and the process metrics can be difficult and frustrating at times. So many numbers and symbols and letters. It is tough to keep them all straight, but they do enable organizations like Lean Acres to experience dramatic improvement. You also have to remember that every phase of a DMAIC project uses a broad set of tools, some of which are admittedly quite boring. Some, however, are quite collaborative and can be fun."

"Like what?" asks the Horse.

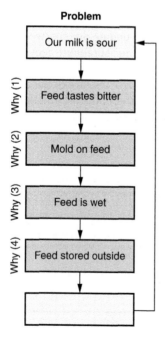

"Like one of my personal favorites from the *analyze* phase, the *5 whys*," answers the Owl. "The *5 whys* is the name of an extremely simple but effective method of conducting a root cause analysis. First, a problem statement is identified. Does anyone want to give it a try?"

"I'll start," the Bull volunteers. "Our milk is sour."

"But all of our milk isn't sour," claims the Cow. She's understandably upset.

"No, it's not," the Rooster comments. "But we're not trying to find the root cause for the good stuff right now."

"That is correct, Rooster," the Owl steps in. "Remember, Cow, the problem statement will often appear to be all-encompassing due to its brevity, but it's a general statement focused on a specific problem. Does that make sense to you?"

"Now it does. Thank you, Owl," says the Cow. "Sorry if I'm still a little touchy about this, everybody."

"Not at all, Cow," the Dog replies. "None of this has been easy, but so far it's all been worth it. I'd say that we have our problem statement. I guess that the next question is *why*, right? Why is our milk sour?"

"I don't think that it has anything to do with the way that the cows actually make the milk. Nothing's changed there since the beginning of time as far as I can tell. Could it be that we don't have enough inspectors at the end of the line to catch it all?" asks the Pig.

"No, Pig," answers the Bull. "Remember what the Owl said. We can't inspect quality into the milk. We have to build it in."

"If that's the case, why don't we take a look at our one and only input?!" recommends the Chicken. "Let's look at the feed!"

"But nothing's different about the feed," the Cow responds, "except for the . . ."

"Except what?" prods the Bull.

"Except, well, now that I think about it, right around the time we started having issues in the Milking Parlour, the girls and I noticed that the feed started tasting bitter. Just a little bit here and there and just a little bitter, but different for sure," admits the Cow.

"Why did the feed taste bitter?!" eggs the Chicken.

"We did notice that there was more mold on it than usual," continues the Cow. "I mean there was always some mold on there, and it gives the

feed a little extra flavor. But a while back the difference became notice-able. At least it did to us."

"And why was there more mold on the feed?" spurs the Horse.

"I think that it has something to do with moisture. The feed has also been coming in wet, and the more water that there is in the mix, the more mold we see, and taste."

"Why is the feed wet?" the Sheep inquires.

"Because it's stored outside the Milking Parlour in open boxes," the Cow replies. "The girls and I, we thought that it would be nice to have room to exercise inside the Parlour. You know, yoga, aerobics, noth-ing high-impact. So about two years ago, we moved the feed outside." She pauses for a few seconds and then looks to the ground and sighs. "Oh no . . ."

The wood chips drift downward into the dirt, and the Cow looks up at the root cause analysis diagram.

"Congratulations!" the Owl says, rattling the group from its collective realization. "You made it to the root cause in four whys."

"But we didn't use all five," the Sheep offers a concerned response.

"And you don't have to," assures the Owl. "We call it the 5 whys to encourage continuous questioning and exploration. It might take a group of animals seven or nine whys to get to the root cause of their problem. It could take another group three whys. The right amount depends on the issue at hand, the participants, and numerous other factors. The goal is to get to a level of granularity where you can enact a relatively simple solu-tion or set of solutions to address the core issue. You happened to dis-cover your root cause in four whys. Now, the next question is *how*. How should we address this cause and eliminate the symptoms?"

Fixin' to Fix It

"Could the answer be as simple as moving the feed inside, or somewhere under cover?" asks the Cow.

"Sure it could," the Owl replies. "All possibilities should be considered in the *improve* phase."

"But we'll need to fix the roof in the Parlour," says the Bull. "It's been leaking here and there for awhile now."

"And maybe we should 7S the Milking Parlour to make certain that the feed is not just thrown in here," offers the Rooster.

"Should we also start inspecting the inputs to our process?" ques-tions the Cat. "Should we start inspecting the feed before the cows eat it? It seems to me that if we get rid of any moldy feed before it touches their lips then we would essentially be removing the cause and eliminating the effect. Isn't that a focus in this Six Sigma approach?"

"It certainly is," the Owl responds. "The emphasis in Six Sigma is to inspect your inputs and monitor your outputs. By calculating and then exploiting the relationship between the two, you will be able to achieve control over your process and be able to accurately predict performance and the effects of any changes you might make."

The animals are understanding the methodology and synthesizing the fundamentals with their own situations, their own experiences. The Parlour grows quiet with thoughts and considerations.

The Dog breaks the silence. "Well, we've come up with a few ideas on how to improve the quality of our milk," he announces. "How do we decide what to start on first?"

"There is another tool that might prove useful," the Owl says. "It's called a *prioritization matrix*, and you can use it to sort out ideas or activities based on a fixed and weighted set of criteria."

"What in the heck does that mean, a *weighted set of criteria*?" the Horse requests.

"What are the characteristics that you care about concerning the improvement actions for the milking process?" the Owl inquires. "How would you evaluate them?"

"By how quickly we can get them in place," offers the Bull. "The faster we can make the change, the faster we will start improving the quality of the milk."

"So *speed of implementation* is a criterion," the Owl comments. "What else?"

"To add to what the Bull said," the Sheep furthers, "I think that we need to consider how hard or easy it will be to implement each solution. It just makes sense to get the easier ones done first."

"Understood," the Owl affirms. "*Ease of implementation* is a second criterion. Can anyone come up with a third?"

"How about the *impact of the implementation*?!" asks the Chicken. "I mean how much benefit we think that the improvement activity will give us! Does that work?!"

"Without a doubt, it does," the Owl says. "Please allow me a few minutes to draft up a template on the Parlour wall incorporating your ideas from the brainstorming sessions that we just had."

"Those discussions were brainstorming sessions?" asks the Pig. "I thought that they had to be more formal, more structured, you know?"

"I do know, Pig," the Owl replies, "and no, they do not. Remember that a brainstorming session is simply a collaborative conversation centered on a theme. You have probably been a part of hundreds through-out your lifetime without ever realizing it. You just had one, and it was very effective. Now, if you will excuse me, please take a break, grab some water, stretch, do whatever you would like. We will be done with the etch-ing soon."

The Owl and the Woodpecker meet at one of the last empty spaces on the Milking Parlour interior wall and begin working. As the Owl is speak-ing and the Woodpecker pecking, a square develops into a table. The team members group behind the pair as they apply the final details to the image.

The Owl steps away from the drawing and engages the team once more.

"Before we decide which idea holds the highest priority, we will need to discuss the importance, or the weight, of each of the criteria. To do this, we will distribute 10 points across the three criteria. We have 10 points in total to work with as a group. For example, is speed of implementa-tion more important to you than the impact of the implementation? If you feel that one criterion holds more weight than another, simply assign it a greater number of points. But remember, we only have 10 points to work with. Would anybody like to start us off?"

"I will," the Horse volunteers. "I'd say that speed is the most critical factor right now, with the issues that we are having at the market and the threat of the Boo-chair. We need these solutions in place *yesterday*! I rec-ommend that we give speed just over half of our points. A weight of six."

Some of the animals voice subtle disagreement, when the Owl intervenes.

"Use this first weight assignment as a starting point," he encourages. "Let us discuss and compare the other two criteria. We can always adjust weights as the full picture develops. Would anyone like to offer a sugges-tion for another criterion?"

"For the ease of implementation," the Cat begins, "I recommend that we give it the lowest score possible, a one. It's not really important how easy the improvements are for us right now. We have to get better, and we

	Speed		Ease		Impact		Total	Order
	Weight:		Weight:		Weight:			
7S the milk shed								
Inspect feed								
Repair roof								
Move feed indoors								

have to do it now no matter how difficult it might be. I guess that I'm also agreeing with a high weight for speed."

"That only leaves three points left over!" cries the Jackass. "Do you really think that the impact of the improvement activity only carries half the weight of the speed of implementation?"

"I might not have before," declares the Cow, "but after this, I have to say that yes, I do. It's like the Cat said, we need to make improvements *now*. The higher-impact activities might take a longer time, and with the limited resources that we have here on Lean Acres, we can't do everything at once. We need improvement *now*. The impact is important and might earn a higher rating in the future, but as for now, we need to move."

"Can we do that, Owl? Over time, can the weighting scheme change on a prioritization matrix?" the Bull inquires.

"Absolutely," the Owl replies. "A prioritization matrix is a wonderful, dynamic tool. As your situation changes for the better or the worse, the weights and rankings can be adjusted to reflect your environment and your strategy to act within it."

"But what about *this* matrix?" asks the Sheep. "We have weights assigned, so what do we do now?"

"Now we rank the activities according to each of the criteria. The improvement activity that will take the least amount of time, for instance, would receive the highest ranking of four. The activity that will take the most time will be scored as a one. Once we have ranked each of the activities across all of the criteria, we multiply the ranking by the weight, and record the product. Then, we add up the weighted ranks for each activity and capture the total score for each. The highest score will indicate the activity with the greatest priority. This will indicate the work that we will engage in first. The lower scores will be ordered accordingly, and you will essentially have a plan of attack. Let us give it a try and see what you come up with."

The animals banter, argue, and evaluate the actions and scores across the matrix. Early decisions are revised, and final designations fall in place.

	Speed		Ease		Impact			
	Weight: 6		Weight: 1		Weight: 3		Total	Order
7S the milk shed	1	6	2	2	1	3	11	4
Inspect feed	2	12	1	1	3	9	22	3
Repair roof	3	18	4	4	2	6	28	2
Move feed indoors	4	24	3	3	4	12	39	1

Calculations are performed, corrected, and assessed. Numbers find their way into the wood through a thin, sharp beak. Before long, they are standing in front of a finished product illuminated by the orange, soft rays of a setting sun.

"I see," starts the Cow. "We need to move the feed indoors first, then fix the roof. Next, we'll start inspecting the feed. When all of that is in place, we'll 7S this place."

"Our actions have a prioritized order now, and we can each understand why," the Pig says.

"And that is the point of the tool," the Owl affirms. "Hopefully, you can all see how this complements the *improve* phase of your Six Sigma effort. Now that we know what we need to do, we can complete the required actions and evaluate the effect on the quality of our milk. If the positive changes we are anticipating do occur, we will need to put controls in place to make sure that any improvements are sustained. If we are going to shift our average from a score of seven to an eight and reduce the variation around it, we will want to ensure that it stays there and even improves over time. Once we tighten up our shot group, so to speak, we want to get better and better until we see one BB hole right in the center where every shot is fired."

Making It Stick

"What do you recommend, Owl?" asks the Dog. "Should we standardize our solutions, making them common and enforced practices like we did with the 7S program in the barnyard?"

"*Standard work* is an excellent option, Dog," answers the Owl. "Write down the procedures that you need animals on the farm to follow when it comes to feed handling, storage, and inspection. You have arrived at the *control* phase."

"Would it be helpful to include pictures, like some of the charts and graphics that we have up on the wall in here?" the Cow queries.

"That is a best practice that many organizations use. They call the instructions that they use *standard operating procedures*, or *SOPs* for short. They can be effective, but when you include images and examples, what you have are *standard work instructions*. These explain how to do the job at a level of detail that enables brand-new workers to do the job, sometimes without any training at all."

"You mentioned inspecting the inputs and monitoring the outputs, Owl. How will we do this moving forward? Will we continue to develop frequency distribution charts in the control phase?" poses the Cat.

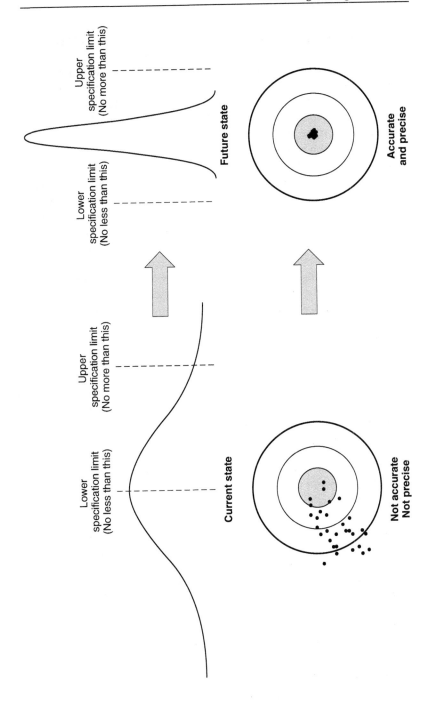

"You will continue to analyze data, Cat, but you will most likely use the calculations we discussed earlier, including defects per million opportunities and capability, and an especially powerful tool called a *control chart*," suggests the Owl. "The control chart will help you to distinguish between *common cause variation*, that which occurs within your process, and *special cause variation*, which is indicative of an external factor acting on your process. It can also help you to pinpoint when a problem may have occurred. This is the point in the project where a *failure mode and effects analysis*, or FMEA, would be useful as well. An FMEA looks at potential things that could go wrong—risks that threaten your success—and evaluates them by the likelihood of occurrence, the severity of the impact if the risk were to actually happen, and the likelihood that we would be able to detect the issue. When we multiply these three scores together, we get what is called a *risk priority number*, or RPN, for each failure mode. These help us to develop an order of attack, and we can develop counteractions that can mitigate or eliminate the negative effects. It becomes a living document, so as failure modes occur and we implement mitigation actions, we can revise RPNs and set new priorities. If you and the Rooster would meet with me after dinner, I would be happy to explain the intricacies of the FMEA, the control chart, and a complementary practice called *lot sampling*."

The Cat and the Rooster agree. The Bull steps forward with a question.

"Owl, will standard work instructions and control charts really help us to sustain the benefits we'll get by executing the actions we've prioritized?"

"They will help, but they will not guarantee it," the Owl responds. "In all of the methodologies that you will be exposed to this week, there is not a single tool or a combination of tools that will guarantee your success. Only you can do that. No matter how complex, robust, or seemingly effective a tool might be, it is *discipline* that determines victory. Standard work instructions will enable workers to follow the appropriate steps in a process, but they must be enforced or they are useless. Control charts will capture and reveal information about your operations, but these will only be facts if they are constructed and analyzed appropriately. The phases of the DMAIC approach provide a framework for your projects and a structure for your thinking. They are intended to delineate the path. All of you must have the discipline to follow it. All of you."

The Owl peers at the horizon. Red is becoming purple, and the sky is welcoming the night.

"You have performed admirably today," states the Owl. "You have defined your issues and your goals, measured your current performance, and analyzed the root causes of your issues. You have developed an action plan of improvement initiatives, and you are focused on methods to control the gains that will be realized. I think that you all understand that the work is not finished here, but rather it has just begun. It will most likely take several iterations of the DMAIC cycle to reach your goals. Follow the framework, utilize the tools, and apply discipline, and you will achieve performance excellence. It is late, and you have all worked a long, hard day. Goodnight. I will see you in the morning at the Hen House."

As the animals disperse, the Owl takes to the darkening air and disappears.

Rest/Reflect/Relate (R³)

1. Has any organization that you have been a part of engaged in a Six Sigma deployment or project series? If yes, what projects received the most attention? If not, why not? What were the barriers, from your perspective?

2. Does your current organization apply the Six Sigma methodology? Why or why not? What are the relevant enablers and barriers?

3. Does your current organization capture and analyze key metrics to assess the performance of its core processes? If yes, what are its core processes and how are they performing? If not, why not?

4. Do you have objective data available to assess your performance? Are you accurate and precise in the products and/or services that you provide? What are the key measures, and how are they captured, updated, and analyzed? Who performs the analysis? If none of this is being done, why not? How would you measure your effectiveness?

Chapter 8

Cracking Constraints

Know your limits. Also know how to break them.

—Geraint Straker

Every member of the Farm Animals Team is lost in the depths of restful sleep. Some have visions of days gone by, and others of things to come. Lean Acres is embraced in a nocturnal peace that could seemingly last forever. But forever comes too soon for most. The Rooster crows out and ushers in the dawn, severing dreams and obliterating fantasies. It is a new day, and there is work to be done. The representatives gather groggily in front of the Hen House with customary greetings and conversations concerning the week's activities. Some of the discussions can be heard over others.

"It seems like we made more progress with the corn harvesting than we did with the milking," the Pig says.

"Yes," the Horse agrees. "At least with our process we developed a future state. We've started making the changes necessary to get there, but haven't seen any significant results yet. It's been a couple of days now!"

"And it could take a few more," interjects the Owl. He stands atop the Hen House roof looking over the team. His wings stretch wide as he

floats to the ground and meets the animals beak to beak, so to speak. "The methodologies that we are using are not intended to deliver instant solutions, but rather they are focused on the application of lasting solutions. Some, like the lean effort, produce gains on a shorter timeline. Others require further, ongoing analysis and improvement actions, like the Six Sigma project that we began yesterday. Remember, we are *starting* the strategic improvement initiatives on Lean Acres this week. Each will have follow-on activities like those that we have brainstormed and annotated in the previous two events that are required to see the effort through. The sponsor for each endeavor will work with the animals that have been assigned on our RACI chart and ensure that the implementation of the solutions that are required to achieve your goals is timely and effective. The work that we are engaging in is not intended to serve as a 'quick fix.' These are elements that will drive a cultural change here on the farm, a new way of working and thinking about work. We are simply getting the ball rolling this week. Moving forward, it will be everyone's responsibility to keep it in play."

"I understand, Owl," the Bull admits, "but sometimes I feel like we are wasting our time. Do we really need dramatic change here or are we just going through the motions?"

Before the Owl can answer, the Dog joins the group and moves to the front. His face is solemn. He is calm, but something is clearly wrong. Every animal takes notice, and the discussion halts.

"Are you okay, Dog?" asks the Sheep.

"Yeah, what happened to you? Is the Farmer talking about taking you to get tutored at the vet again?" the Pig jibes.

The Dog looks up from the ground and slowly surveys the team. Then he speaks.

"I heard humans talking this morning," he begins, "out on the porch."

"Who was it?!" calls the Chicken. "A salesman?! A delivery person?! The suspense is driving me crazy!"

"I don't know who it was for sure, Chicken," the Dog replies. "But I have an idea, and I hope that I'm wrong."

"Dog," presses the Bull, "please tell us. Who do you think that it was? Who was the Farmer talking to?"

The Dog pauses a moment and looks back toward the house. "I went out on the porch to sniff around on my way here," he offers. "The scent was horrible, something I won't describe. And then I saw it. There were fresh, wet red drops of paint on the floor."

The silence that follows is initiated with a collective gasp. Hearts freeze and spirits drop as the Cat speaks the unspeakable name.

"The Boo-chair," she whispers. "The Boo-chair was here again?"

"Yes, Cat," the Dog responds, "I'm afraid he was. If anyone here is wondering about our efforts, about transforming Lean Acres and improving all that we do, let the fresh red paint remind you. We grew our Strate-Tree for a reason, and we have to see it through. Our livelihoods, our very existence is at stake."

"You have made an excellent start," assures the Owl. "So far, we have leaned the corn harvesting process, and we are working toward a six sigma quality level for our milk. The next branch on the Strate-Tree indicates that we need to get a larger volume of eggs to the market and that we need to get them there devoid of cracks in their shells. Can anyone describe the current state of affairs in the Hen House, specifically with the egg production process?"

"It's pretty cut and dry," the Rooster starts. "As we discussed when we developed our goals, we're just not getting enough eggs to the market, and quite a few of them that do get delivered have cracks in their shells. As far as the way we do our work, it's basically laid out like this: The chickens lay all of the eggs, the pigs and the sheep gather them, the cats inspect them for shell integrity, and then they are packed in baskets and cushioned with straw. The Farmer uses a refrigerated delivery service, the same one that picks up the milk, to get the eggs to the market. It shows up here every day at four o'clock and delivers the eggs to market the following morning. There's different places throughout the process where the eggs stack up from time to time. With all of that, well, *inventory* I guess you'd call it, I can't believe that we're not making enough green paper.

The Chicken is mortified. The Rooster approaches her and holds her gently with his wing around her shoulders.

"If I may attempt to summarize your situation, I believe that you are producing a large quantity of eggs and that you have a good deal of inventory, but some*thing* some*where* is restricting your throughput, or the number of eggs that are actually sold at the market," the Owl states. "Am I right?"

"That's it," answers the Pig. "Some*thing* some*where*. How do we tackle this one? Do you have a theory?"

"Actually, I do," the Owl replies, "and it was developed by a human they call Eliyahu Goldratt. It's called the *theory of constraints*."

Step 6: Academics

Working Through the Chain

The animals are curious and they wait for the lesson to begin.

"Think of the egg production process as a chain. Each activity that occurs in succession is a link in that chain, and the entire chain needs to be strong enough to handle the task at hand. However, the chain as a whole is only as strong as the weakest link. If that link breaks, the chain can not pull its weight or do its job. The capability and the capacity of your entire process, or linked set of activities, is thus determined by the ability of its weakest activity. Thus, improving any other activity besides the weakest, or the *constraint* as it is called, would simply be a waste of time, effort, and resources. The theory of constraints helps us to target the weak link and improve the process as a whole. It is all about managing the activities in your process or, on a larger scale, the processes in your system, all in order to achieve the highest output volume, or *throughput*, possible."

"But we're already producing so many eggs!" the Chicken hollers.

"Throughput is not analogous to production, Chicken," the Owl explains. "In this methodology, we consider three basic categories. There is *throughput*, which is the rate at which your process generates green paper for Lean Acres through the sale of eggs at the market. The second category involves *inventory*, and this is defined by the investment of green paper that the Farmer makes in materials and labor that are used to create the eggs that are sold at the market. This also includes the cost of the eggs that are sitting in between activities in your process, like the corn in the harvesting effort. Unless the eggs have been sold, they are inventory as well. Finally, we come to operating expenses. *Operating expenses* is defined by the green paper that is spent to facilitate the processing of the eggs, from laying through delivery."

"Once again, Owl," the Jackass interjects, "this sounds complicated. How do we fix the throughput, the inventory, and the operating expenses all at once?"

"You do not," the Owl responds. "You take them on one at a time based on potential gains. First we aim for optimizing our throughput. Then we reduce our inventory, and finally, minimize our operating expenses. In our effort today, we will not focus on the amounts of green paper in each category because none of us knows how much the Farmer actually gets from the people or spends on the farm. But we can focus on our throughput and our inventory as measured in number of eggs."

"So is there an overarching structure that we can follow, like the four lean principles or the DMAIC framework?" questions the Bull.

"There is indeed," replies the Owl. "Please come around the side of the Hen House with me, and I will be more than happy to walk through it with you."

The animals shuffle behind the Owl as he leads the way. As they round the corner they immediately notice a fresh etching in the boards.

"It looks like that thing the Farmer uses to look at the leaves on our crops from time to time," the Cow comments. "You know, the circle of glass with the handle, oh, what's it called again?"

"A magnifying glass, Cow," the Cat responds. "It helps him to get a closer look at the crops and to find the cause of any problems."

Identify the Need

"Much like the theory of constraints," adds the Owl. "What a wonderful analogy. Let us explore the magnifying glass a little further. The first two steps are called the *path to discovery*, and they involve justification and assessment. The primary step requires the identification of the need for exploration. Why are we looking at the egg production process, for example? Is it driven by our strategy? Is it a response to the voice of the customer? Is it both? These questions must be answered before pressing onward to be sure that your effort is focused in the appropriate area, one of significant impact."

"What about after that?" the Horse queries.

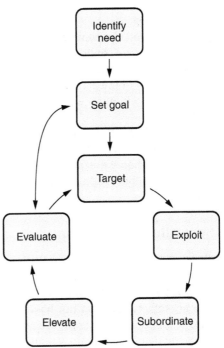

Set the Goal

"Next, we set a goal for performance improvement," the Owl continues. "To do this, we must first baseline our current performance by evaluating each activity in the process by the three criteria: throughput rate, inventory levels, and operating expenses. Once we compare these data with the need that we identified in the first step, we can establish a SMARTER goal that will drive our effort. At this point, we will then enter the *cycle of improvement*."

"What's that?" the Rooster asks.

Target the Constraint

"This improvement cycle consists of five steps that should be repeated until the goal is met. It begins with the third step overall, *targeting the constraint*. With the information that we have aggregated and analyzed while setting the goal, our constraint—or the most limiting activity in our process—should be quite clear. There are times when more than one constraint arises of equivalent value, but this is rare. The next phase will include the exploitation of that constraint."

Exploit the Constraint

"How in the heck do we explode the constraint, or whatever you said?" presses the Pig.

"We *exploit* the constraint by ensuring that we are getting the most out of it," the Owl continues. "This is an area where other methodologies like lean and Six Sigma can be applied to maximize productivity, utilization, or the efficacy of the activity."

"Can we add more animals to the job?" inquires the Sheep. "Would that help?"

"It can, but that is not an option at this point in the cycle," offers the Owl. "We want to get the most out of the activity without increasing operating costs when we exploit the constraint. Once this has been accomplished, we subordinate everything else, and I mean everything, to the constraint."

Subordinate Everything

"You mean slow down other activities to the pace of the weak link?!" the Chicken shrieks. "Are you crazy?!"

"Not yet," the Owl answers with a grin. "Listen, pushing more eggs into an activity that can not handle its current load could cause problems like excess inventory and damaged product, right? And all of that extra and damaged inventory requires more animals, or greater operating expenses, to handle it. If every step moves at the rate of the slowest, we reduce variability in our process, inventory levels, and resulting operating expenses. We establish a balanced and even flow of products with appropriate buffers, or *inventory caches*, in place to cushion our throughput should another activity fall behind. In this methodology, we call this the *drum–buffer–rope*, with all of the activities, including material release, tied to the slowest, which in turn sets the tempo. The buffers guarantee continuous throughput despite potential issues, and never allow the constraint to *starve*, or run out of incoming goods. We are managing the process based on the constraint at this point."

"Do we only subordinate the other steps in the process?" questions the Cat.

"No," the Owl replies. "At this phase, we also look for rules, beliefs, practices, or assumptions that might limit the performance of the constraint. We look for them, and we do our best to mitigate or eliminate them."

Elevate the Constraint

"What does *elevate* mean, Owl?" asks the Dog.

"In the next step, after we have exploited the constraint and subordinated everything else to it, now we elevate the constraint. This means that we shift some of the work to another area in the process with additional capacity, or increase the number of animals working on this activity. It is not ideal to increase operating expenses like this, but it certainly is an option that could help you achieve your throughput goal."

"Why don't we just do that right away?" goads the Jackass. "Why go through all the trouble if we're just going to put more animals on the task?"

"Because you might not need to, Jackass," the Owl answers. "By engaging in exploitation and subordination, you might eliminate root causes thereby reducing resource requirements, and thus operating expenses, rather than increasing them."

"And we don't have any animals to spare, Jackass," enforces the Dog.

"Well, what do we do after all of this?" the Rooster requests. "Will we be done after we've worked through the cycle?"

Evaluate Results

"Maybe," the Owl offers, "but it is a cycle. The final step in an iteration is to evaluate your results against your goal. Have you achieved it? If not, you will need to reengage."

"Looking at the same constraint?" wonders the Horse.

"Rarely. Typically, addressing a constraint in this manner advances its performance beyond some of its peer activities, and other constraints arise as you continue to manage and improve the entire process. There will always be a 'slowest' activity. The cycle is engaged until the goal is satisfied. Then the methodology can be applied to another need."

"This doesn't sound as complicated as the Six Sigma approach. Is there math involved?" the Pig inquires.

"First," starts the Owl, "it is not as complicated as the Six Sigma approach. But you must remember that each approach is specific to a certain need. If we are looking to eliminate activities that customers perceive as non-value-added, we apply lean. If variation or centering is our issue, we use Six Sigma. In this case, where throughput is our main concern, the theory of constraints is the appropriate vehicle. Second, yes, there is math involved, but only basic calculations. Does that answer your questions, Pig?"

"Yes, it does," the Pig replies. "Thanks, Owl. Let's get started."

Step 7: Action

Present Problem

"To do that, we will need to start with our first step by identifying the need. Why are we looking at the egg production process? Why should we care?" the Owl asks.

"Because we have a strategic objective. I mean, it's on the Strate-Tree and all, right?" suggests the Sheep.

"You're right, Sheep," joins the Dog. "And the only reason that it's part of the Strate-Tree is because the voice of the customer demanded it."

"Great reasons all around!" states the Owl. "Now, what should our goal be? Is our initial estimate appropriate, or do we need to revise our strategic plan?"

"How can we know?" the Horse asks.

"To begin, we will need to review the egg production process as it is now," the Owl replies. "The Rooster gave us a detailed description earlier, and the Woodpecker captured it for us. Please take a look to ensure that the process map has been drawn accurately."

The animals collect around the image and carefully review each detail. The Rooster pushes his way to the front of the group as he escorts the Chicken for a better view.

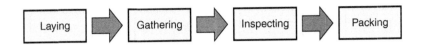

"This is it!" declares the Chicken. "This is how we do it every day!"

"And what is your daily quota? How many eggs did you aim to produce before the Strate-Tree was developed?"

"We always try to get 1680 eggs out every week, and that's 240, or twenty dozen, each day, four dozen per hour from eleven in the morning till the truck shows up at five. My girls need quality time in the morning to rest and relax. Even with only six hours of work, we always make more than that, so I can't say that I know what the problem is," the Rooster responds. "We can't start packing in the first hour because that's when we kick off the laying, gathering, and inspecting. This is the real 'production' piece, and we don't do any of that stuff in the last hour because we're busy packing out the last load. I mean, sure, we fall behind in some areas in the process, but we try to make it up in others. Yesterday was a shining example. The cats keep records of our work. They show that our production rates are outstanding, but we're only getting about ten dozen eggs to the market each day when we have the demand for at least twenty. Sometimes we make enough eggs to hit the strategic target of 480 eggs, but for some reason on those days we end up throwing a bunch away."

Capturing Capacity

"That is good information, Rooster, but I must caution you that high production rates that are not directly correlated to high throughput rates cause more harm than good," cautions the Owl.

"What do you mean?" asks the Rooster.

"Making a lot of something indicates activity. Delivering a lot of something to customers, responding to their requirements, that indicates results," answers the Owl. "First, we will need to see the constraint in our process. Cat, would you mind consolidating the records from your brothers and sisters? I would like to see the best daily output per process step. We will use this number as our capacity. Woodpecker, I need your assistance once again."

The Owl and the Woodpecker meet along the side of the Hen House and go to work revising the existing image while the Cat meets with her family members. After she returns, she joins the hushed conversation between the two birds. Several minutes pass before the modification

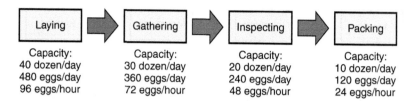

Laying	Gathering	Inspecting	Packing
Capacity:	Capacity:	Capacity:	Capacity:
40 dozen/day	30 dozen/day	20 dozen/day	10 dozen/day
480 eggs/day	360 eggs/day	240 eggs/day	120 eggs/day
96 eggs/hour	72 eggs/hour	48 eggs/hour	24 eggs/hour

is complete. The Owl and the Cat step away from the drawing and the Woodpecker flies up to the roof.

"What do you think of this?" the Owl questions the group.

The animals read over the fresh details, and the Pig speaks.

"Why did you label each activity with its capacity? Why didn't we consider the cycle time?"

The Owl responds, "Remember, cycle times are critical measures in the lean methodology, just as variation is key to Six Sigma. When applying the theory of constraints, we are most interested in throughput, or the output from each activity and from the process as a whole. The capacity that we have identified per each activity in this process is indicative of the maximum number of eggs that each step can handle in a single day of work. There are times when an inverse relationship is present, and the constraint is the activity with the lowest capacity and the highest cycle time, but not always."

"So the best that we can do in a day is forty dozen, right?!" questions the Chicken.

"Wrong," returns the Owl. "The best you *could* do in a day is forty dozen eggs, but that would require substantial improvements."

"Could that be our goal? Forty dozen eggs off to the market each and every day?" the Cat asks.

"It certainly can. It is an aggressive goal, but it aligns with the maximum capacity within your current process. It is entirely up to you," says the Owl, "as long as the goal provides for your customers."

"What exactly do they want?" prods the Bull. "We haven't seen the Mice yet today, and . . ."

A micro explosion of straw erupts from the floor in the middle of the group. Dust and stalks fly into the air, blinding the team members for a moment. As it settles, three mysterious but familiar forms become visible. The Mice have returned, and within seconds their chanting begins.

Forty dozen is what we need.

On forty dozen eggs we'll feed.

We don't want splits, we don't like cracks.

If you send them forward, we'll bring them back.

We want more eggs, and we will pay.

Forty dozen eggs each day.

The rhyme ends, and the Mice stare upward beyond the faces of the animals. A crow caws from overhead, and the animals look to the sound. When they glance back at the Mice, they realize that they are gone. Their consult is valued. Their presence is unsettling.

"Forty it is," declares the Rooster optimistically. "We can do it. We'll modify the branch for this goal and press forward."

"What is our throughput rate as of today?" the Cow inquires.

"Carefully consider the diagram," remarks the Owl. "Currently, you have the capacity to release ten dozen eggs for shipment to the market per day."

The animals are surprised, to say the least. Some are downright upset.

"What do you mean by that, Owl?" blares the Jackass. "We can get 480 eggs laid every day, but you're suggesting that we can only get 120 on the truck?"

"No, Jackass," begins the Owl. "I am not suggesting that. I am stating it as a fact. A process can not outperform the slowest step within it. This is the essence of the theory of constraints. No matter how many eggs you produce in front of the packing activity, you will still only be able to pack ten dozen eggs per day. Your process, your chain, is only as strong as its weakest link."

"And our weakest link, or our constraint, is packing," says the Dog. "I think I get it. The step in our process with the lowest capacity, the lowest throughput rate—that's our constraint. If any other steps in the process move at a faster rate, all we'll end up doing is piling up eggs at different points. If all of the activities move at the same pace, then we won't accumulate excess inventory."

The Jackass interrupts. "Maybe, but I just don't see it as far as production is concerned. Is the constraint really a problem? We hit our production quota by four o'clock just like we always do, and in the last hour we pumped out forty-eight eggs for the packers. Sure, we had a slow start, but we made up for it in the end."

Egg-regious Effects

"Let us take a look at that," suggests the Owl. The Woodpecker is at the ready position. "Your current quota is forty-eight eggs per hour for the combined steps of laying, gathering, and inspecting. The greatest amount of eggs that you have been able to produce from these three activities just happens to be forty-eight eggs per hour. The capacity of your entire process is 120 eggs each day, or twenty-four eggs per hour. This of course assumes that the bottleneck, or your constraint, really is a problem. If you will take a moment, please review the previous diagram and let me know if that number looks familiar."

"It matches the capacity of the packing activity," says the Cow.

"Very good," the Owl continues. "Now let us look at your production numbers from yesterday. You laid, gathered, and inspected six in the first hour, eighteen in the second, two dozen in both the third and fourth hours, and wow, forty-eight during the last. That is 120 eggs all together, and like you said, Jackass, all by four o'clock."

The Woodpecker finishes and steps away from the drawing.

"So what's the problem, Owl?" asks the Jackass. "We made enough. We had a rough start, and that happens from time to time. But we pulled through in the end just like we always do." He beams at each face in the group, confident that his opinion is truth.

The Owl responds. "Remember our strategic goal, Jackass. Simply making enough eggs will not save Lean Acres from the Boo-chair. We have to sell more eggs at the market. Let us go over the second piece of this process. Let us include the data from packing."

The animals move closer around the Owl as he continues. "In the first hour of packing, from noon to one o'clock, you could have finished twenty-four eggs. However, you only sent a half dozen over from production. This means that in the first hour of packing, you only finished half of a basket. You could not do more or optimize the capacity because you *starved* this step. That is what it is called when you send an amount of inventory forward in a process to the constraint that is less than the constraint's capacity. The packing activity *needed* to take on more inventory in order to achieve its quota, but you did not feed it enough. You starved it, and while you improved production, you starved packing again from one to two o'clock."

"But we made up for that later," argues the Jackass.

"Did you, now?" returns the Owl. "We'll see. In the third and fourth hour of packing, you presented inventory levels that matched the

Demand: 240 eggs/day • Quota: 48 eggs/hour • Capacity: 120 eggs/day • Adjusted quota (existing capacity): 24 eggs/hour

11 am	12 pm	1 pm	2 pm	3 pm	4 pm	5 pm
6	18	24	24	48		
Output: 6 Quota: 24 Diff: −18	Output: 24 Quota: 48 Diff: −24	Output: 48 Quota: 72 Diff: −24	Output: 72 Quota: 96 Diff: −24	Output: 120 Quota: 120 Diff: 0		

Capacity: 48 eggs/hour

Production: Laying → Gathering → Inspecting

constraint's capacity. This is what is called *balanced*. I'm not talking about balancing your constraints with the demand, but rather balancing the capacity of your entire process by producing to the capacity of your constraint. You fed the packing activity just as much as it needed, no more, no less for two iterations. And in the final hour before the truck arrived, it looks like you really maxed out production at forty-eight eggs."

"Well, we needed to make up for the slow start," retorts the Jackass.

"Did it work?" the Owl ponders. "You produced twice as many eggs as the packing activity could handle in the last hour. You gorged the constraint. And what happened to the additional eggs? Did they make it on the truck?"

"No," the Pig answers. "Actually they went right into the compost heap."

"So all of that extra work, that extra push," the Chicken wonders, "all of that was for nothing?!"

"Worse than nothing, I'm afraid," the Rooster replies. "It looks like it was all a waste of product, effort, and time. Look at the diagram."

"So when we starve the constraint, we bring our throughput down for the entire day, and there's no way to make it up. If we try to gorge the constraint later, the additional inventory beyond the constraint's capacity ends up on the compost pile," offers the Horse.

"Yeah, okay, but what if we have an awesome start?" proposes the Jackass. "What if we max out our production capacity from the get-go?"

"That would look like this," answers the Owl as he nods to the Wood-pecker. In moments a new image takes shape with different numbers and shocking results.

"See!" rants the Jackass. "On our best days we can hit it! 120 eggs on the truck! That's what I'm talking about."

"I see what you mean, Jackass," the Cat begins, "if what you're talking about is a huge amount of waste. We could get ten dozen on the truck if we went full throttle, but we'd end up throwing just as many away."

"Well, what's the right answer?" questions the Pig. "How can we get as many eggs as possible to the market and minimize our losses?"

The Owl responds, "The only way to optimize throughput is to create a balanced system where the constraint is consistently fed inventory at the rate of its capacity, never more and never less. We want to nourish the constraint with a balanced diet and avoid starving and gorging at all costs. Woodpecker, please show us what said system might look like."

The chips and splinters take to the air as the Woodpecker takes to the boards. The result reflects the truth in the Owl's statement.

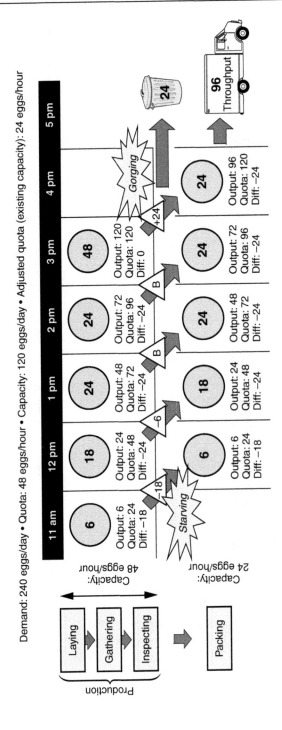

Demand: 240 eggs/day • Quota: 48 eggs/hour • Capacity: 120 eggs/day • Adjusted quota (existing capacity): 24 eggs/hour

Demand: 240 eggs/day • Quota: 48 eggs/hour • Capacity: 120 eggs/day • Adjusted quota (existing capacity): 24 eggs/hour

Demand: 240 eggs/day • Quota: 48 eggs/hour • Capacity: 120 eggs/day • Adjusted quota (existing capacity): 24 eggs/hour

Delving Deeper

"But now that we can see our constraint, what do we do about it?" asks the Horse. "I understand the effects of it now and the concepts that could help us to optimize our throughput today, but 120 eggs each day won't cut it for long. How do we increase our throughput?"

"We engage in the next phase of the cycle," the Owl answers. "We have identified the need, set our goal, and we can see and understand the constraint. The time has come to exploit it. To do this effectively, we will need to explode the packing activity into its basic components in a separate process map. Now, what are the steps involved in packing?"

"The pigs and the sheep perform that work," comments the Cat. "Perhaps their representatives would describe it best."

"The work is best described by those who do it," affirms the Owl. "So what exactly do you and your family members do?"

"I can tell you that the inspectors put the good eggs on the packing table," the Sheep begins. "Then we go and get a basket and bring it back to the table. Then we go over to the bin to get some straw. Next, we return to the table where we pack the bottom and put the eggs on top."

"Yeah," inserts the Pig. "Then we go back to the bin for more straw, come back to the table, cover the eggs, and finally we stage the basket for pickup by the back door."

As the Pig finishes his sentence, the Woodpecker completes a new process map.

"How does this look?" the Owl asks.

"Well, that captures it," replies the Pig, "but it looks too simple. It really doesn't show how much running around we do when we're packing the eggs."

"No, it does not," agrees the Owl. "And transportation is a form of waste in which methodology?"

"From lean, right?" attempts the Bull.

"Absolutely right," responds the Owl. "In order to examine and improve the magnitude of transportation involved, we can use a lean tool, the *spaghetti diagram.*"

The Pig likes the sound of this, and his stomach rumbles violently.

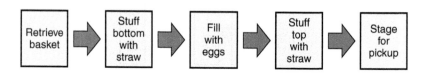

"But I thought that we were using the theory of constraints on this one," argues the Cow.

"We are," the Owl replies. "Now that we have identified our constraint, we are working to exploit it. This could mean attacking the issues with multiple options from our armory, including lean, Six Sigma, and other improvement approaches. The theory of constraints helps us to measure, evaluate, and target the problem.

"We can integrate the other methodologies at this point to get the most out of the current process that we possibly can without adding more resources to the equation. Woodpecker, please draw us a floor plan of the Hen House and include the relevant structures from the process description."

A few minutes pass before the carving is complete. The animals huddle close to the wall.

"Is this an accurate depiction of the workplace layout?" the Owl inquires.

The Rooster looks the floor plan over with extreme care before answering.

"Yes, I believe that it is. Nice work, Woodpecker."

The Woodpecker does not speak, but he nods to the Rooster in thanks.

"Tell us about your packing process again, please," the Owl requests. "Only this time, include distances when you describe your routes. The Woodpecker will capture the information as he develops the image further."

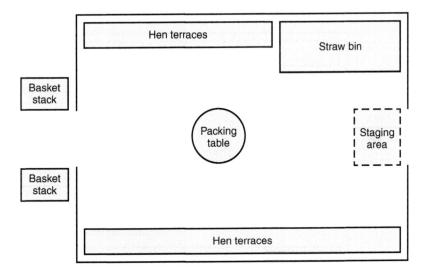

"All right," says the Pig. "We start at the packing table and go out to get a basket. That's about thirty feet. Then we come back and put the basket on the table, that's another thirty feet. Then we go get some straw, it's about ten feet away, and come back to pad the bottom of the basket and load the eggs. Then we make a second trip to the straw bin and come back to the table to cover the eggs. When all that's done, we take the basket to the staging area and then come back to the table about twenty feet away."

"How much is that all together?" inquires the Sheep.

"140 feet," the Rooster reports. "And at ten baskets that's 1400 feet traveled every day in the packing step alone."

The tapping stops, and the team members look at the changes.

"What a mess!" cries the Chicken. "I mean, I've always said that you guys are all over it, but I didn't mean it literally!"

"The lines spread out across the Hen House," the Bull observes. "Sometimes it looks like they are piling up on each other."

"Like spaghetti noodles on a plate!" announces the Pig. He is upset about the image, but excited by the thought.

"Exactly," enters the Owl. "By tracing our steps in everyday activities, we can grasp the complexity of workplace requirements and the extent of transportation that we engage in. The star represents the starting and end point at the table, and the numbers indicate the stops that you are mak-ing, or *touch points*, around the Hen House. Depicting this on a spaghetti diagram can help us to see the problem and to design an improved state."

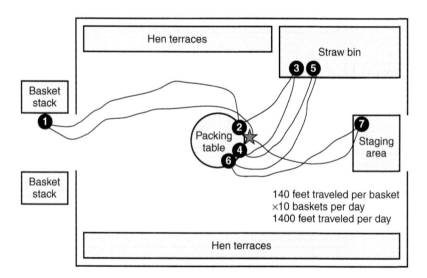

"How do we improve this process?" the Dog asks.

"By thinking practically," answers the Owl. "Without fundamentally altering the process itself, what can we do to decrease the distances traveled by the pigs and sheep?"

"We could move the baskets inside, right next to the packing table," the Bull suggests.

"But we just designated spaces for the baskets outside the front door when we 7S'd the barnyard!" the Jackass blurts. "Can we change that?"

"Yes you can. It is *continuous* performance improvement," repeats the Owl. "Your organization and your environment will evolve as a whole. What was great yesterday might not be good enough for today. My recommendation is to embrace any chance to change as a welcome opportunity for improvement. If that means modifying your 7S program in order to achieve a strategic objective, then make it so. Now, if we move the baskets near the packing table, what else can we do?"

"We could move the baskets and the table closer to the straw bin," offers the Horse.

"And closer to the staging area," adds the Cat.

"If we do that," starts the Pig, "we would only have to walk about two feet to grab a basket, a foot to gather some straw, three feet back to the table for the eggs, and three feet back to the straw bin. You know, we could bring the basket with us on the second trip to the straw bin and just cover them right there. Then it's about three feet to the staging area and two feet back to the table. Holy smokes, how much distance does that make, Rooster?"

"Fourteen feet per basket," the Rooster returns. "That's only 140 feet at ten baskets per day, or one-tenth of the way we do it now."

"One-tenth!" shouts the Chicken. "How in the heck did we do that?"

"Through a very elementary lean application, Chicken," the Owl asserts. "If we had more time today, imagine what we could generate if we applied all of the principles. However, we are on a tight schedule. Woodpecker, will you show us the proposed future state?"

The Woodpecker flies across the wall, beaking the boards. Following a flurry of taps, ticks, and tacks, the Hen House is redrawn with a new layout. The animals like what they see, especially the Sheep and the Pig.

"How much would you say that this solution could increase the capacity of the packing activity?"

"I think that we can all safely agree that this at least doubles it," the Rooster answers. "We should be able to get at least four baskets through every hour. If everything goes well during the day, we could even satisfy our demand level." His team members nod their agreement. "What do we do now?"

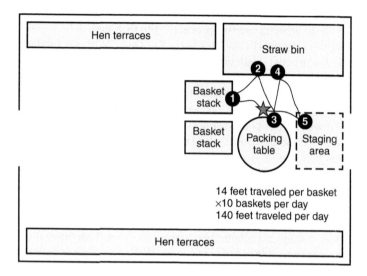

14 feet traveled per basket
×10 baskets per day
140 feet traveled per day

Protected Pace

"We continue to improve the egg production process by further improving the capacity of the constraint. We will need to be able to satisfy the demand even if we have a bad day. You should always work to establish capacity that is greater than demand. This is the real world, and variation is everywhere. We should make our processes robust enough to handle it. To do this we will advance to the next step in the cycle and subordinate everything to the decisions we have just made in redesigning the packing process," responds the Owl.

"What do you mean again by *subordinate*?" the Dog asks.

"Subordinating means to make something secondary," the Owl replies. "For example, we just subordinated a rule that we established while engaged in the 7S effort regarding the placement of baskets. We previously determined that the best place to store the baskets was on either side of the front door to the Hen House, remember? But the distance that caused the pigs and sheep to travel during the packing process proved to be an enabler of the constraint. In order to impact this aspect of the process and increase its capacity, we moved the baskets, therefore changing an established policy. Rather than absolutely conforming to a rule that limited our throughput just because it was a rule, we changed it to accommodate improved performance. If there is something acting on the constraint from the outside, we need to mitigate or eliminate its power to restrict the constraint's capacity. We need to subordinate the other activities in the process to the constraint as well. Does it really make sense for the chickens to operate at their full capacity, laying forty dozen eggs each day, if we can only pack ten dozen? What happens to the 360 eggs that don't make it into baskets? Tell me about all of that inventory. What does it do for you?"

"They do pile up something awful between the stations," remarks the Sheep.

"I've always thought those piles might be causing the cracked shells," the Cat interjects. "The eggs pile up so high that the weight just crushes those on the bottom, and sometimes they just roll off the top and onto the floor."

"They stack up after inspection, too," says the Pig. "Maybe that's how some cracked eggs make it to the market. It's all of that extra inventory, just like it was with the corn!"

"We do not always require a tool or a method for root cause analysis," comments the Owl. "It can be as simple as a progressive conversation."

"But I think that it's nice to have some extra inventory around," states the Pig. "Each step doesn't always run exactly at capacity, and it's a good thing to have some stashed to the side just in case."

"What exactly happens to the remaining inventory at the end of the day?" asks the Owl.

"All of those eggs, all of them, off to the compost heap!" the Chicken cries. "What a world! What a world!"

"It is okay, Chicken," assures the Owl, "there is a solution."

"Would a pull system work? You know, similar to the one we used in our corn harvesting effort," queries the Cow.

"That is an outstanding option," the Owl declares. "With your constraint at the end of the process, a pull system would enable the last step to dictate the egg flow and the production pace."

"Even with all of this in place, we're still not meeting our daily quota," the Jackass blares. "We're only gonna get 240 eggs out each day. We need to get twice that to hit our quota, and three times that to satisfy our strategic goal."

"Do not lose heart, Jackass. We have two remaining phases in our improvement cycle. The next concerns *elevation*. We will elevate our constraint in order to increase its capacity," the Owl announces.

Greater Gains

"How do we elevate the constraint?" the Rooster asks.

"By making any other changes necessary in order to defeat it," the Owl replies. "Our victory is declared when packing is no longer a constraint.

What is required in order for this step to achieve our daily quota of forty dozen eggs per day?"

"Can we place additional animals at the packing station?" the Horse inquires.

"The sky is the limit," the Owl responds.

"Well, then that might be our solution," the Pig asserts. "If one of us can get twenty baskets out in a day, two of us, a pig and a sheep, should be able to finish forty. Right, Sheep?"

The Sheep thinks the proposition over carefully and then nods to the Pig with confidence.

"Make it happen, you two," orders the Dog. "It looks like we've arrived at the final step in the theory of constraints model, Owl. How do we evaluate in this methodology?"

"This phase requires that you simply compare your results to your goal and calculate the difference. If it is zero, you have completed the cycle. If the throughput that you have achieved falls below your goal, engage in the cycle again," the Owl recommends.

"So, we must be done then! Our throughput rate is equal to our daily quota! Great work! Great work all around!" the Chicken celebrates.

"Not so fast," warns the Rooster. "We did break the constraint, and packing is no longer the issue. However, look at our process map. Even with our enhanced performance, we are still limited to a total output of twenty dozen eggs per day. *Inspecting* has risen as a new constraint, and it's anchoring our entire system."

"And our strategic goal is set at 720 eggs per day," adds the Bull. "What do we do about that?"

"We'll need to utilize the improvement cycle again." It is the Cat who replies. "Isn't that correct, Owl?"

"Indeed it is," he remarks. "We are beginning the strategic improvement journey this week, and it will never end. It is the same with each of our efforts here, at the Milking Parlour, with the corn, and tomorrow's initiative at the Shearing Shack. You have selected measures that will

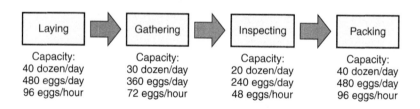

Laying	Gathering	Inspecting	Packing
Capacity:	Capacity:	Capacity:	Capacity:
40 dozen/day	30 dozen/day	20 dozen/day	40 dozen/day
480 eggs/day	360 eggs/day	240 eggs/day	480 eggs/day
96 eggs/hour	72 eggs/hour	48 eggs/hour	96 eggs/hour

need to be analyzed, tested, and proven. You have designated activities that will require phased execution. No matter how good you become, there will always be an opportunity to increase efficiency or speed, improve quality, reduce inventory and lead time, or to make progress in areas you have not even considered yet. Performance excellence is not about a destination or a specific achievement. It is about a journey, a quest for perfection that continuously redefines itself. Your strategy sets your direction. These methodologies provide the means to progress. As it has been with your previous efforts, there is more work ahead of you to optimize the egg production process. Continue to apply the theory of constraints and its unique approach and you will achieve your goals. We have worked through the day once again, and dusk is upon us. Go back to your families and enjoy your evening. You have all earned it. I will meet you tomorrow at dawn near the Shearing Shack. We have one more day to deploy your strategic performance improvement program. Bring your energy and your enthusiasm, and they will in return bring you results. Good evening."

The team members stand together as the Owl flies overhead, gliding into the soft night. His shape is enveloped by the sky, and before long he is gone. The animals review the etchings on the outer walls of the Hen House, realizing their advancement and understanding the approach. Each returns to their respective pen with a satisfied spirit and an increased portion of hope. The moon presses the horizon, and the population of Lean Acres Farm drifts off to sleep.

Rest/Reflect/Relate (R³)

1. What are the constraints that prevent you from satisfying your internal customers (fellow employees, managers, and so on) at work? Are there specific steps or activities that slow or stop progress?

2. Are these activities clearly indicated by piles of inventory, or are they more difficult to detect? Remember, even in *invisible processes* (information transactions, for example) inventory exists. This can be in the form of pending decisions, unanswered requests, and so on.

3. Constraints are often enabled by policies and regulations, equipment, or people. What is the primary enabler for your constraint?

4. How would you recommend exploiting your constraint? How would you elevate it? What resisting forces would you need to mitigate or eliminate in order to break the power of your bottleneck?

5. What is the next constraint? What do you think would arise as the new challenge?

Chapter 9

Business Process Reengineering for Ewe

I do not think there is any thrill that can go through the human heart like that felt by the inventor as he sees some creation of the brain unfolding to success.

—Nikola Tesla

The Rooster lifts his voice as the light of the morning sun greets the night. It is the last day of the Owl's visit, and the animals rise against their sleeping stupors to engage the morning. As feed troughs are invaded and water pails drained, the animal team members make their way toward the epicenter of this day's work, the Shearing Shack. It's a long building with a low roof that sits next to the Milking Parlour. The Sheep and the Pig are talking right outside the front door.

"The Owl inside?" calls the Horse.

"Yes, he is," returns the Pig, "and the Woodpecker too. This whole thing's a mess, so maybe we should try to start early."

The Pig leads the team as they shuffle into the shack. The Owl is standing in the center of the floor facing the door, and the Woodpecker is beside him.

"Good morning!" he calls to the group. "Are you ready for our final day of strategic improvement deployment here on Lean Acres Farm?"

"Final day?" asks the Bull. "I thought you said that we were going to continue working on these projects in the weeks to come."

"I did," replies the Owl, "and you will. This week we are deploying our efforts, or getting them started. The results will come as you progress through the key steps of each methodology and transform your processes in accordance with your strategic direction. Some will take longer than others, but if you maintain the discipline and an aggressive approach, you will get there. So, who can tell me about the Shearing Shack? What goes on in here?"

The animals look to the Sheep and the Pig. Shocking to most, it is the Sheep who speaks.

"Shearing means shaving all of the wool off of each sheep in the flock and gathering it in bags for delivery to the market. We do it every day because the sheep on Lean Acres replace our wool, in full, overnight. Shearing is a resource- and labor-intensive process that lends itself to low volume and *flat* bags of wool," she offers.

"Well said, Sheep," the Pig comments. "The other pigs and I, we operate the shears and stuff the bags as the sheep move through the building, in one door and out the other. We store the bags of wool wherever we can, and they usually pile up all over the place. We don't have enough shears, only two for all of us to share, so between trading those back and forth and passing the bags forward, well, it's a mess. Let's just leave it at that."

"So, how many sheep are being sheared at any given time?" the Owl questions.

"Well, one at a time, of course," responds the Sheep. "We sheep are modest animals, and frankly, it just wouldn't be proper for one of us to see another in the act of being sheared. It's shameful to even think about it!"

"But you all do stand in the fields as bare as the day you were born," interjects the Bull. "What's the problem?"

"A freshly sheared sheep is a beautiful thing, and quite natural," the Sheep begins. "Being sheared is a personal experience, and we mean to keep it that way. It's the act, not the result that, well, rubs us the wrong way."

"What do we need to do, then? Do we need more pigs on the shearing detail?" suggests the Dog.

"We don't have any more," the Bull replies. "The pigs, all of them, have been dedicated to different areas around the farm. We don't have any more to spare."

"It doesn't matter anyway," adds the Pig. "We've tried bringing a few extra pigs over now and then to help, but it just makes the whole process more cumbersome. We've got too many pigs involved as it is that could be used in other areas around Lean Acres. Actually, we've tried improving the existing process several times in the past with no luck. Look, we only have two sets of shears, we have limited space in which we can operate and store the bags, and the sheep won't come in unless they have privacy. We need to do more with less, all the while sending fluffier wool to the market."

"We'll improve this process when you-know-who over here flies," the Jackass belts, gesturing toward the Pig. "The only way we can make this one any better is to start from scratch, eh, Owl?"

"I believe that you are correct, Jackass," answers the Owl. "About the second part, that is."

The Jackass is smiling to himself, but his expression turns to confusion as the Owl's words fall upon his ears.

"Starting from scratch," the Owl goes on, "designing the shearing process the way that you want it to be without any dependency on the structure, sequence, or flow of the current state is a viable option."

"How can we do that?" enters the Cat. "Do we somehow adapt the steps in the other methodologies, or is this something new, a different way of engineering a solution?"

"It's a different way of *reengineering* a process," the Owl offers. "A human named Dr. Michael Hammer developed an approach that allows for the systematic design and implementation of a brand-new way of working. It is called *busy-ness process reengineering*."

Step 6: Academics

The animals settle around the Owl as the lesson begins.

"Busy-ness process reengineering, or BPR as some like to call it, was built upon the idea that sometimes gradual improvement is not enough,"

continues the Owl. "The focus of this methodology is the fundamental and at times radical rethinking and redesign of critical organizational
processes, particularly those that deliver value directly to the customer.
By improving the efficiency and efficacy of these critical processes, we can
improve our customer satisfaction ratings, which in turn should enable
an increase in revenue, or the green paper from the market."

"This approach sounds a bit more creative than the others," the Cat
comments. "Is there any formal structure to it?"

"There certainly is, Cat," the Owl replies. "If I may direct your attention to the shack wall at my right, you will see the Woodpecker's latest
work."

The team members take note of a solitary image engraved in the
wooden boards of the shack's interior wall. A circle of overlapping arrows
stands bold and alone in the growing morning light. There are words in
each segment of the circle detailing specific actions that seem to drive
others.

"As you can see," states the Owl, "this methodology, like the others
that we have applied throughout this week, has an ordered and iterative
sequence of steps to guide our journey toward improvement. First, we
target the process to be reengineered, and then we analyze its current

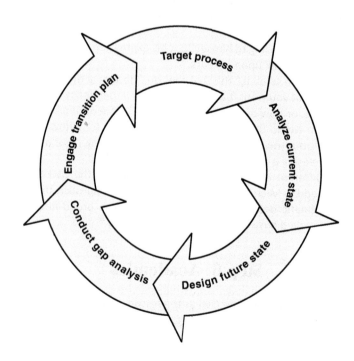

state of operations. Next, we will design the future state and analyze the difference between the *to be* and the *as is*. Once we have detailed the differences, we will build a plan to transition between the two. When that plan is complete, we will engage in the required activities to make our future state a reality. And, as always, we will start the cycle again, perhaps on a new process as we press onward with continuous performance improvement."

"How do we do all of that?" asks the Rooster. "I get the gist of the methodology, but what are the specifics of each activity in the cycle?"

"That is a great question, Rooster," the Owl responds. "Let us all take a look at each of the steps, one at a time."

Target the Process

"When we target the process, we consider our strategy and the voice of the customer," says the Owl. "An effective strategy should be driven by the voice of the customer, as well as a few others. That integration will drive performance improvement across any farm. So these two factors, the voice and the strategy, should not be discrete or disparate. However, it is important to constantly and consistently listen to the voice in order to maintain awareness of your customers' current needs. Remember that this is the pulse of your organization, the reason for your existence as a farm, and frequent checkups can facilitate better health. This will enable us to identify the processes that need to be redesigned, and at the same time understand *why* we are improving them. When we have completed this phase, we examine the process that we have targeted."

Analyze the Current State

"Should we calculate the capability of the process, or use a value stream map?" questions the Bull.

"Both are valuable," states the Owl, "but in this case we will most likely use a tool called a *process map.*"

"Is that like a value stream map?!" the Chicken inquires.

"It is indeed," the Owl returns. "A process map captures the individual activities that occur and the sequence that they follow. The two differ in that a value stream map portrays a high-level view of the work performed whereas a process map can explore the tactical details and specific steps carried out by individual animals. And while we are capturing process-centric issues, we will also discuss problems that are external to our work flow, such as material, equipment, and work space dilemmas."

"Like with the shears?" the Pig queries.

"Like with the shears," the Owl confirms. "And we might engage in some root cause analysis as well."

"Will there be any math in this one?" the Sheep inquires.

"We will look at *takt time* again," the Owl responds, "and we will have some very basic calculations as we attempt to balance the workload. And there will be some addition as we examine root causes. All in all, it is simple stuff, and nothing to be afraid of."

The Sheep and a few others look relieved, if only slightly.

"When we have the information captured and consolidated, then we get to be completely creative as we work on what we are to be," proposes the Owl.

Design the Future State

"What do you mean by that?" asks the Dog.

"I simply mean that the sky is the limit, to put it into winged vernacular," the Owl responds. "In this stage we will develop a future state from scratch exactly the way that we want it to be. Actually, that is why some call it the *to be* state. The only restrictions that we place on our design are the available skill levels of our animals, the number of animals that we have available, and the resources and equipment that they currently use. Otherwise the solutions that we generate could be too costly, or the technology we would require might not exist. We ground ourselves in reality but shoot for the stars, and unconventional ideas often lead to dramatic improvement. The result is a process map that details how we are going to perform the shearing process in the future."

Conduct a Gap Analysis

"And how in the heck do we get to this future state, Owl?" blares the Jackass. "I mean, look at this place and listen to the Pig. It would take a miracle for this process to get better."

"No miracles here," the Owl returns. "In this phase we will discuss the actions that will be required to progress from our current state to our future state. This will include a force field analysis as well, and culminate in the development of a transition plan depicting *what* we need to do, *who* will do it, *when* it needs to be done, and *how* we will know it is done."

"And when we have that, we're done, right?" assumes the Cow. "I mean, that should fix the problem, whatever it is."

"But we haven't actually transformed the process yet," claims the Cat. "There has to be more to this."

Engage the Transition Plan

"There is," assures the Owl. "In the final step of the busy-ness process reengineering cycle we will actually execute our plan. Remember what Antoine de Saint-Exupéry said: 'A goal without a plan is just a wish.' Like each of the other approaches and efforts that we have worked on this week, success will require deliberate project management and concerted effort from all of you. Accountability will be essential, and the results could be remarkable. Please take a look at the wall behind you and you will see what I mean."

The animals suddenly become aware of two things. The first is a new silence. There had been a light tapping echoing throughout the duration of their discussion. It has now ceased. The second is a new image. The Woodpecker is resting on the floor beneath the fresh words, cleaning his beak.

Twenty eyes review the list. Scrutiny and optimism appear, vanish, and then resurface in different expressions across the team. The Sheep turns to the Owl.

"This is what we need here," she says.

"What do you need?" the Owl queries.

"All of this," the Sheep replies.

"The Sheep is right," declares the Pig. "We can see it from the top level through the branches of our Strate-Tree, and now we can see it clearly from the ground level. How do we make this work for us?"

"By stepping into the BPR cycle," the Owl recommends. "Is everyone ready?"

"Let's get 'er done," asserts the Bull.

BPR Benefits

- Improved efficiency, efficacy, and flexibility to changing customer needs
- Higher utilization of animals and equipment
- Improved information and material flow
- Reduced labor requirements
- Improved communication
- Improved morale
- Reduced work space requirements
- Improved safety

Step 7: Action

Know the Need

"We all know why we're here," says the Dog. "We carefully developed each of these initiatives as we grew our Strate-Tree."

"And when we did that," interjects the Cat, "we were very careful to ground our decisions in the voice of the customer and the voice of the farm."

"Are the voices still saying the same thing you heard at the beginning of this week?" the Owl inquires.

"It's only been a few days now," cries the Rooster. "What could possibly have changed in that time?"

"Maybe nothing," continues the Owl, "but a deliberate and constant effort to listen to those voices drives meaningful and focused effort."

"I think I hear you, Owl," starts the Dog. "I don't hear any change from the voice of the farm. We need to sell more wool, and we need to use fewer resources doing it. Our mission and vision are still the same, and we're working our tails off to stop the Boo-chair from getting Lean Acres."

"As far as the voice of the customer is concerned, how different could that be?" brays the Jackass.

"I don't know about the wool," says the Cow, "but the Mice sure helped us to set our improvement targets during our other initiatives. I mean, we thought we had it right after the strategic planning we did, but something changed. It seems like listening to them on a regular basis might help us to be more flexible and able to deliver what they want, when they want it, and how they want it."

As the Cow completes her comment, the animals nod toward her and each other.

"Where are those Mice, Owl?" the Bull asks.

An eerie silence descends upon the gathering, but the team members are ready this time. Nerves spark and hairs rise. They quickly search under claw, paw, and hoof, through the straw and along the rafters. They are filled with anxiety, prepared for a startle at any given moment. The Jackass opens his mouth to speak, and a shrill, dissonant voice seems to escape his lips.

Never fear.

We are here!

The Mice announce from behind the Jackass's ears. The Jackass bolts into the air in fright and the Chicken faints. The Cat loses one of her lives to a heart attack, and the Bull, the Horse, and the Pig are in a panicked pile on the ground. The Mice do not budge as the Jackass completes his last lap around the shed and the other animals recover from the sudden fright.

"Settle down," barks the Dog, "all of you settle down."

The Mice are giggling to themselves as they ride back into the fold. The Rooster revives the Chicken as his teammates return to the group.

"Alright now, Mice, you've had your fun," the Bull presses. "What do our customers want from the Shearing Shack? What do they want of our wool?"

"It says 210 bags of wool per week on our Strate-Tree," the Pig announces. "That's thirty per day!"

The Mice respond harmonically.

Forty bags of wool per day, 280 bags per week.

Fluffy and light, and soft to the cheek.

Not so flat.

We don't like that.

"Forty bags, are you crazy?" belts the Bull.

The Mice stare back with empty, dark eyes. The Bull realizes that they just might be.

"Let's see," inserts the Rooster. "Forty bags per day with 180 minutes of work time available. According to the takt time formula, that's one bag every four-and-a-half minutes. Yep, they're crazy."

"Crazy or not, the demand has increased," the Sheep says. "The Mice aren't making this up. They just carry the voice of the customers to the farm, and I'm grateful for it." The Mice stare at the Sheep as she talks, and their gaping jaws twist into sweet, adoring, and yet disturbing smiles. "What should we do?"

"We will need to update our Strate-Tree," the Rooster states, "but for now I think we need to take a look at our current performance. We need to see if we are hitting the mark, or if not, how much we need to improve. Is that right, Owl?"

"It certainly is, Rooster," the Owl responds. "What does the process look like now? How do you shear sheep here on Lean Acres?"

Map and Measure

"The pigs actually *do* the shearing," the Dog offers. "Wouldn't the Pig be the best animal to tell us about the process?"

"I believe that he would," the Owl replies. "What can you tell us, Pig?"

The Pig steps forward a few paces and then turns to face the ranks.

"Like I said," begins the Pig, "it's a mess in here, total chaos, and I'm not even sure that we have a process."

"If the work is being performed and products are delivered, you have a process" assures the Owl. "Sometimes it can be difficult to see the steps through the conditions and circumstances. At times like this, a process map is a useful tool. There are many different symbols to use, but we will only need one today. This will be a rectangle. Rectangles will represent the discrete activities that are required as you shear a sheep. As you explain the details of the shearing process, the Woodpecker will develop a process map that we can use to further our reengineering journey. So, Pig, how do you shear the sheep here on Lean Acres?"

"Alright then," the Pig continues. "The sheep enter the shack one at a time through the front door. We can only move one sheep through the process at a time because, well, let's just say that they are very modest. We've tried to work through this issue by forcing groups into the shack, but it was too stressful for everyone. The pigs couldn't maintain control, and the sheep were so stressed out that their wool began to thin."

The Sheep's cheeks hold a slight hue of red. The animals can see that this is a hard requirement. The Pig goes on with his description.

"The sheep that enters the Shearing Shack walks forward through four stations and then out through the back door. We have a pig waiting on the left inside the door, and their job is to shear the left side of the sheep. The first pig gathers all of the wool into a bag and walks the bag forward to the second pig. Oh yeah, and we only have two sets of shears. The first pig continues down the line to the third pig to hand those off and then returns to the first station. Meanwhile, the sheep moves on to the second pig, who handles the wool on the right side of their body. The second pig continues to fill the bag with wool, and then takes it to the third pig in the line. Now the second pig shares shears with the fourth, so they have to go down to that station, hand off the shears, and then return to their original position. The sheep walks forward to the third pig, who handles the wool on the top. This pig gathers the wool, walks the bag forward to the fourth pig, then back to the first pig to drop off the shears, and then finally back to their place in the line. The fourth pig works on the belly. When the work there is complete, the fourth pig puts the last bit of wool into the bag, applies the Lean Acres label, threads the tie-string through the top of the bag, ties it shut, and shakes it to fluff up the wool. The wool tends to get smooshed down a little bit during the first three steps and while its being marched from one station to the next. Finally, the pig stacks the bag up wherever there is room, walks the shears back to the second pig, and then returns to their position. We try to put our most experienced workers in this last slot because it requires the most effort. It hurts morale a bit because they complain about the extra work. 'Why work harder if this is the reward?' they say. I've never heard a good answer for this, but this is the way we've always done it. I'll tell you what, when one of our star performers is sick or tasked elsewhere, our production numbers plummet. The skills and ethic that it takes to run that station really make it a potential single point of failure. I'd like to get to a more evenly distributed workload, but I just can't see how we can get there. Oh yeah, and the sheep is done once their belly is sheared and they exit the shack through the rear door. Then the next gal comes in the front and we do it all over again."

As the Pig pauses for a breath, the animals watch the Woodpecker work across the planks of the interior wall. Boxes are joined with arrows as the map evolves, and dotted lines separate tasks performed by different workers. The Owl speaks quietly with the Pig, and within moments he joins the Woodpecker. Numbers appear under the boxes as the Pig calls out over the rapid succession of driving and precise impacts. Mere minutes pass before the pair steps away from the boards. The sawdust curtain settles and parts. A new image is revealed to the team members, who immediately move closer to study its detail.

"A process map is more detailed in its depiction of activities than the value stream map," explains the Owl.

"What is that, Rooster? A fifteen-minute flow time?" the Pig asks.

"Seventeen minutes," responds the Rooster. "And with the way we run the shack now, with one sheep at a time, that's twelve and a half minutes longer than our takt time allows."

"That sure is a lot of boxes," comments the Horse. "Why did you label some with a VA above them? Is that like the value-added steps that we talked about during the corn harvesting effort?"

"Spot on," replies the Owl. "According to the subject matter expert, the Pig, these steps are where the actual work gets done. If you focus on these while you are reengineering, you will be more likely to create an efficient and effective future state."

"Why are there lines between some of the steps?"

"The lines enable us to delineate the specific steps performed at different stations or by different animals throughout the process," the Owl responds. "We call them *swim lanes*, and they also allow us to capture, analyze, and understand the flow and timing between parallel activities."

"Oh, I get it!" announces the Chicken. "The sheep walk through while the pigs are passing bags! I see what you mean!"

Several animals inspect the map and nod.

"Speaking of that, it looks like a lot of *transportation* going on there," comments the Cow, "and a lot of work in general. How in the world

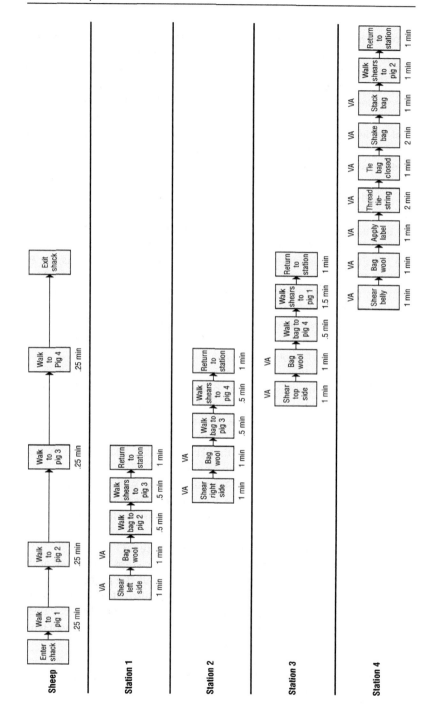

Sheep

| Enter shack | → | Walk to pig 1 | → | Walk to pig 2 | → | Walk to pig 3 | → | Walk to Pig 4 | → | Exit shack |

.25 min   .25 min   .25 min   .25 min

Station 1

VA   VA

| Shear left side | → | Bag wool | → | Walk bag to pig 2 | → | Walk shears to pig 3 | → | Return to station |

1 min   1 min   .5 min   .5 min   1 min

Station 2

VA   VA

| Shear right side | → | Bag wool | → | Walk bag to pig 3 | → | Walk shears to pig 4 | → | Return to station |

1 min   1 min   .5 min   .5 min   1 min

Station 3

VA   VA

| Shear top side | → | Bag wool | → | Walk bag to pig 4 | → | Walk shears to pig 1 | → | Return to station |

1 min   1 min   .5 min   1.5 min   1 min

Station 4

VA   VA   VA   VA   VA   VA   VA

| Shear belly | → | Bag wool | → | Apply label | → | Thread tie-string | → | Tie bag closed | → | Shake bag | → | Stack bag | → | Walk shears to pig 2 | → | Return to station |

1 min   1 min   1 min   2 min   1 min   2 min   1 min   1 min   1 min

could you do all of that with fewer pigs? If anything, it sounds like you need more."

"I don't know, Cow," sounds the Horse. "Looks like there could be a lot of standing around or *waiting* going on there, too."

The Woodpecker tears new shapes into a fresh section of wood, but the Owl calls for the group's attention.

"What other issues can you think of?" the Owl asks. "Let us brainstorm for awhile."

"Well, we already know that we have too many pigs working in here. We really need them to do other chores around here," offers the Bull.

"And we don't have enough shears for everybody to have their own set," the Pig sounds.

The animals continue to identify the issues that affect the shearing process, and the periods of silence between suggestions extend as more items are listed. Eventually, the well appears to be dry, and the Owl addresses the team.

"Thank you all for your contributions," he begins. "This is a fine list of problems that we are facing here in the Shearing Shack."

The team reviews the Woodpecker's carvings on the wall.

"Why did you arrange our ideas in a circle?" the Cat inquires.

"Because we are about to engage in root cause analysis," responds the Owl.

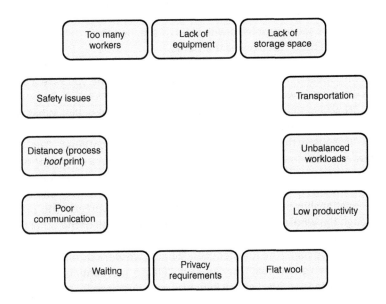

"Are we supposed to ask *why* five times for each of these problems?" the Jackass shouts. "How long is this going to take?" He rolls his eyes and gawks at the group.

"That type of root cause analysis would take some time, Jackass, but that is not what I am recommending," the Owl replies. "When you have a long list of potential problems or solutions, exploring each in depth might not be a viable option, and simply prioritizing them will not help. The ideal answer is to discuss and document the number and types of cause-and-effect connections that these items share. We can do this with a tool called the *interrelationship digraph.*"

"What's this about an inter-spatial giraffe?" asks the Cow.

"An *interrelationship digraph,*" repeats the Owl. "It will be easier to understand if you build one yourselves. To begin, we need to pick one of the issues from the circle."

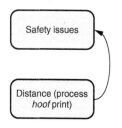

"Let's do *distance,*" votes the Sheep. No one argues against her.

"Alright," responds the Owl, "*distance* it is. Next, we need to ask a series of questions as we move clockwise around the circle. For this issue, we need to know if *distance* causes *safety issues,* if *safety issues* causes *distance,* or whether there is no relationship between them. If *distance* does cause *safety issues,* then we would draw an arrow from *distance* into *safety issues.* Technically, we say that *distance* is the driver and *safety issues* is the outcome."

"It does cause problems with safety," the Pig offers.

"How's that?" challenges the Horse.

"We have to run around all day dodging teetering heaps of bags while carrying shears, that's how," the Pig returns. "Anytime you take a step in this place when we're working, you're taking a risk."

"Now I understand," the Horse admits. "Thanks, Pig. What if the opposite were true?"

"If it were the other way around," the Owl continues, "we would draw an arrow from *safety issues* into *distance.* If there is no relationship, then there is no arrow. Once we have answered these questions for *distance* and *safety issues,* we would advance one block further and explore the relationship between *distance* and *too many workers.* You proceed through the whole circle and compare each item to all of the others. How does that sound?"

"Not too bad," the Rooster calls. "Should we work through this now?"

"That is a great idea," the Owl says. "Please, just continue your discussion, and the Woodpecker will annotate your decisions."

The animals press through the exercise, moving across every possible pairing of problems. Arguments flare now and then, but the Owl knows that this is a normal aspect of healthy group dynamics. Passion is the key to performance improvement, and he smiles as the team storms, norms, and ultimately performs. When the last arrow is carved and the conversations give way to the quiet of midday, the Owl returns to the front of the group.

"What do you think?" poses the Owl.

"I think it looks like a tangled mess," answers the Cat. "We were counting on this exercise to reveal something. I'm just not sure what or how."

"I can answer both," the Owl assures. "The interrelationship digraph will reveal the primary driver and the key outcome. That is the *what*. And you say that you were 'counting on this exercise.' That is precisely what we will do. That is the *how*. Simply count the number of arrows going out from each box and the number of arrows coming in. The issue with the most arrows going out is your *driver*. This is the cause of your problems. And the box with the highest number of incoming arrows is your *outcome*. This is the issue that you will most likely face as the other problems occur. Woodpecker, would you please show them?"

The Woodpecker takes flight, and in moments the picture has been transformed with new numbers, words, and shapes. The animals step closer.

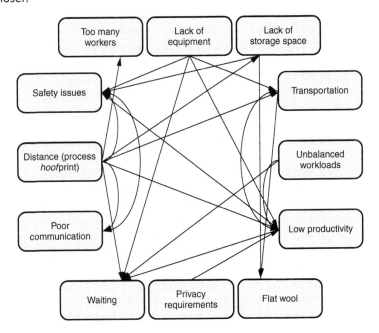

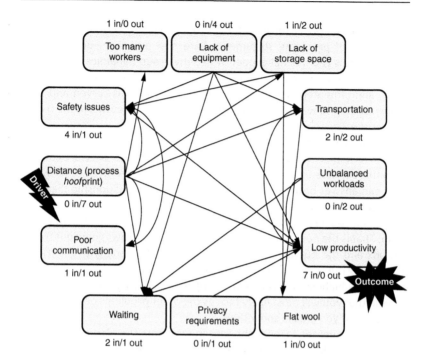

"So the distance between our stations—the hoofprint of our process—causes the low productivity that we've been fighting in here?" the Pig wonders. "It makes sense. I don't know why we didn't think of that before."

"Most of the tools that we use rely on your experience, Pig," the Owl says. "They simply provide structure and order, a way to organize and examine that which you already know."

"I just always thought that if we came up with a better storage system, some shelves or something, that that would solve our problems," says the Pig.

"Do not give up on that idea," the Owl encourages. "The results of the interrelationship digraph exercise reveal the main culprit, but that does not mean you should let the others off the hook. It simply shows us the best place to start from a cause-and-effect perspective. If we could only work on one of the issues we are facing in the Shearing Shack, the dispersed physical layout of the process is the winning candidate. Improvements in that area will most likely affect improvements in others. The remaining issues can also be addressed at your discretion."

"Well, we know what the problem is, but what can we do about the layout?" sounds the Jackass. "How are we going to change it and still give the sheep the privacy that they need? You all heard the Pig. We've always done it this way."

"But the Boo-chair wasn't always watching," the Dog reminds the team. "We can't afford to continue down the same path, or else we might just end up getting cut. What is the next step, Owl? We need something completely different here. How do we transform the shearing process?"

Shoot for the Stars

"My advice to you is to start from scratch," the Owl responds. "How can we deliver twice as much wool with half as many pigs? Let your imaginations flow."

"Maybe we could get some new shears," the Cat declares. "Why don't we get two more sets?"

"We've tried, but there isn't another shipment due in to any stores in Perfection until next year. Someone was running with a set in the factory, things happened, and, well, the whole situation got messy real fast. New equipment just isn't an option for us right now."

"What if we just moved the stations closer together?" suggests the Rooster. "That would reduce the distance and cut out a lot of the transportation. Heck, the pigs could just hand the shears and the bags to each other instead of walking clear across the shack. Think of all the space that would open up for staging our shipments."

"That would just be improper," poses the Sheep. "We may be a quiet bunch, but our modesty is absolute."

"Noted, Sheep," the Bull interjects. "What if we blindfolded the sheep before they enter the shack? That way they wouldn't see each other no matter how close the stations are."

The group considers this option carefully, but the Cow interrupts their thoughts.

"That might cause some safety issues," she states, "and it could slow them down considerably as they move from one station to the next."

"I agree with the Cow!" the Chicken blurts. "Another accident could cost us another set of shears! Then we'd really be stuck in a corner with nowhere to turn!"

"What was that, Chicken?" the Dog requests.

"I said we'd really be stuck in a corner with nowhere to turn!" repeats the Chicken.

"That gives me an idea," continues the Dog. "Turning the sheep. Let me gather my thoughts here."

The Dog walks away from the group toward the front door of the Shearing Shack. He paces back and forth and then carefully studies the floor. He begins stepping around the area in a square formation, pausing every now and then to look to his right and then to his left. A few minutes pass before he returns to share his proposal.

"I don't have this fully developed," the Dog begins, "but let me try to explain what I'm thinking. What if we don't march the sheep through the shack?"

"What do you mean, Dog?" the Pig questions. "Where else are we supposed to shear them?"

"In the shack, of course," the Dog replies, "but maybe we don't need to move them through it. What if they walk through the process in a consolidated area, right here by the front door? That would leave a ton of room for bag storage and staging."

"We'll never fit the entire line in that space!" the Jackass says. "No matter how close we put the stations together, they'll at least end halfway through the shack. At that point, what's the use in turning the sheep around?"

"You're right, Jackass, we won't fit the line in that space," the Dog answers, "not like it is today. But what if we gave it some corners, so to speak? What if we wrapped the line into the shape of a horseshoe, bringing the sheep in and sending them out the same door?"

"That would create a huge area for wool storage separate from our production area," comments the Pig. "But how could that help us with our other challenges? We still don't have enough shears, we need to free up a few pigs, and the sheep need their privacy."

"I've been thinking about the first two things you mentioned, Pig, and I'm pretty sure that the first two take care of themselves," the Rooster interjects. "If we only have half of the number of shears that we need now, but we are reducing the pigs in the process by half, the issue is resolved. Am I missing something here?"

"I don't think so, Rooster," adds the Cat. "Addressing those two issues independently certainly would be confusing. I still don't understand the horseshoe idea though, Dog."

"I recommend that you explain your concept visually," the Owl says. "The Horse has left an excellent print here in the dirt. Would you feel comfortable walking the team through your proposal using this?"

"That'll work just fine," the Dog replies. "My idea only addresses the space issue, but I'm sure we can tackle the others as we work through this together."

The animals gather around the fresh horseshoe impression, and the Dog begins to speak.

"If we bring the sheep in and work them around the path of this curve, we could consolidate the four separate stations and virtually eliminate the distance between them."

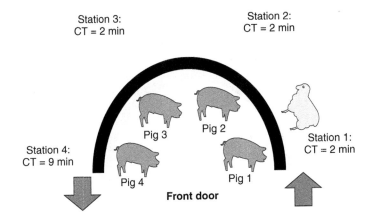

Station 3:
CT = 2 min

Station 2:
CT = 2 min

Pig 3

Pig 2

Station 1:
CT = 2 min

Station 4:
CT = 9 min

Pig 4

Pig 1

Front door

"How would we do that?" asks the Horse.

The Dog scratches new shapes into the dirt at their feet with his paw.

"Let me show you what I mean. We have four stations altogether, and I'll throw the cycle times for each in here as a reference. The pigs could still perform their functions as they do today, but the first and the second pig could share shears, and the third and fourth pigs could do the same. It trims our flow time down by a few minutes, frees up a heck of a lot of storage space, and might help us out with the safety problems we've been having. The sheep will still have to move through the process, but the pigs will be able to stay in place."

"I have a question. Why do you have the sheep moving around the horseshoe counterclockwise like that?" the Sheep queries.

"I just figured that since most animals are right-hooved, -clawed, or -pawed, it would make sense for the pigs to bring the wool forward from their right side."

"It does make sense, Dog" the Owl interjects. "Also consider the horse and dog races, and that thing called NASCAR that the Farmer likes to watch on the television. Which way do the dogs, horses, and cars go around the track?"

"Counterclockwise," the Dog says.

"Again, in most animals on earth this is a natural tendency," the Owl continues. "It is best to take advantage of this inclination in your process design."

"Not bad, Dog," the Cat offers. "This would enable us to perform at a slightly improved rate with limited equipment and resources and in a much smaller area."

"We've reduced the process hoofprint, improved our communication and safety, and that should positively impact morale—what else is there?" asks the Horse.

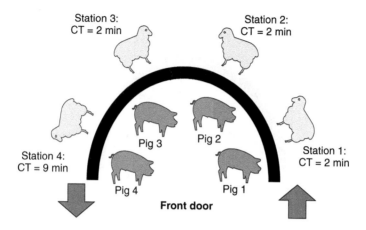

Station 3:
CT = 2 min

Station 2:
CT = 2 min

Pig 3

Pig 2

Station 4:
CT = 9 min

Station 1:
CT = 2 min

Pig 4

Pig 1

Front door

"Remind me. How has your flow time changed?" the Owl inquires.

Each team member returns their gaze to the diagram on the floor and runs the numbers through their heads. It is the Rooster that has the answer first.

"We are at seventeen minutes per bag in our current state, and fifteen minutes for our future state. Our takt time to get forty bags out in the three hours that we have available each day is four and a half minutes, and we're running at over three times that. Do we need to try a different design?"

"Not necessarily," the Owl returns. "How could you continue with this construct? What else could you do differently?"

"If we could fill each station working toward continuous flow as we sheared the sheep, we would definitely get closer," the Cow suggests. "I mean, sure, our first piece would still take fifteen minutes, but we could get one bag produced every nine minutes after that, right? How many is that in a day, Rooster?"

"That would be nineteen bags altogether. That's almost twice as many as we make now," the Rooster claims.

"But the sheep at the third station would have to turn and face the other direction," the Pig asserts. "Just so we could get at her right side."

"That shouldn't be a problem, right Sheep?" the Dog insists.

"No, turning around is not a problem. We are quite capable of that, but what about our privacy?" she insists. "We can't live in shame, and you've all seen what happens to our wool when we're stressed out."

The animals are stumped by this recurrent challenge. This has been a cultural consideration on Lean Acres since any one of them can remember, and no one wants to discount the needs of the sheep.

"If the sheep need privacy," starts the Owl, "why don't we just give it them?"

"Because the way we do it severely hinders our production, Owl," the Bull responds. "You know that better than any of us."

"Providing privacy might not be the issue here," the Owl continues. "Like you said, it might be the *way* that you are making this provision. Clean-slate thinking is absolutely required for dramatic improvement in the busy-ness process reengineering methodology. Is there any other way to provide the sheep with the privacy that they require?"

The animals look around the shed, at the ground, and at each other. Silent personal debates abound within their skulls as possibilities ricochet between their ears. The Pig is looking up at the Farmer's house when the idea strikes like lightning.

"Dog?" he asks. "What do you call those things that the Farmer hangs over his windows? You know, those blankets that he pulls shut at night. What do you call them?"

"You mean the *curtains*, Pig?" the Dog answers.

"Yes! The curtains!" the Pig exalts. "Could we set up some curtains around the horseshoe, protecting the sheep from each other's view like this?"

The Pig hooves new shapes into the design to illustrate his thought.

"You know, there's a few old sets in the barn loft," the Cat says. "We could use those."

"And we could hang them from the rafters in here," suggests the Horse. "They're not out of reach. What do you think of the idea, Sheep?"

The Sheep carefully studies the design in the dirt and considers multiple scenarios. At last she looks to her teammates.

"This could work," she announces. "It's actually an improvement to our current situation. None of us likes standing in the open while being

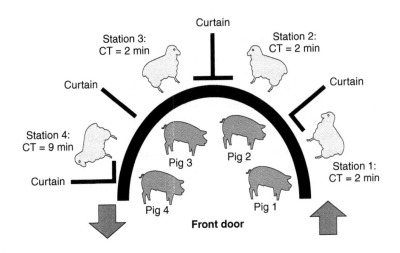

sheared. I think that this idea actually offers us increased privacy, and my sisters will be excited about that."

Celebration erupts throughout the team, but again it is short-lived.

"I don't want to be the bearer of bad news, but we're still not meeting the customer demand," the Jackass reminds them.

"Thank you, Jackass," the Owl responds. "You are absolutely correct. If we look at the horseshoe design as it is now, what is the biggest problem that you see?"

"It looks like station 4 is a constraint in our process," the Horse states. "But we absolutely have to perform each of those steps. I think that we'd all agree that they are *value-added*."

"In a case like this," the Owl replies, "we will not attempt to reduce the cycle times of individual activities yet, because, frankly, we might not need to. The workload throughout the shearing process is unbalanced. If we take the value-added steps from our process map, adjust the height of the boxes so that they represent the amount of time they require, and then stack them on top of each other per each station, we would end up with a workload balance chart like this."

The Woodpecker hammers at the boards that compose the wall with furious velocity. The animals shield their eyes as the splinters and chips sail into their feathers and hair. The sound of impact stops just as suddenly as it began, and through the settling dust the team views an unsettling image.

"Holy cow!" the Bull shouts.

"Is that really how much work the pig at station 4 is doing?" asks the Cat.

"Unfortunately, it is," remarks the Pig. "But we have to perform each of those steps. Again, they're value-added. It's true. Straight from the Horse's mouth. This will cause a huge amount of waiting at the other stations, but what can we do?"

"When the redesign of specific steps is not an option, there is a way to deal with an unbalanced workload," assures the Owl.

"And that is?" begs the Dog.

"To balance it, of course," the Owl returns. "This means reallocating steps from stations that exceed takt time to those that have additional capacity, or space between the top of the column and the dotted line. Are there activities that are currently performed at this station that could be done earlier in the process? For instance, could you apply the label to the bag at any station besides the fourth?"

"I don't see why not," the Pig says. "And we could lace the tie-string before the bag gets to the last station too."

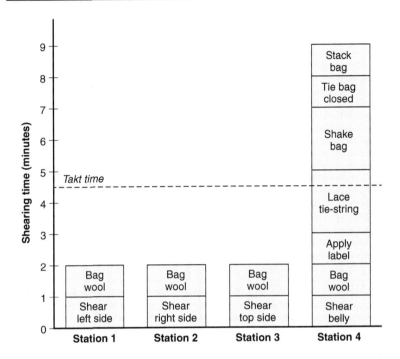

"We'll still have to shake the bag at station 4, right?" the Rooster questions. "The wool should be fluffed up right before it's put on the truck."

"Yes and no," offers the Pig. "We only shake the bag because the wool tends to get packed down as it moves between the stations. With the distance reduced so much, I think we'd be fine doing it at station 3."

"This is good news," comments the Owl. "What would those changes look like, Woodpecker?"

A storm of chips and taps produces a revised chart.

"Whoa," the Horse exclaims. "Did we really just bring all of the stations below takt time, just like that?"

"You did indeed, Horse. You did indeed," confirms the Owl.

"But we didn't reduce the amount of work we're doing," the Pig announces. "I mean, sure, it looks good on the chart, but what did this really do for us?"

"We'll still get our first piece out in fifteen minutes," declares the Rooster, "but we'll get one bag out every four minutes after that versus the nine minutes that we were working before. That's forty-two bags in a three-hour shift. I think we might have our answer here."

"How did that happen?" snorts the Pig.

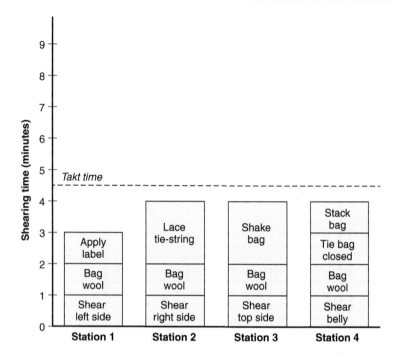

"I think that it has to do with some of the stuff we learned in the Hen House," starts the Cow. "The fourth station was our constraint, and by shifting the additional workload—the things that pushed us over takt time—we reduced its effects on the process as a whole. Right, Owl?"

"I could not have said it better myself," returns the Owl. "By balancing the workload across the horseshoe, you have accomplished two results. The first is that you have, as the Cow stated, reduced the process flow time and increased your throughput. The second is that you have reduced wait time for stations 1 through 3, thereby increasing the value-added time that each animal, pig and sheep alike, is contributing to the effort."

"Okay," the Bull says, "I'm feeling pumped up now. What's next?"

"We're still using four pigs," the Cat points out.

"But we have four stations!" declares the Chicken. "How can we run four stations with only two pigs?!"

"Do we have to run four stations?" the Owl asks.

"You see the process," the Horse responds. "It takes that many to get the work done."

"There is a way to know for sure," interjects the Owl. "With two key pieces of information, flow and takt time, we can calculate the number of workers that are needed to work on a process. We just happen to have both of these data points for our theoretical new process, and to get to the answer we simply divide the flow time by the takt time."

$$\text{Number of workers needed} = \frac{\text{Flow time}}{\text{Takt time}}$$

"So, the flow time of our new process is the time that it takes one sheep to move through the line, or the sum of the cycle times for each station, right Owl? That's fifteen minutes," the Dog offers.

"Right indeed," responds the Owl. "And if you remember, our takt time is one bag every four and a half minutes."

"Okay, okay," the Rooster announces, "I've got this. Fifteen divided by four and a half is roughly three and a third. Does that mean that we need three and a third pigs on the line?"

$$\text{Number of workers needed} = \frac{15}{4.5} = 3.33$$

"Not quite. Whenever we run this calculation, any decimal or fractional remainders are rounded up to the next whole number. At three and a third, the formula is telling you that you need four pigs to run this process effectively at the rate dictated by your takt time," clarifies the Owl. "If that is the case," continues the Owl, "I recommend that we take another look at the work itself. We have significantly reduced the distance between activities. How does that affect the cycle time for the individual activities that are performed at each station? Also, are there other ways to lower these times?"

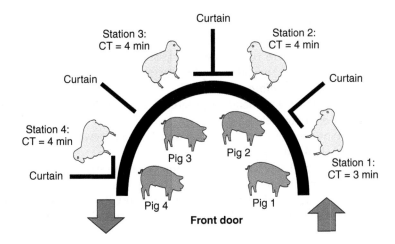

The animals consider the proposition carefully, and the Cow is the first to speak.

"If we kept the materials that we needed at each station, like the labels and the tie-strings, at the points where they were actually used, would that help?" she offers

"That's not half bad, Cow," the Pig says. "It would help a lot. Probably cut the time in half for each activity. The only reason the first two steps took a whole minute was because the pigs had to go and get the labels and the strings from where they're stored along the far wall. We also counted some of the time that it took to transport the bag in the tying phase, so that time would drop, too."

"Why don't we see that transportation in our process map, Pig?" the Bull inquires.

"I just never thought about it as being a separate activity," the Pig replies.

"And many animals think that way as well," the Owl interjects. "Additional steps that we perform on a regular basis, those that are required to complete our core functions, are often discarded during a mapping exercise. They are the known but unrecognized, and we call these steps *hidden fact-stories*. These occur where work is done but not identified as a distinct activity. It is extremely important that these areas are called out and documented so that the true components, sequence, and flow of your process can be analyzed."

"That being said," starts the Rooster, "why is it that you spend two minutes shaking the bag at the third station?"

"Like I mentioned earlier, the wool tends to get packed down a bit as we carry it from one station to the next. The pounding of our hooves takes its toll on the stuff."

"But we're just handing it off now, right?" the Cat comments. "There shouldn't be any issues due to transportation."

"You know, you're right," the Pig agrees. "We should still give it a shake at the end, but I would say that thirty seconds should be ample time to fluff the wool up before we store it."

"You are making tremendous progress," announces the Owl. "Take a look and see for yourselves."

The Woodpecker chisels the final details on his newest picture, and the animals look closely.

"What do we have now, Rooster?" the Dog requests.

"With this configuration, we could get our first piece out in eleven and a half minutes, and each piece after that every three and a half minutes," the Rooster reports. "That means we could produce forty-nine bags of wool each day."

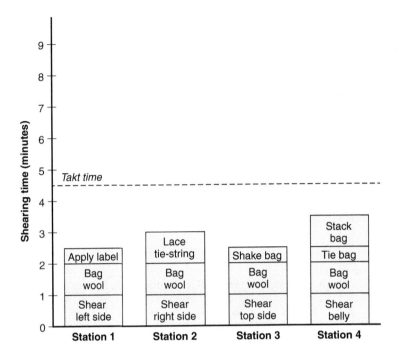

"Is there anything else," the Owl asks, "any other steps that might be reduced or eliminated from this process?"

"I have a question," the Horse says. "Why does it take a minute to bag the wool at each station?"

"After we shear the wool from the Sheep, it takes a while to pick it up off of the ground, pull the straw out of it, and pack it into the bag," explains the Pig.

"Well, why do we let it fall to the ground if it makes all of that extra work?" continues the Horse.

"How else could we do it?" the Pig challenges.

"Why not shear the wool directly into the bag," the Horse responds. "I mean, it only takes one hoof to work the shears. Why not hold the bag in the other and just let the wool fall into it?"

"Because . . ." the Pig begins and then pauses. "Because we never thought of that before," he admits. "That could work, and it would eliminate the bagging step altogether."

The team is gaining momentum and realizing the benefits as the process design evolves iteratively. The Woodpecker captures their ideas, and the next image takes its place on the Shearing Shack wall.

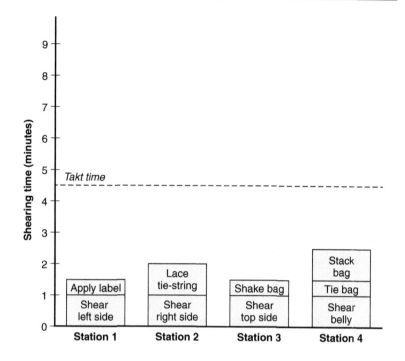

"First piece out in seven and a half minutes, the others coming at two and a half minutes each for seventy total bags in a day," calls the Rooster.

"But again," reminds the Sheep, "we're still using four pigs and running four stations. I wonder if we could balance the line again and maybe eliminate one of the stations."

"We have room for that," the Dog says. "If the space between the tops of the columns on our chart and the takt time line are additional capacity, we definitely have the room to consolidate steps. Does anyone have any ideas?"

"Could we shear the left and right sides of the sheep at the first station?" the Cow proposes.

"Why would we do that?" asks the Jackass.

"Well," the Cow continues, "that could balance the work between stations 1 and 4. Then we could combine the steps that are performed at stations 2 and 3, and hey, that consolidated station would be balanced with the other two at two and a half minutes."

The Woodpecker completes the amended chart. The team members review each of the three stations.

"It's the exact same output with one less station," realizes the Rooster. "With this configuration we'd only have to share shears between two pigs

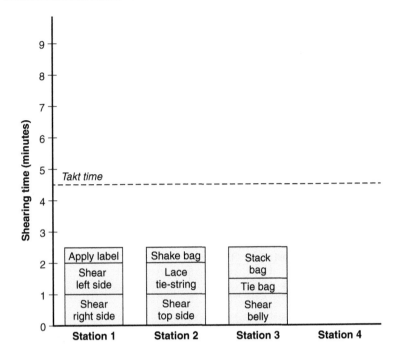

while the third had their own, or we could try to run two of the stations with one pig working at our required resource limit."

"Should we run the formula again to see how many pigs we should use?" questions the Cow. "We've made some pretty big changes, and the cycle times look pretty low."

"It looks like our flow time is down to seven and a half minutes now," the Rooster confirms. "Seven and a half divided by four and a half is about one and two-thirds. Holy smokes. We can do this with two pigs."

$$\text{Number of workers needed} = \frac{7.5}{4.5} = 1.6667$$

"And we still have a bunch of additional capacity," says the Bull. "Can we merge the three stations into two without violating takt time?"

"Let's see," offers the Pig. "We have to tie the bag and stack it at the last station, but we could lace the tie string at the first. If we do that and then combine the activities of the second and third stations, well, what would that look like?"

"Please show us, Woodpecker," the Owl requests.

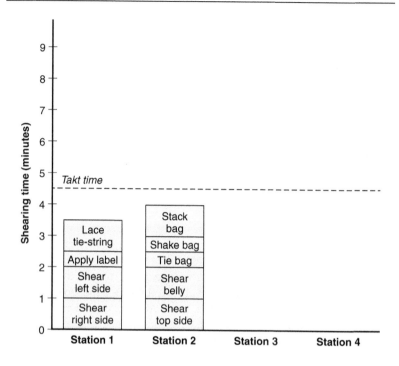

Familiar rapid tapping takes hold in the shack. Two columns form where there once were three, and all of the animals smile at the results.

"This will produce fewer bags of wool in the end," starts the Rooster, "but we will be able to meet the customer demand with some room to spare, as the chart indicates. We'll get our first piece out in seven and a half minutes, that's about ten minutes faster than our current process, and each subsequent bag will come out every four minutes after that, less than half of the time that it takes now. That's roughly forty-two bags of wool each day."

"Is it okay to run faster than the takt time, Owl?" asks the Cow. "Are we in danger of building up excess inventory?"

"That is a fantastic question, Cow," the Owl answers. "Takt time is an ideal target, and when we produce exactly at that rate we are assuming that variation will not occur in our process, product, or environment. But you all know from our experience at the Milking Parlour that variation is natural and will happen. Pigs will drop shears, sheep will flinch while being trimmed, sometimes it rains—you understand. It is always best to produce at a rate slightly faster than the demand to account for these issues. However, as with everything else we are doing here on Lean Acres, you must monitor the situation constantly to ensure that you are balancing the

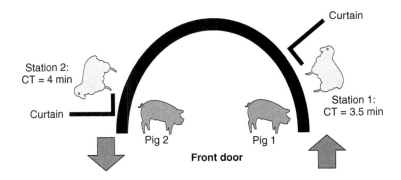

utilization of excess capacity with the variation and takt time. We can not run forward blindly, but must be vigilant in controlling the processes that satisfy our customers."

"What does this mean for our horseshoe, Dog?" the Cat inquires.

"It's much less complicated now, that's for sure," the Dog responds as he scratches a new design into the dirt. "We'd only need two curtains to protect the sheep, each pig would have their own shears, and we'd be darn close to continuous flow. Just a little drag, about thirty seconds is all, between the two stations."

"I'll tell you what, though," interjects the Bull, "this saves space, improves safety and communication, increases the fluffiness of our wool by allowing us to store the bags in rows that are one high rather than in piles, optimizes our equipment utilization, more than doubles our output, and we can do it with half the number of pigs. I like it. I like it a lot. And now I get the whole *reengineering* piece. This is a completely new approach to shearing, and I know we couldn't have gotten here without applying the discipline of this methodology. The only question I have is, how do we get this solution in place?"

"Yes," the Owl responds. "The *how* is the next step. Let us talk about gaps between the current and future states, the gaps between the *now* and the *next*, and what we need to do to bridge them."

Plot the Path

"What's this gonna take? More fancy charts and diagrams, Owl?" bellows the Jackass.

"We could employ various tools, Jackass," the Owl returns. "Different matrices, radar or spider charts like the one we designed during our 7S effort, and other pictorial applications often meet the needs of assorted organizations. However, in our case, I believe that a simple discussion will suffice. Please join me by the wall to begin. The Woodpecker has built the template for our conversation."

The group shifts its collective attention to the section of boards behind the Owl and recognizes a fresh carving.

"We have two states to consider," the Owl continues. "The first is our current state, or where we are now. This is the hill on the left. The second is our future state, or where we want to be. This is, of course, the hill on the right. We have key attributes of each listed to guide our discussion. Imagine that these two hills are separated by a valley. The depth of the valley represents the differences in resources and rules between the two hills. And you can think of the width of the valley as the time required for transformation. These are symbolic representations, so do not worry about scaling them appropriately. We need to identify the activities that will enable the most effective and efficient required changes to the resources and rules that we operate with now. The resources include everything that you need to run the process: animals, equipment, materials, you name it. The rules involve regulations and guidance as well as the way you work each step in the process. These actions will serve as the foundations of a plan that will support our process as we transition from the current to the future state over time, improving performance with every step forward. The question that you must answer is this: What activities will be required to enable your transition from the current to the future state over the least amount of time? Consider what the actions are, who will perform them, when they should take place, and how long they should take. It would also be helpful to come up with a goal for each, or a way to report that the action is complete. The Woodpecker will record the details in a simple table for you."

"According to the RACI chart, this is ultimately my responsibility, and I accept that," states the Pig. "But I sure could use some help."

"We can all pitch in," replies the Dog. "We just need to zero in on the key elements of the plan."

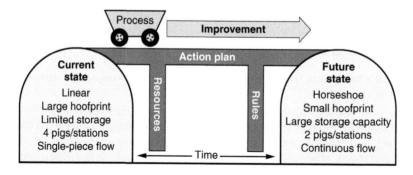

"What do you mean, like training the pigs to work in the new configuration?" the Bull asks.

"That will definitely help the transition along," the Owl agrees.

"I'll take that one on," declares the Pig. "We can be a rough crowd, so it's best that this comes from within. What's today?"

"The last day of June," announces the Rooster.

"Alright," the Pig progresses, "I'll start tomorrow and should be done in about five days. I need to walk each pig through both stations to guarantee some flexibility. I guess I'll be done when they have all been trained."

"And we'll need to train the sheep too," the Cat states. "They'll need to understand the new route and the reasoning for it."

"I can handle that," volunteers the Sheep. "The Pig is right. The training should come from one of our own, and they will also need to know that their privacy has been preserved. That is critical. If it's okay, I'll do my work concurrently with him, and will need to go through it with every sheep."

"You certainly can perform two activities at the same time, Sheep," the Owl answers, "especially if they are complementary, but only if they do not require the same resources."

The Sheep is pleased, and she smiles behind a wave of red blush.

"We're going to have to rearrange the Shearing Shack before we do any of that," says the Horse. "We'll need to permanently frame the horseshoe, reposition the supplies, designate the storage area, and ultimately, 7S the Shearing Shack. I guess that's how we'll know when we're done. The 7S program will be established. I'll need some help, and about five days to do it."

"We probably shouldn't start training till that's all taken care of, Sheep," the Pig figures. "So we'll move our start date out to the sixth."

"What about sharing our ideas with everyone else?" the Cat questions. "When should we tell the rest of the farm about our plan? When should they be involved?"

"Tomorrow would be ideal," the Owl responds. "And you might want to make it a continuous effort on a daily basis throughout implementation. This way everyone will know what you are planning, what you are doing, and what the results of your actions are."

"But shouldn't we wait until the solution is in place?" the Cow queries. "I mean, what's the point in letting the cat out of the bag, if you'll excuse the expression, Cat."

The Cat raises an eyebrow but allows the comment to pass.

"Because we want to develop buy-in across the entire organization, not just within specific functional areas like the Shearing Shack or on your team," the Owl suggests. "You never know, there may be some great ideas out there that we have not considered. Take advantage of the diversity on your farm. Expose problems and solutions to as many animals as possible. After the new process is up and running, your communications should take place in the form of strategic reports and on a more periodic basis."

"How do we test and prove the process? When do we do that?" the Rooster asks.

"I would guess as soon as possible," the Dog replies.

"That would be starting on the eleventh, right?" continues the Rooster. "That's when the animals should all be trained and the Shack should be ready to go. What do you say, Pig, start it then and run it for about five days? Would that be enough to pilot the new configuration?"

"Yeah," the Pig responds, "I think that would work just fine. Good idea, you guys, and good catch. Can anyone think of anything else we'll need to do to get our solution in place, to achieve our future state?"

"We have actions in place to facilitate the transition for all resources and rules. The communication plan is included along with training plans, and we have a pilot run scheduled to test it all out. I think we've really got something here, Pig," the Horse comments. "I think we've got a robust plan that is manageable and accountable. What more could we ask for?"

"How would you like a tool that will enable you to schedule, track, and assess the discrete but integrated actions you have planned?" the Owl inquires.

"Sounds great," the Dog replies. "What is it?"

"It is called a *Gantt chart*," offers the Owl, "and that is *Gantt* with two *t*'s. This is a basic project management device that captures specific actions, the owners of those actions, start and end dates, goals to achieve, and planned and actual durations and sequencing for each activity. Most of the information is displayed as text, but bars on this chart help to visually assess the timing of the plan as a whole."

The Owl signals the Woodpecker, and he finishes the final touches on the Gantt chart. The animals follow its flow across the wood, reviewing specific assignments and sequences chiseled in place, and confirming that the plan will work with each other and themselves.

"I like this Gantt chart!" the Chicken states. "Even though the work won't be easy, the plan is easy to read and easy to understand!"

Fly Forward

"What's next, Owl?" calls the Bull. "Is that it? Are we done?"

"Not yet, Bull," the Owl responds, "but your assumption is one of the most common causes of failures in improvement efforts. Developing

Action	Owner	Start	End	Goal	1	2	3	4	5	6	7	8	9	10	11	12	13	14	15
Share plan	Cat	July 1st	July 15th	100% awareness	█	█	█	█	█	█	█	█	█	█	█	█	█	█	█
Arrange Shack	Horse	July 1st	July 5th	7S program established	█	█	█	█	█										
Train pigs	Pig	July 6th	July 10th	100% trained						█	█	█	█	█					
Train sheep	Sheep	July 6th	July 10th	100% trained						█	█	█	█	█					
Pilot run	Pig	July 11th	July 15th	Fill 100% of demand											█	█	█	█	█

the solution and the plan are never enough. As with the other methodologies that I have presented this week, you must engage the plan and continue your journey of continuous performance improvement by regularly measuring and analyzing the key metrics such as cycle and flow time, and especially throughput rates. This will support further improvement efforts as you continue to optimize your process. In accordance with your plan, you start tomorrow, but the initiative will never end. Your performance will never be good enough for Perfection."

"That's kind of a downer," the Sheep mumbles.

"It is more like a *driver*," returns the Owl. "Customer satisfaction is momentary at best. As soon as you make improvements and they feel the impact, they will want more. That is the nature of the consumer since the Beginning. To survive and thrive, Lean Acres will have to constantly raise the bar in order to keep a safe distance from and maybe one day overtake the Boo-chair. Who is to say that *he* can not be *cut*?"

The team members are shocked by this proposal. Most are pleased by the possibility.

"We never even considered that before," remarks the Dog, "turning the tables, making the Boo-chair our target instead of living as his. We can do that?"

"You certainly can," the Owl replies, "and to truly achieve your vision you will have to."

The Owl bounds to the windowsill above the team members' heads with one fell swoop of his powerful wings. He looks out across the fields and beyond the woods that surround them. Night is coming, and he is leaving.

"I have truly enjoyed my time with you this week," he says, "but as much as it pains me, I must be moving on. Lean Acres is more than a farm. You are a diverse family of unique individuals, and a stronger family for it. You know why you need to get better. The threat has been announced through every building and pen. You all know who wants to purchase this farm and what you need to do so that the Farmer will not sell. Because of the Strate-Tree that you have grown, you know where to focus and what to improve, including by how much. We initiated efforts across each of your key areas, or your branches, and discovered new ways to explore, analyze, and solve problems. Engage the methodologies I have taught you where appropriate and, at times, together. While this is the end of my visit, it is the beginning for the new Lean Acres. You will become lean in your operations, not in numbers. You will base decisions on data, not assumptions. And you will focus on results, not activities. Remember the three D's: discipline, diligence, and determination. These are the keys to your success. Until we meet again, I bid you a fond good night. Farewell."

As the Owl turns to take flight, the Chicken cries out.

"When will we meet again, Owl?! When will you be back?!" she calls, choking back tears.

The Owl does not turn, but looks over his shoulder and replies, "You already know my answer, Chicken. It depends." He smiles warmly at the group and then he is gone. Onward and upward, out and away he sails into the dark blues and swelling black that is the night sky. The animals disperse slowly in ones and twos, upset at the loss of their facilitator but encouraged by their newly formed future. No one knows exactly what will come, but they do have a plan, as does the Owl. He will return.

Rest/Reflect/Relate (R³)

1. Have you engaged in reengineering a process before? If so, what went well? What didn't go so well? Was the solution sustained? Why or why not?

2. Are there processes that you participate in or encounter in your life that require dramatic improvement? What are they? Who performs them? What do they provide? To whom?

3. Do you have any thoughts or ideas concerning a redesigned future state for these processes? What would it look like in each situation?

4. Which of the tools or concepts referenced in the Shearing Shack example seem to be the most applicable to your situation/ environment? How would you use them?

Chapter 10

You Reap What You Sow

You don't get something for nothing
You can't have freedom for free
You won't get wise
With the sleep still in your eyes
No matter what your dreams might be

—Neil Peart

Welcome back! Innovation here. I hope that you enjoyed our visit at Lean Acres Farm. I hope that our trip helped you to realize that there are significant levels of complexity in the seemingly most simple surroundings. If I were to bring an observer to your world for a week, just imagine what we would discover.

In the time that it took you to turn the last page, six months have passed on the farm. The methodologies introduced by the Owl have become a part of the farm's culture. They have not adopted a new program. Rather, they have adapted and incorporated performance improvement—lean, Six Sigma, the theory of constraints, and business process reengineering—as a new way of life. They have also successfully integrated the approaches with each other. By using the framework of the DMAIC project management model, all of their efforts progress through a standardized set of phases, including tollgate reviews. The differentiation between approaches occurs in the *measure, analyze,* and *improve* phases based on the problem at hand and the tools that provide the best solution, but this does not limit their flexibility. If a constraint is identified, they might use tools from the lean, Six Sigma, or business process reengineering methodologies to exploit it. As the animals reengineer a process, lean concepts such as *continuous flow* and *pull* could be incorporated. The intent and purpose of each approach is distinct, but the methods and effects are complementary.

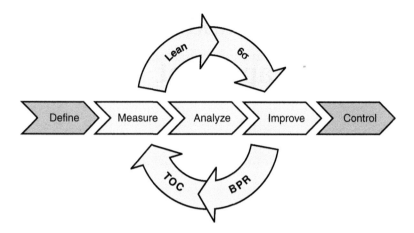

The animals embrace this and are prospering for it. The Strate-Tree has been pruned and has grown new branches bearing fresh fruit. Their efforts have evolved with increased target performance levels and even new root causes to attack, and they continue to drive progress toward achieving Lean Acres' vision. As of today, they have captured seventy percent of the total market share in Perfection.

Their newest effort involves the feeding process on the farm. This is an activity that flows across all pens, yet for some reason each performs the task in a different way. The animals believe that addressing a common chore performed in each functional area could yield significant results, and they are right.

As for the Farm Animals Team, they have continued to transform as well. They are no longer referred to as the F.A.T. They are now the Farm Improvement Team, or F.I.T. for short.

Later today, in a few hours in fact, the Boo-chair will return to Lean Acres. With stains smeared on his clothes and a crooked smile spread around his face, he will stand on the Farmer's porch. With dripping red gloves he will rap on the Farmer's door. And with a guttural voice he will offer his final dreadful bargain. The Farmer will answer today, and the twisted grin will be forced into a frown. The Farmer will reject the Boo-chair's offer and ask the Dog to help him find his way off of the property. The Dog will do so with pleasure.

The Farmer doesn't need green paper from the Boo-chair because the people and the businesses of the state of Perfection are giving him more of their own. They like his products now more than ever before, and they can get more of what they like faster and cheaper from Lean Acres than anywhere else. As the customers' requirements change, Lean Acres is able to fulfill their needs. They like this. They like this a lot.

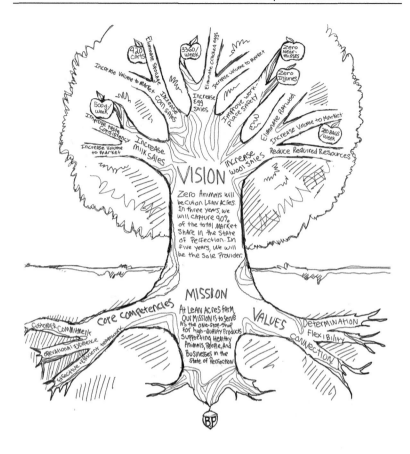

Now the Farmer is making plans of his own. He plans to expand Lean Acres by purchasing neighboring properties and growing his workforce. Will he see the Boo-chair again? Absolutely. And he will see him soon. Only this time, the Farmer will be making the offer.

I can not say good-bye because we will meet again. You will realize that I am all around you if you take the time to see, and that I am within you if you will only look. Take a chance and let me out. You will be amazed at what we can do together.

Rest/Reflect/Relate (R³)

1. Are there similarities between the animals, processes, and issues at Lean Acres and those (including the animals) at your place of work? If so, what are they? If not, what are the differences?

2. Is your Farmer engaged in daily operations, including improvement efforts? Is it a help or hindrance?

3. Has a formal pursuit of performance improvement been initiated on your farm, either currently or in the past? Is it working? How do you know?

4. If you were to lead the next press toward performance excellence, how would you begin? How would you sustain it?

Posttest:
What Have You Learned?

1. The *lean* methodology is focused on reducing or eliminating _____ in a process.

   a. Variation

   b. Waste

   c. Work

   d. People

2. In order, the five principles of lean are:

   ___ Pull

   ___ Flow

   ___ Value stream

   ___ Perfection

   ___ Value

3. When engaging in a project using the *theory of constraints*, one is looking to increase:

   a. Inspection

   b. Inventory

   c. Operating expenses

   d. Throughput

4. The Six Sigma methodology is focused on reducing or eliminating _____ in a process or product.

   a. Variation

   b. Waste

   c. Work

   d. Expenses

5. _____ is an improvement methodology that proposes radical transformation of current processes and a fundamental shift in operations in order to increase efficiency and efficacy.

   a. Six Sigma

   b. Lean

   c. Business process reengineering

   d. Theory of constraints

6. From a project perspective, the individuals or groups who have interest in or are impacted by the results of an improvement effort are the _____.

7. Which of the following is not one of the 7 S's?

   a. Salvage

   b. Standardize

   c. Security

   d. Safety

8. Which of the following is not one of the nine "wastes":

   a. Motion

   b. Transportation

   c. Injury

   d. Reporting

9. A process running at a Six Sigma performance level produces a yield of:

   a. 95%

   b. 99%

c. 100%

d. 99.99966%

10. Which of the following factors does the theory of constraints *not* focus on?

    a. Operating expenses

    b. Inventory

    c. Throughput

    d. Efficiency

Now turn to the Test Answer Key once more and compare your pretest score with this one. Hopefully, you will see measurable improvement!

Afterword

You made it! Or . . . you skipped ahead to this page. If you did read through *Lean Acres*, I sincerely hope that you had fun and that you now have a better understanding of continuous *performance* improvement, including its application in everything that we do. Feel free to join the Lean Acres community at http://www.leanacresonline.com, and on Facebook and LinkedIn (search for "Lean Acres"). The F.I.T. and I will post updates, share stories and experiences, and answer any questions you might have.

As I stated in the beginning, I'm not trying to grow a base of experts with this particular work. There are plenty of great books on the shelves that delve into specifics at considerable length. But a bunch of Owls can't run a farm. It is more important that the people who actually *do* the work grasp the spirit of these approaches, the intent of these methodologies, than it is that they master specific tools (for example, FMEA or interrelationship digraphs).

As a continuous performance improvement zealot, I am constantly looking for ways to improve the results that I deliver. That being said, I have an online survey set up to capture, analyze, and act on feedback from you, the customer. This survey will *not* be monitored by an administrative crew. I will personally review each submission and respond at your request.

Go to: http://leanacresonline.com/leanacressurvey and answer a few questions.

It's short and sweet, and I'll thank you for your time by sending you a package of useful performance improvement tool templates in electronic format for your use. While you're there, feel free to explore the rest of the site as well. The Farm Improvement Team will be posting their own blogs and might even respond to some of your queries.

Thank you again for visiting Lean Acres with me. From my perspective, it was a blast. Based on the information I get from you, we just might go back for another visit.

Test Answer Key

1. b. Waste

2. Value, value stream, flow, pull, perfection

3. d. Throughput

4. a. Variation

5. c. Business process reengineering

6. Stakeholders

7. a. Salvage

8. d. Reporting

9. d. 99.99966%

10. d. Efficiency

References

Breyfogle III, Forrest W. *Implementing Six Sigma: Smarter Solutions Using Statistical Methods*, 2nd ed. Hoboken, NJ: John Wiley & Sons, 2003.

Galsworth, Gwendolyn. *Visual Systems: Harnessing the Power of a Visual Workplace*. New York: AMACOM, 1997.

George, Michael L., David Rowlands, Mark Price, and John Maxey. *The Lean Six Sigma Pocket Toolbook*. New York: McGraw-Hill, 2005.

Goldratt, Eliyahu M., and Jeff Cox. *The Goal: A Process of Ongoing Improvement*, 3rd ed. Great Barrington, MA: North River Press, 2004.

Hirano, Hiroyuki. *5 Pillars of the Visual Workplace*. Portland, OR: Productivity Press, 1995.

Kaplan, Robert S., and David P. Norton. *The Balanced Scorecard: Translating Strategy into Action*. Boston: Harvard Business School Press, 1996.

Kubiak, T. M., and Donald W. Benbow. *The Certified Six Sigma Black Belt Handbook*, 2nd ed. Milwaukee: ASQ Quality Press, 2009.

Pyzdek, Thomas. *The Six Sigma Handbook: A Complete Guide for Green Belts, Black Belts, and Managers at All Levels*. New York: McGraw-Hill, 2003.

Rother, Mike, and John Shook. *Learning to See: Value-Stream Mapping to Create Value and Eliminate Muda*. Cambridge, MA: The Lean Enterprise Institute, 2003.

Tapping, Don, Tom Luyster, and Tom Shuker. *Value Stream Management: Eight Steps to Planning, Mapping, and Sustaining Lean Improvements*. New York: Productivity Press, 2002.

Westcott, Russell T. *The Certified Manager of Quality/Organizational Excellence Handbook*, 3rd ed. Milwaukee: ASQ Quality Press, 2006.

Womack, James P., and Daniel T. Jones. *Lean Thinking: Banish Waste and Create Wealth in Your Corporation*. New York: Free Press, 2003.

Yamamoto, Tsunetomo. *Bushido: The Way of the Samurai*. Justin F. Stone, ed. Minoru Tanaka, trans. Garden City Park, NY: Square One, 2001.

About the Author

Jim Bowie is a strategic performance improvement expert. He has more than 18 years of experience leading continuous improvement efforts in diverse environments and industries around the world including federal, commercial, and nonprofit organizations.

Jim is a former United States Army infantry officer and an Operation Iraqi Freedom veteran, holds a Master of Business Administration, is Kaplan & Norton Balanced Scorecard Certified, a Certified Lean Six Sigma Master Black Belt (including ASQ Certified Six Sigma Black Belt), an ASQ Certified Manager of Quality/Organizational Excellence, a Certified Lean Master, a Certified Project Management Professional, and a certified facilitator. Mr. Bowie's expertise was also recognized as he was selected to serve as a member of the Board of Examiners for the Malcolm Baldrige National Quality Award in 2010 and 2011. His educational track has included Salisbury University, Villanova University, University of Tennessee, Yale School of Management, Auburn University, and he is currently pursuing his doctoral degree.

Jim resides in the Washington, DC, area with his beautiful wife and four amazing children.

You can stay connected with Jim on LinkedIn. Simply go to www.jim-bowie.com and select "Add Jim Bowie to Your Network." You can also stay in touch with the Lean Acres community at www.LeanAcresonline.com or by joining us on Facebook.

Index

Belong to the Quality Community!

Established in 1946, ASQ is a global community of quality experts in all fields and industries. ASQ is dedicated to the promotion and advancement of quality tools, principles, and practices in the workplace and in the community.

The Society also serves as an advocate for quality. Its members have informed and advised the U.S. Congress, government agencies, state legislatures, and other groups and individuals worldwide on quality-related topics.

Vision

By making quality a global priority, an organizational imperative, and a personal ethic, ASQ becomes the community of choice for everyone who seeks quality technology, concepts, or tools to improve themselves and their world.

ASQ is...

- More than 90,000 individuals and 700 companies in more than 100 countries
- The world's largest organization dedicated to promoting quality
- A community of professionals striving to bring quality to their work and their lives
- The administrator of the Malcolm Baldrige National Quality Award
- A supporter of quality in all sectors including manufacturing, service, healthcare, government, and education
- YOU

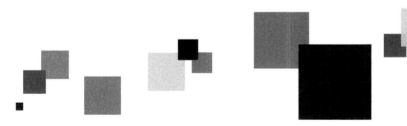

Visit www.asq.org for more information.

ASQ Membership

Research shows that people who join associations experience increased job satisfaction, earn more, and are generally happier*. ASQ membership can help you achieve this while providing the tools you need to be successful in your industry and to distinguish yourself from your competition. So why wouldn't you want to be a part of ASQ?

Networking

Have the opportunity to meet, communicate, and collaborate with your peers within the quality community through conferences and local ASQ section meetings, ASQ forums or divisions, ASQ Communities of Quality discussion boards, and more.

Professional Development

Access a wide variety of professional development tools such as books, training, and certifications at a discounted price. Also, ASQ certifications and the ASQ Career Center help enhance your quality knowledge and take your career to the next level.

Solutions

Find answers to all your quality problems, big and small, with ASQ's Knowledge Center, mentoring program, various e-newsletters, *Quality Progress* magazine, and industry-specific products.

Access to Information

Learn classic and current quality principles and theories in ASQ's Quality Information Center (QIC), *ASQ Weekly* e-newsletter, and product offerings.

Advocacy Programs

ASQ helps create a better community, government, and world through initiatives that include social responsibility, Washington advocacy, and Community Good Works.

Visit www.asq.org/membership for more information on ASQ membership.

*2008, The William E. Smith Institute for Association Research

ASQ Certification

ASQ certification is formal recognition by ASQ that an individual has demonstrated a proficiency within, and comprehension of, a specified body of knowledge at a point in time. Nearly 150,000 certifications have been issued. ASQ has members in more than 100 countries, in all industries, and in all cultures. ASQ certification is internationally accepted and recognized.

Benefits to the Individual

- New skills gained and proficiency upgraded
- Investment in your career
- Mark of technical excellence
- Assurance that you are current with emerging technologies
- Discriminator in the marketplace
- Certified professionals earn more than their uncertified counterparts
- Certification is endorsed by more than 125 companies

Benefits to the Organization

- Investment in the company's future
- Certified individuals can perfect and share new techniques in the workplace
- Certified staff are knowledgeable and able to assure product and service quality

Quality is a global concept. It spans borders, cultures, and languages. No matter what country your customers live in or what language they speak, they demand quality products and services. You and your organization also benefit from quality tools and practices. Acquire the knowledge to position yourself and your organization ahead of your competition.

Certifications Include

- Biomedical Auditor – CBA
- Calibration Technician – CCT
- HACCP Auditor – CHA
- Pharmaceutical GMP Professional – CPGP
- Quality Inspector – CQI
- Quality Auditor – CQA
- Quality Engineer – CQE
- Quality Improvement Associate – CQIA
- Quality Technician – CQT
- Quality Process Analyst – CQPA
- Reliability Engineer – CRE
- Six Sigma Black Belt – CSSBB
- Six Sigma Green Belt – CSSGB
- Software Quality Engineer – CSQE
- Manager of Quality/Organizational Excellence – CMQ/OE

Visit www.asq.org/certification to apply today!

ASQ Training

Classroom-based Training

ASQ offers training in a traditional classroom setting on a variety of topics. Our instructors are quality experts and lead courses that range from one day to four weeks, in several different cities. Classroom-based training is designed to improve quality and your organization's bottom line. Benefit from quality experts; from comprehensive, cutting-edge information; and from peers eager to share their experiences.

Web-based Training

Virtual Courses

ASQ's virtual courses provide the same expert instructors, course materials, interaction with other students, and ability to earn CEUs and RUs as our classroom-based training, without the hassle and expenses of travel. Learn in the comfort of your own home or workplace. All you need is a computer with Internet access and a telephone.

Self-paced Online Programs

These online programs allow you to work at your own pace while obtaining the quality knowledge you need. Access them whenever it is convenient for you, accommodating your schedule.

Some Training Topics Include
- Auditing
- Basic Quality
- Engineering
- Education
- Healthcare
- Government
- Food Safety
- ISO
- Leadership
- Lean
- Quality Management
- Reliability
- Six Sigma
- Social Responsibility

Visit www.asq.org/training for more information.